The Wars Against Napoleon

Debunking the Myth of the Napoleonic Wars

General Michel Franceschi
and Ben Weider

Translated by Jonathan M. House

SB

Savas Beatie

New York and California

The Wars Against Napoleon: Debunking the Myth of the Napoleonic Wars

Cataloging-in-Publication Data is available from the Library of Congress.

ISBN 13: 978-1-932714-37-1

10 9 8 7 6 5 4 3 2 1
First edition, first printing

SB

Published by
Savas Beatie LLC
521 Fifth Avenue, Suite 3400
New York, NY 10175
Phone: 610-853-9131

Editorial Offices:

Savas Beatie LLC
P.O. Box 4527
El Dorado Hills, CA 95762
Phone: 916-941-6896
(E-mail) editorial@savasbeatie.com

Savas Beatie titles are available at special discounts for bulk purchases in the United States by corporations, institutions, and other organizations. For more details, please contact Special Sales, P.O. Box 4527, El Dorado Hills, CA 95762. You may also e-mail us at sales@savasbeatie.com, or click over for a visit to our website at www.savasbeatie.com for additional information.

In memory of Arthur-Lévy, visionary and pioneering proponent
of the thesis of Napoleon as peacemaker,

and Colonel Émile Gueguen

The Emperor.

Contents

Illustrations

A section of color illustrations may be found following page 132.

Maps

Preface

$\mathcal{T}$his study reflects the total unity of ideas between two men dedicated to the defense of the memory of Napoleon I, a memory too often distorted when it is not completely falsified.

General Michel Franceschi, an eminent member of the International Napoleonic Society, worked at my side on this noble mission, in complete agreement with my views. Unfortunately, history is not an exact science. Written by humans, it perforce reflects their frame of mind as well as their opinions. History is also the echo of the authors' emotions, especially when those emotions are as strong as those of the Napoleonic era, one of the most agitated periods in history.

The general upheaval provoked by the Revolution of 1789 released strong emotions and exacerbated political confrontations. As a gifted architect of the new world that resulted, Napoleon was immediately exposed to the unavoidable opposition of the former regime. In consequence of this, his image has fluctuated over time between the two extremes of mythological adoration and visceral condemnation.

These antagonisms remain alive more than two centuries later. Personalities do not always reach the state of serenity necessary to write serious history with as little bias as possible. Numerous would-be historians have not bothered to present events as the product of a logical chain of causes and effects. Instead, their presentation is often limited to the forcible demonstration of a prejudice, a sham performing the function of proof. Gratuitous assertions take the place of reason, and accusations replace historiographic analysis. In short, the history of Napoleon is often written wrong side up. This book proposes to return that history to its proper place.

Although Napoleon is admired in the majority of foreign nations, paradoxically he is the victim of systematic disparagement in France, undoubtedly because the French are both judges and participants. Derision competes with imposture and mystification is rivaled by falsification. The most prestigious page in the history of France is thus reduced to a series of caricatures of Napoleon, to negative clichés about his acts, and to spiteful tales masquerading as history.

As a suspicious Corsican immigrant, Bonaparte is presented as an adventurer in the expedition to Egypt, a murderer of crowds on 13 Vendemiaire, a coup plotter on 18 Brumaire, and an assassin in the case of the Duke d'Enghien. Napoleon is depicted becoming Emperor only as a tyrant and enemy of liberty, all under the hideous mask of a conquering megalomaniac, insensitive to the bloodshed required to satiate his inexhaustible ambition and satisfy his insatiable passion for war.

This book is aimed precisely at this last imposture. It rejects the abominable portrait of Napoleon the unrepentant swashbuckler, dreaming of bringing the world under his martial sway. It lays bare a personality in which incomparable genius was completely compatible with innate compassion. It stresses realistically the explosive ambiance of the post-revolutionary period, an ambiance from which it was impossible to escape. It recalls the prodigious civil works accomplished against remarkable odds under the Consulate and later continued with difficulty under the Empire because of the hostility of European monarchs. It displays convincingly the constant efforts of Napoleon to avoid armed conflicts, reconciled with the difficulties evoked by his efforts to recast Europe. Finally, it demonstrates that all the wars of the Consulate and the Empire were imposed on the new France simply because it disturbed monarchical Europe, a Europe preoccupied with buttressing its privileges. "Napoleon must be destroyed!" was its motto, to paraphrase Cato the Elder's celebrated injunction regarding Carthage.

If nothing else, readers will not close this book with feelings of indifference. Admirers of Napoleon will be strengthened in his convictions, and detractors shaken in their hostility and prejudices.

In any event, the cause, the image of Napoleon will emerge cleansed of his bloody stain.

*   *   *

This book is the result of a close and intimate relationship with General Michel Franceschi of Corsica. General Franceschi is the special historical consultant for the International Napoleonic Society, and his devotion to correcting the errors that now exist about Napoleonic history had made this book a reality.

I equally wish to thank Jean-Claude Damamme, the special representative for French speaking countries of the International Napoleonic Society, for the massive efforts he continues to make in correcting Napoleonic history and eliminating numerous errors.

Special thanks must also go to a number world famous Napoleonic historians for their help, support, and dedication. Among them are David Chandler of London, England, who was also a professor of military strategy at the Sandhurst Military Academy, and Dr. Donald Horward, who dedicated his life to this subject as head of the Napoleonic and French Revolutionary Studies at Florida State University. Dr. Horward is now retired, and has been replaced by Professor Rafe Blaufarb.

I also thank Prince Charles Napoleon, a great friend and supporter.

My profound thanks to Theodore P. "Ted" Savas, Director of Savas Beatie LLC, and to his outstanding staff. Ted has worked closely with General Franceschi and me to ensure that the production of this book would be a major event for Napoleonic experts. Ted's dedication and devotion to publishing first class books are very much appreciated, and I acknowledge as well the professionalism of his organization.

My executive secretary, Rowayda Guirguis, had been essential in verifying a myriad of details in the production of this book.

Last but not least, I wish to acknowledge my dear friend of many years, Colonel Émile Gueguen, a retired French Army officer and former paratrooper. Now deceased, Colonel Gueguen was the most decorated French soldier of modern times. During the German occupation of France, he created an underground cell known as "Le Marquis de Saint Laurent." After World War II, he fought in French Indo-China, Tunisia, and Algeria. He was twice wounded and received an unprecedented twelve awards of the famous and most cherished "Croix de Guerre." For this distinguished service, President Jacques Chirac made Colonel Gueguen a Grand Officer of the Legion of Honor. This book is respectfully dedicated to his memory.

Ben Weider

Among the numerous conventional images concerning Napoleon, that of the megalomaniac conqueror drunk on glory is fixed in the collective imagination. Indefatigable warrior, Napoleon supposedly sacrificed world peace to his insatiable personal ambition. A bloodthirsty ogre, he bled France white to achieve his ends.

But is this historically accurate? We do not believe it is.

The oversimplification of this widely-held opinion, to which even sophisticated people succumb, is explained by the excessive attention focused on the uncommon man who was Napoleon, overlooking the convulsed situation in which he was forced to act for self-defense.

It is anti-historical to overlook the basic fact that Napoleon arose as the heir to the French Revolution of 1789, an unprecedented sociological and ideological upheaval. The adoption of the Declaration of the Rights of Man and Citizen, the abolition of privileges, the substitution of merit for hierarchy, the replacement of absolute monarchy by the democratic idea—all these appear today to be natural human values. At the time, however, they appeared to the defenders of the established order as dangerously subversive ideas. Such ideas threatened too many established situations and compromised too many private interests. The man who became the champion of these ideas would by the same token become public enemy number one for monarchical Europe.

This situation inevitably involved the entire continent, indeed the entire world. Yet, an application of intellectual rigor in analyzing the facts reveals that in fact Napoleon was the person *least* responsible for the situation. This assumes one takes two precautions: First, not confusing causes with effects, and second, not observing those facts through the distorted lense of today. It is to this simple yet powerful exercise that we will proceed.

Part One presents the intractable belligerent situation toward which the First Consul found himself inexorably forced upon his arrival in power, and from which he was never able to escape.

Part Two brings to light the fundamentally pacifist character of Napoleon's politics, founded on his intangible principle of avoiding conflicts.

Finally, validating the first two sections, Part Three demonstrates that wars that he never sought or declared constantly intruded on him (and thus the history of Napoleon).

The focus of our study is on the period of the Consulate and the Empire, after Napoleon had acceded to his responsibilities. The rich earlier period of General Bonaparte will be considered only as opportunity presents itself.

Combatants

 French

 Prussian

 English

 Russian

 Austrian

 Spanish

 Army Headquarters

 Infantry Corps   Cavalry Corps

 Infantry Division   Cavalry Division

 French Attack

 French Attack and Withdrawal

 Allied Retreat

 Allied Attack

 Allied Attack and Withdrawal

 City or Town

 Road Network

Watercourse

 Legend for Maps

Petko Cartography 2007

Part One

An Irreducible Belligerent Situation

Upon his accession to supreme power in November 1799, First Consul Bonaparte inherited an explosive general situation whose origins traced back to 1789. He found a military situation that had deteriorated markedly by comparison to that which he had left upon his departure for Egypt in May 1798. The bad news coming from France had in fact prompted his return home.

Established at the instigation of Pitt, the British prime minister, the Second Coalition against France included Britain, Austria, Sweden, the Kingdom of Two Sicilies, Portugal, and the Holy Roman Empire.

Going from defeat to defeat, the armies of the Directory had been forced back upon the national borders, losing all the gains made by Bonaparte at Campoformio. France thus found itself under direct threat of a general invasion.

Having scornfully rejected Bonaparte's offer of negotiations, the Coalition partners were constrained by force of arms to sign the treaties of Lunéville with Austria in February 1801 and Amiens with Britain in March 1802. We will return in Part Three to the episodes of this war, marked notably by the legendary victory of Marengo on June 14, 1800, achieved by Bonaparte in person, and by the brilliant success of General Moreau at Hohenlinden on December 30 of the same year.

Ending nine years of uninterrupted wars between the new France and the European monarchies, the Treaty of Amiens was received everywhere with indescribable enthusiasm. Europe appeared finally to have achieved a durable peace.

Unfortunately, this was but a grand illusion to which even Bonaparte succumbed for a time, as he later declared at Saint Helena: "At Amiens, I believed fully that the futures of France, of the Empire, and of me were settled. For myself, I could now focus solely on the administration of France, and I believed that I could produce prodigies."

It is easy to understand the smug optimism of the young First Consul, surrounded by glory and already adored by the people. He would not long remain on this little cloud, staying only the time necessary for a cruel recall to order by inexorable international realities.

Three sources of conflict, tightly entangled with each other, combined to lead inevitably to war, the bedrock of the entire history of the Empire:

— The thirst for revenge of the defeated;
— The inflexible monarchist reaction to newborn democracy;
— The implacable Franco-English rivalry.

The Thirst for Revenge of the Defeated

The repeated military reverses suffered at the hands of French armies had left in the spirit of the defeated a lively sense of humiliation, principally in Austria. These defeats had been punished by significant territorial amputations. It is natural that an irrepressible thirst for revenge animated the vanquished, waiting only for an opportune moment to wash away the outrage of their cruel defeats and recover their former possessions.

For Austria, the territorial losses had been considerable. By the Treaty of Lunéville, signed in its own name but also in its role as head of the German Empire, Austria paid dearly for the defeats suffered in its incessant wars against France in Italy and Germany. The Holy Roman Empire had to recognize the Rhine as the natural frontier of the new France. France finally saw the realization of an old dream vainly pursued for centuries. Had it not been said that "when France drinks out of the Rhine, Gaul will be at an end?" The Holy Roman Empire confirmed the loss of the Belgian provinces and recognized the republics of Batavia (Holland) and Switzerland. In addition, France gained a degree of influence in German affairs, in order to remove the threat from the east.

Yet, as a token of peace, France gave up its fortified places on the right bank of the Rhine.

In Italy, Lunéville confirmed the Austrian losses of the Congress of Rastadt on November 30, 1797. Its frontier was fixed at the Adige River. Austria had to recognize the Cisalpine and Ligurian Republics and consent to exchange the Grand Duchy of Tuscany for the archbishopric of Salzburg.

In short, morally bruised and considerably amputated, Austria came out of the war filled with a vengeful rancor.

The Treaty of Amiens put an end to the war between France and Britain. Spain and the Netherlands were also associated with this peace. Britain returned to France the Antilles and the trading ports of the Indies. France retained Trinity, seized from Spain, and Ceylon, taken from the Netherlands. It restored the Cape of Good Hope to the Dutch. Above all, France promised to evacuate Egypt and restore Malta to its Order within three months. This last clause was to constitute a seed of discord ultimately fatal to the peace.

Britain only accepted the peace because she was momentarily isolated in Europe and especially under the pressure of the businessmen of the city, who feared a major economic crisis. Yet it was certain that, at the first favorable juncture, Britain would attempt to refurbish its tarnished image, even more so because it would never pardon France for its decisive support to the "rebels" during the American War of Independence.

As for the other great European powers, notably Prussia and Russia, they were no longer concerned by territorial issues. However, they shared in varying degrees with the other monarchies in their hostility to the Republican France produced by the Revolution.

The Inflexible Monarchist Hostility

"The sovereigns of Europe would all like to come
to my funeral, but they dare not unite."

— Napoleon, 1809

An ideological confrontation without mercy reinforced the effect of territorial conflict.

Upon his arrival in power on November 9, 1799, Bonaparte inherited a new France that was drowning in the blood of the Bourbon monarchy. This contagious political upheaval had panicked all the monarchs, who feared with good reason for their thrones. The "Liberation" wars of the Revolution reinforced the gravity of the threat. In the First Coalition, the monarchies had forged an inflexible doctrine, ratified by the Conference of Angiers of April 6, 1793. The representatives of Britain, Austria, Prussia, and Russia had scheduled nothing less than the annihilation of Revolutionary France.

In the name of Britain, Lord Auckland declared a desire to "reduce France to a mere cipher in politics." Not to be outdone, the Austrian Marcy-Argenteau wished to "crush France by terror, exterminating a large segment of the active party and virtually all of the government party of the nation." Nothing less! His compatriot Thugut had even proposed a bewildering partition of spoils: to Britain, Dunkirk and the colonies; to Austria, Flanders and the Artois; to Prussia, Alsace and Lorraine. An unusual variant was to give Alsace and Lorraine to the Duke of Bavaria, in return for annexing his own duchy to Austria. This visceral hatred by the Austrian representatives owed much to the Revolution's decapitation of Marie Antoinette, an Austrian archduchess. Russia wanted to benefit itself in Poland. Its plenipotentiary Markov ably summarized the purpose of the Coalition's war which they would pursue with an implacable determination to Waterloo:

> All actions against France are permissible. We must destroy anarchy. We must prevent France from ever regaining its former preponderance. It appears that these two goals can be accomplished at once. Let us take possession of those French provinces that seem

convenient. . . . That accomplished, let us all work together to give whatever remains of France a stable and permanent monarchical government. She will become a second-rate power that will no longer threaten anyone and we will eliminate the hotbed of democracy that thought to set fire to Europe.

This piece of bravado is well worth an extended citation.

It is true that the monarchy of the tsars was more exposed than the others to the contagion of human rights. Its social system constituted an insult to human dignity. An arrogant aristocracy held the peasantry in serfdom, a situation very close to slavery.

The Emperor Napoleon did not yet exist at that time. Thus, these autocrats were engaged in a gross deception when they later claimed that it was only Napoleon as an individual, and not France as a whole, that they opposed.

Ten years after their first conference, the hatred of the European monarchs was not attenuated in the least. Quite the contrary. The easy victories of the French revolutionary armies owed much to their enthusiastic reception by the populations concerned and to the inhibiting effect on the enemy combatants who opposed the "liberators."

The autocrats of Divine Right tottered more than ever on their shaky thrones. To save their regimes, they needed at all costs to extirpate "the French evil" at the root, smother the Revolution once and for all, and return the French people to their places so that no other people would try to imitate them.

An experienced diplomat, the Count de Hauterive, expressed perfectly the inexorable nature of the confrontation between monarchical Europe and the new France:

One must kill the other. Either France must perish, or it must dethrone sufficient kings so that those who remain can no longer form a coalition. The coalition will have destroyed the French Empire the day it forces that Empire to retreat, because in that march than can be no stopping.

Words of premonition . . .

From 1789 to 1815 the fierce will of the European monarchs to cut down Revolutionary France never failed, and ended by becoming a malignant obsession. Neither the institution of the Empire with its monarchical pageant nor the matrimonial alliance with the Hapsburgs impaired this visceral hostility in the least, a fact that, one must note in passing, constituted the greatest Republican homage rendered to the imperial regime.

In early 1813, his ministers Rumiantsev and Nesselrode would persuade the conquering tsar that "Holy Russia" was charged with a divine mission to deliver Europe from Napoleon. This fanaticism was in large measure shared by the other courts.

We must consider not a coalition but a crusade against France, where public opinion responded in like manner. The "Song of Departure," the most popular of the epoch, immortalized French hostility to monarchy: "Tremble, enemies of France, kings drunk on blood and conceit, the sovereign people are on the march. Tyrants will fall to the grave. The Republic calls. . . ."

It only needed the inextricable religious question to take the general hostility against Consular France to its greatest height of convulsions. Among the outrages perpetrated by an unbridled Revolution, the tragic persecution of Catholics and the de-Christianization of the country provoked the opposition of the papacy and of all those whom Europe counted as devout. One excess provoked another. Bonaparte as heir to the Revolution was not far short of being considered the antichrist whom humanity would not rest until it had eliminated as quickly as possible and by any means necessary. Later, after he became emperor, his courageous emancipation of the Jews was unlikely to lessen this Catholic hostility toward him, which rivaled in intensity the Catholic abomination of Great Britain.

The Implacable Franco-British Rivalry

The bitter antagonism between France and Britain obviously did not begin with the Consulate, but existed throughout the tangled history of the two countries. The Hundred Years War comes instantly to mind. It would be more accurate to speak of a conflict of a thousand years, in which even today some sequels exist, although fortunately not military ones.

Britain had quietly encouraged the disorders of the Revolution in order to weaken France. The records of a Russian diplomat include the following information: "The English agents Clark and Oswald are members of the Jacobin Club. It would have been more honorable [for Britain] to make war on France than to foment the troubles and massacres that have horrified all humanity."

At the time of the Consulate, three interconnected conflicts nourished the hostility between the two powers: the old territorial dispute in Europe, a pitiless economic rivalry, and the inexorable race for world hegemony.

The Territorial Dispute in Europe

The Franco-English territorial conflict in Europe is as old as the two countries, but the expansion of Revolutionary France in the last decade of the 18th century greatly exacerbated it. France historically sought to secure itself by establishing its borders along the natural frontiers (the Rhine River, the Alps and the Pyrenees) and, by the mid-1790s, the French revolutionary armies had firmly secured these borders. The French revolutionary government extended its control to the neighboring states (Switzerland, Italy and Low Countries), where a series of republics formed a buffer zone around France. These conquests, however, collided with two fundamental principles of British diplomacy.

The first is that of the "European balance," the fixed foundation of all British foreign policy that, even in our time, has not lost any of its validity. Albion has never tolerated and will never permit any European power to dominate the continent to an excessive degree. This principle goes both to the security and the prosperity of Britain. Each time that a country has been about to achieve such domination, Britain has mobilized all its forces and all its subsidiaries to oppose that country with military coalitions. That was precisely the situation with regard to the Consulate in 1800.

The second principle, a corollary to the first, is the postulate that Great Britain finds its security to be incompatible with the occupation of the North Sea coastline by any great power. This is the famous "pistol aimed at the heart of England." Britain will not forget that she has already been invaded twice from this coastline, by Julius Caesar and William the Conqueror. Thus, the Convention had annexed Belgium in 1795 and the Treaty of Luneville had effectively placed the Netherlands under French sovereignty. By the time Bonaparte came to power, France and Britain had been long engaged in a protracted war, with neither side willing to concede. Moreover, the French presence in these strategic regions also constituted a threat to close off the flourishing British trade with Europe.

The Pitiless Economic Reality

The commercial competition of France had become a great matter of uneasiness for the merchant classes of Britain.

Leading all nations in the Industrial Revolution, Britain at the start of the century was the foremost economic power in the world. Yet, post-Revolutionary France was at the point of economic takeoff. She was regaining her losses and checkmating British exports in Europe. The French-British free trade treaty of 1786 had already given way to a more protectionist system, aimed at protecting French industry against foreign competition and ensuring its supplies of raw materials and tropical products. In 1793 this commercial competition transformed itself into economic warfare by forbidding the export of grains to enemy nations and the importation of all products from those same nations.

The Directory had violated the practice according to which the flag protected the merchandise on board. English products transported in neutral bottoms were declared fair prizes for seizure by privateers. A draconian law of October 1798 had further hardened the preference given to French goods.

In sum, the economic war had ended by blending into the military conflict. The escalation of such measures would not stop until it reached its logical conclusion in the disastrous continental blockade.

The Race for Global Hegemony

For some time previously the Franco-British rivalry had reached beyond the oceans to develop on a planetary scale. Henceforth it would assume the character of a race for global hegemony to obtain cheap raw materials, protected commercial markets, and secure strategic positions. The Russian ambassador to London in 1803, Voronzov, left this edifying testimony of an experienced diplomat: "The system of the English cabinet will always aim to destroy France as its sole rival, and to reign despotically over the entire universe."

At the accession of Bonaparte, Britain scarcely bothered to hide its ambition to dominate the world. She was in full colonial expansion. In this enterprise, she collided with Spain and the Netherlands but above all with France, which Britain wished to deprive of her remaining colonies in order to build an immense empire. Britain had recently expelled the French from Canada. France had taken her revenge by contributing to the independence of the United States of America. Now Albion coveted Martinique and Guadaloupe. She struggled with France for control of the India trade, the Seychelles Islands, Maurice, and La Reunion. In this overseas confrontation, Britain benefited decisively from its maritime superiority, while France enjoyed a strong position only on the European continent. In effect, a new Punic War was under way on a global scale.

Britain showed itself most aggressively in the Mediterranean. The control of this waterway of primordial importance determined British mastery of its communications with its empire in the Indies. At one point Britain had occupied Toulon, sole French naval base in the Mediterranean, followed soon thereafter by Corsica, which it attempted to annex to the British crown. In response, France made Britain nervous in Egypt from 1798 to 1801, already at the initiative of Bonaparte. Sovereign at Gibraltar since the Treaty of Utrecht in 1713, Britain also maintained the land and naval forces that it continued to reinforce on the Balearic Islands, at Malta, at Naples, in Sicily, and as far as Livorno.

This provocative domination of the Mediterranean by a foreign power had long constituted a humiliating infringement on the legitimate presence of France in this sea that washed a thousand kilometers of its continental coastline as well as Corsica. Matters could not possibly remain indefinitely in that state.

Thus, at the start of the Consulate, the situation in Europe was nothing less than explosive. Moved by a strong emotion of vengeance and fearing for their economic survival, the European monarchies only waited for an auspicious occasion to strike down the Republic in France and restore the Ancien Régime to the frontiers of 1789. In full imperialist expansion, Albion was in an excellent position to coalesce the hatreds of France in order to strike the hereditary enemy with whom it had disputed world supremacy for so many years.

Inscribed by fate and programmed in spirit, the war against France was thus unavoidable except by surrendering without conditions, which the French dignity could not tolerate.

At this stage in our discussion, one may say that Napoleon was already condemned to perpetual warfare from the moment of his arrival in power.

The non-recognition, real or simulated, of this tragic reality is at the origin of many of Napoleon's errors of judgment, too often depicted as the work of a warmongering tyrant.

We shall see that, on the contrary, he made every effort to avoid the war for which he had neither taste nor interest to provoke, nor time with which to adjust. He was to fight only when constrained to do so, always in a state of legitimate defense of France.

Part Two

Napoleon: A Builder in Love with Peace

*U*pon his accession to power, Bonaparte, in a letter addressed to British King George III, wrote: "Peace is the most basic of necessities and the first of glories." This noble maxim expresses the purest essence of the policy of Napoleon Bonaparte.

His elevation to the rank of the greatest captain of all time, as well as the inevitability of the wars he fought, have eclipsed the peaceful creative genius that was his primary characteristic. Clichéd caricatures have blurred his image, beginning with his personality.

A Fundamentally Peaceful Nature

The strong and abrasive character of Napoleon is indisputable. He rejected demagoguery and formed the most contemptible of prejudices, as does any self-respecting politician. Confronted by intolerable duplicity he did not always control his natural impulsiveness. It was to this that he owed the implacable enmity that cost him so much, notably with regard to major officials such as Talleyrand and Fouché. Anger caused him to make several unfortunate decisions, of which the most fatal was on the catastrophic question of Spain. Yet one must note that his public tantrums were sometimes deliberately calculated to obtain a political effect.

That said, contrary to appearances, Napoleon was a sensitive soul as opposed to the "Corsican ogre," the image produced by false propaganda often based on fallacies.

Consider this remark that he confided to Pierre Louis Roederer: "There are within me two distinct men: the man of the mind and the man of the heart. At my core, I am a man of the heart."

Numerous witnesses, both public and private, to this aspect of Napoleon Bonaparte's personality support this idea.

Napoleon was severely traumatized by the atrocities of the Revolution, notably the horrible massacre of the Swiss Guards at the Tuilleries Palace, which he witnessed on August 10, 1792. From that day onward he contracted a severe aversion to all forms of uncontrolled popular violence and to any system of extremist government.

We know many other examples of the tenderness of his soul. He always exhibited an unfeigned nausea at the spectacle of a battlefield after the fight. At Austerlitz he was to express the great suffering he felt at the deaths of so many humble soldiers, whether French or enemy. "May all this misfortune rebound on the perfidious island dwellers [i.e., the British] who caused it."

His horror of war caused him on at least three occasions to commit the same serious strategic error. At Wagram, at Borodino, and after Bautzen, despite the pleas of his marshals he gave up the pursuit of the vanquished in order to halt the bloodshed. "Enough blood has been spilled!" he exclaimed after Wagram. In these three circumstances, he knowingly violated his own unchanging goal in war, which was to destroy the enemy's army so as to discourage him from recommencing the conflict.

In visiting the battlefield of the dreadful butchery of Eylau, a battle he could not have avoided, the tears, which ran down his cheeks, did not escape General Billon, who heard him say, "What a massacre! And for what result? A spectacle well formed to inspire in princes the love of peace, the horror of war. . . . A father who loses his children finds no charm in victory. When the heart speaks, even glory has no more illusions." When speaking of his intrepid veterans, he frequently used the expression "my children," containing a true affection that accentuated his legendary ear pinching. Once could repeat many examples of this type of remark.

We possess testimonies of his unfathomable sadness at the loss in combat of the best of his companions, such as Desaix at Marengo (1800), Lannes at Essling (1809), or Duroc at Markersdorf (1813).

Upon his return from the island of Elba, Napoleon fainted with emotion at the news of the suicide of his former chief of staff, Berthier, even though that general had abandoned him. He endured the torture of never again seeing his four-year-old son, the tragic Eaglet, of whom he had been inhumanly deprived. He tried to let nothing show, but Carnot found him in tears before the child's portrait. Still, he did not attempt to trade the child for the Duke d'Angouleme, whom he had at his mercy in the Rhone Valley. Such an act of gangsterism was repugnant to Napoleon's morals.

Yet many critics will argue that Bonaparte acted like a true barbarian at Jaffa in March 1799, during the expedition to Egypt. Well, let us not avoid this question.

In that ill-fated circumstance, Bonaparte was forced, in violation of his conscience, to submit to the horrible way of that ferocious war by replying in kind to the frightful military customs of his enemies.

He confronted the Ottoman army of Pasha al Jezzar, whose nickname "the butcher" summed up his legendary cruelty. One of his pastimes was the decapitation of Christians. In war, he took no prisoners. When Bonaparte sent a negotiator to the garrison of Jaffa to offer the defenders their lives in exchange for surrender, the only reply was the decapitated head of the emissary. Thus, matters were clear in all their frightful simplicity. Neither side would grant quarter to the other. Such requests were unlikely to encourage compassion in the hearts of Bonaparte's soldiers, who retained the abominable memory of the horrible massacre of several hundred of their comrades during the insurrection in Cairo a few months before. The French also knew that any straggler or stray would be mercilessly killed after frightful tortures and mutilations.

Jaffa fell after two days of furious combat. Despite Bonaparte's instructions to spare the population, even those who were actively involved with the defenders, the sack of the city was atrocious, involving odious crimes despite the intervention of officers. Among these, General Robin did not hesitate to risk his life while cutting down his own soldiers.

An appalling misunderstanding occurred with regard to the last defenders who had taken refuge in the citadel. Their fate normally would have been sealed by their original refusal to surrender. Yet, to "calm as much as possible the fury of the soldiers" with regard to women, children, and the elderly, Bonaparte sent his aides de camp, Eugene de Beauharnais and Crozier. Listening only to their hearts, the two young officers violated the mutually accepted rule against offering pardon to combatants. They accepted the surrender of some 1,500 combatants, mainly Albanian, in exchange for their lives.

Confronted with a fait accompli, Bonaparte found himself in a nightmarish issue of conscience. Already suffering from a shortage of provisions for his soldiers, he was unable to feed this additional mass of humanity under any circumstances. Nor could he spare sufficient soldiers to guard them, being cruelly undermanned as a result of operations. Simply to abandon these men to their fate would be to condemn them to a slow and horrible death in the desert. Finally, in the rigid oriental mindset, any measure of clemency would be perceived as a weakness of will that would probably encourage even more ferocious resistance in future combats.

It was thus that Bonaparte was obliged to resolve his moral crisis by taking the terrible decision to exterminate the prisoners under indescribable conditions. He at least made the decision with the backing of his principal subordinates, after a very long deliberation. When waging war, one must have the force to overcome one's scruples or else change one's profession.

This is the tragic reality of the Jaffa affair. It undoubtedly reinforced Bonaparte in his horror of war.

By the same token, we need to wring the neck of another misconception that clings to Napoleon, that which labels him as a slaver because he reestablished slavery on Guadeloupe on May 20, 1802. Let us examine this matter more closely.

It is important to remember first that at that time France had already been engaged for several months in a slave rebellion in the colony of Santo Domingo. A former black slave, the phenomenal Toussaint Louverture, had led the island in an uprising and seized power. At first, Bonaparte succeeded in concluding with him a form of protectorate, and named Louverture captain general in March 1801. Very quickly, however, Toussaint Louverture's dictatorial and violent conduct endangered the future of the colony. An expeditionary force debarked on the island in January 1802 to reestablish the situation.

The key here is not to know the outcome of this affair but the conditions that prompted the intervention itself. The French navy, which controlled the colonies, had recommended the expedition. The lobby of sugar and coffee traders had pressed the First Consul closely to reestablish slavery, abolishing the convention of 1194. Bonaparte was fiercely opposed.

In the spring of 1802 the affair shifted to the Antilles. The Treaty of Amiens, signed on March 25, 1802, with Britain, returned to France both Martinique and Guadeloupe.

Therein lay the problem. Because the British had occupied it, Martinique had not benefited from the previous abolition measure. The competition between the two islands had been shifted to the detriment of Guadeloupe, to the point of provoking a collapse in production and an extremely serious social crisis that was resolved only with difficulty.

Bonaparte's first impulse was to give it in turn the benefits of abolition. The navy and business circles counseled strongly against this. Because the neighboring British colonies had remained slave economies, the same cause would produce the same ill-fated effects in Martinique. Bonaparte therefore sought a solution by maintaining the status quo on Martinique, but the Senate vetoed this in the same of the sacrosanct "republican" equality.

Bonaparte thus found himself confronted with a terrible dilemma, a sort of choice between cholera and the plague, between misery in economic chaos and a return to some more temperate form of slavery. Shouldering his responsibilities as a statesman, he decided against his own conscience to choose the latter measure advocated by the government.

These are the facts that no fallacious argument can twist.

Can one in good faith criticize the First Consul for having chosen the lesser evil? Does one accuse of infanticide the physician who, in a tragic childbirth, must sacrifice the life of the child to save that of the mother?

Can one dare to accuse Bonaparte, the heir of the Revolution and the emancipator of peoples, of slavery?

In truth, inveterate detractors depict him as the scapegoat in this affair. Bonaparte is less guilty of slavery than the king of England or the tsar of Russia, who did not abolish slavery in their colonies or serfdom in Europe. Napoleon at least suppressed serfdom in Poland in 1807, and during the Hundred Days of 1815 he proposed to abolish slavery. It is also worth remembering that President Thomas Jefferson had not sought an abolition law so as to avoid ruining the American economy, because slavery still existed in most of the Americas. As for Guadeloupe, Bonaparte shared the responsibility for this decision with the representatives of the people who voted without soul-searching to reestablish slavery. This measure was supported by all the governments that followed Napoleon until 1848, the year of definitive abolition. And, for good measure, let us add that serious historians barely mention this event if they do not neglect it completely.

Crimes, even crimes of state, were always repugnant to Napoleon. The abominable accusation that he was responsible for the "assassination" of the Duke d'Enghien on March 21, 1804, is completely unfounded. Napoleon had legitimately ordered the arrest of the Duke d'Enghien because of severe allegations against him. His past service fighting in enemy ranks against the French army did not argue in his favor. His abduction in Baden outside French borders is a ridiculous criticism given the severity of the offense. The arrest was ordered on the basis of legitimate right of pursuit. A legally constituted independent court judged him. Capital punishment was voted unanimously on the basis of laws then in force, not for his unproven participation in the Cadoudal conspiracy but rather for five other counts of treason and dealing with the enemy, all subject to the death penalty. Savary directed the odious summary execution alone. Owing nothing to Napoleon's will, this decision had been inspired by the regicides in his entourage to stop definitely the temptations to restore the monarchy, as General Monck had done in Britain a century and a half earlier. On the contrary, the First Consul had reserved to himself the political power of clemency, which he undoubtedly would have granted were it not for the strange "sleeping" failure of his State Counselor Real.

By contrast, Napoleon had miraculously survived an uncounted number of assassinations organized almost openly by the British government or the Count of Artois, the future Charles X. He ultimately succumbed on Saint Helena to arsenic poisoning, now scientifically proven, perpetuated by the same people who accused him of assassinating the Duke d'Enghien.

But Napoleon, the Corsican, never gave in to the temptation for vendetta. He repeatedly rejected offers for contract killings that could rid him of his mortal enemies.

He did not even indulge in easy vindictive measures. At Tilsit, for example, he did not ask Tsar Alexander I (who could have denied him nothing) for the head of the Corsican Charles Pozzo di Borgo, an enraged intriguer who spouted his hatred of Napoleon at the court of Saint Petersburg.

Napoleon's great tolerance often reached the stage of weakness. Josephine abused his patience for years. He pardoned many corrupt acts by his companions in the name of long friendship, including Bourrienne, for example. He refused to try for high treason senior officials such as Talleyrand, reported to have "betrayed all those who had bought him," or even the detestable Fouché, who said to Talleyrand after becoming vice chancellor that "this [ruthlessness] is the sole vice that he lacks." What a poor "jailer" Napoleon was.

And what can one say about Napoleon's excessive patience with the constant disloyalty of that criminal, Bernadotte, who ended by using the Swedish army to fight against France?

Napoleon even made some exceptions to the sacrosanct reasons of state. It was thus that, on two occasions, he succumbed to the pleadings of women at his feet to pardon their husbands, Polignac for the Cadoudal conspiracy in 1804 and the prince of Hatzfeld for felony at Berlin in 1806.

Contrary to appearances, political moderation was a constant in Napoleon's behavior. As early as the Italian campaign, he restrained the "bitter end" policy of the Directory, which was determined to strike down the Hapsburgs and the papacy. At Campoformio, he allowed the court of Vienna to have a reasonable way out, while he spared the pope in the central Italian states.

Upon his accession to the Consulate, his first concern was to avoid any institutional excess. His famous motto was "Ni talons rouges, ni bonnets rouges" (neither aristocrats nor revolutionaries.) He was not a man for historic ruptures, but rather wished to continue the traditional France. The Empire was a synthesis of the republican ideas of the Revolution and the heritage of the Ancien Régime. It is striking today to compare the result to the somewhat monarchical and imperial character of the Fifth French Republic.

To avoid bloody revolutions, Napoleon did not seek to inspire people to rise against their despots, something those despots attempted in vain against him. Except for the justifiable exception of the Bourbons in Naples, even when he occupied their capitals Napoleon did not attempt to overthrow the old absolute monarchies. The state of servitude, in effect semi-slavery, that the arrogant aristocracy of Saint Petersburg imposed on the Russian peasantry would certainly have justified a campaign of social liberation.

The primary cause of Napoleon's final fall undoubtedly traces back to his excessive benevolence with regard to the ruling dynasties. He acknowledged as much later while biting his nails on Saint Helena: "Although many people speaking in the name of their sovereigns have called me the 'modern Attila' or 'Robespierre on horseback,' deep down they all know better. If I had been what they claimed, I might still be ruling, whereas those monarchs would definitely no longer be on their thrones!"

In all the wars that were forced upon him, Napoleon displayed a restraint for which one might well reproach him. More than once he failed to achieve victory because he wished to halt the bloodshed, naively believing that the enemy would be grateful for his clemency. This was true, for example, at Austerlitz, Friedland, Wagram, the Moskva River (Borodino), and Bautzen. At the Tilsit negotiations after Friedland, one could not distinguish between the speech of the conqueror and that of the conquered. The truce accorded to the Coalition members after the victory of Bautzen became an obvious fool's paradise.

Out of horror of violence, Napoleon abdicated twice, in 1814 and again in 1815, to protect the people, who remained loyal and determined to defend the country from the throes of civil and foreign war.

Is this the portrait of the "bloody ogre" that a hideous propaganda has attempted to portray?

The Consulate's Prodigious Work of Peace

The extraordinary balance sheet of the Consulate merits consideration here because it eloquently illustrates the overarching peaceful preoccupations of the First Consul.

Extinction of the Hotbeds of War

As previously discussed, the deceptive treaties of Lunéville and Amiens, those forced fruits of the first war imposed on Bonaparte, constituted the most spectacular conquest of peace by the Consulate. But they did not lead to the general peace to which all France aspired after nine years of incessant conflict. Other hotbeds of war persisted in continental Europe, in the Mediterranean, in the Iberian Peninsula, and in the Atlantic.

In continental Europe, a first treaty of friendship between France and Bavaria, signed on August 14, 1801, opened the era of French influence in Germany.

The Treaty of Paris, concluded on October 8 of the same year, ended a state of war with Russia. After joining the Second Coalition, Russia's army had suffered a grave reverse in Switzerland during the summer of 1799. The First Consul had magnanimously returned home 6,000 Russian prisoners held in France, along with their arms and new uniforms. At a stroke, Tsar Paul I had become a fervent admirer of Bonaparte. He had taken the initiative to form a league of neutrals with Sweden, Denmark, and Prussia, thereby restricting British commerce in Germany and the Baltic. He paid for his reversal of attitude with his assassination under horrible conditions on March 24, 1801. With at least the passive complicity of his son and heir, Alexander I, Britain took the necessary steps to strangle at birth a Franco-Russian alliance that would have been catastrophic for British interests. To leave future opportunities open, Bonaparte nonetheless proved generous: France renounced its claims to the Ionian Islands and, to please Alexander, spared the hostile Kingdom of Naples, which had participated in the Second Coalition.

In the Italian peninsula, the Treaty of Florence of March 18, 1801, put an end to war with Naples. The Kingdom of the Two Sicilies closed its ports to the British and permitted French occupation of Taranto, Otranto, and Brindisi.

In the Mediterranean, France was at war with the Regencies of Algiers and Tunis, who supported Turkey since the Egyptian expedition. Negotiations with Algiers led to an accord on December 17, 1801. The Regency restored to France its trading posts and accorded special rights to the Compagnie d'Afrique. All the same, the acts of piracy on the coast of Provence did not completely end, because of a sad issue of payment for wheat supplied by the Directory.

With Tunis, the peace was signed February 23, 1802. Taxes on merchandise were reduced to three percent.

This normalization of relations with Algiers and Tunis was made possible by the Peace Treaty with Turkey, concluded at Paris on October

9, 1801, and ratified on June 25, 1802. France restored Egypt, militarily lost since September, and recognized Turkish suzerainty over the Ionian Islands. Another treaty signed on June 26, 1802, established most favored nation status and reestablished former concessions, opening the Black Sea to French commerce.

In the Iberian Peninsula, the question assumed a completely different form. Bourbon Spain constituted a key piece on the diplomatic chessboard. Alliance with it carried a valuable aid against the British in three theaters: the Mediterranean, Portugal, and the Americas.

The Treaty of Lunéville initiated the consolidation of Franco-Spanish friendship. To please the Spanish king Charles IV, Bonaparte transformed the Grand Duchy of Tuscany into the Kingdom of Etruria and offered it to a Bourbon de Parma, a relative of Charles IV. This friendly gesture encouraged Spain to sign the Treaty of Alliance of Aranjuez on March 21, 1801. The crown princess of Spain, married to the King of Etruria, was proclaimed "Queen of Etruria." Spain ceded Louisiana to France and Charles IV confirmed the Franco-Spanish convention of January 29, 1801. He then prepared to wage war against Portugal, the faithful ally of Britain.

What followed was a sham confrontation, known in history as the "War of the Oranges." On April 16, 1801, General Leclerc entered Spain at the head of an army corps. On May 19 Spanish troops crossed the Portuguese frontier. Three days later the Regent of Portugal yielded to the councils of London even though Britain could provide no aid. The Treaty of Badajoz of June 6, 1801, ratified at Madrid on September 29, granted to France an enlargement in Guiana, an indemnity of 20 million francs, and most favored nation status. The moderation of these provisions must be emphasized. Bonaparte had made no effort to conquer Portugal, but solely to close to Britain the port of entry into the Iberian Peninsula, a port that could form a second front to take France from the rear. We shall see, unfortunately, how this moderation did not pay.

In the Atlantic, Bonaparte sought two peaceful actions: the reestablishment of the former Franco-American friendship and the resolution of the question of Santo Domingo.

The Alliance of 1778 linking France to the young United States of America had suffered under a wartime rivalry, encouraged by Britain.

Bonaparte seized the occasion of George Washington's death in December 1799 to initiate a process of improving relations between the two nations. He decreed ten days of national mourning. Touched by this tactful gesture, the United States sent a delegation to Paris. Long negotiations culminated in the Treaty of Mortefontaine of October 3, 1800, which normalized relations between the two countries and included significant clauses concerning maritime rights. These clauses favored the neutral powers against the British blockade.

The Alliance of 1778 could not be restored fully because of Louisiana, ceded to France by Spain. The loss of this strategic province blocked American expansion to the west. This contained the seed of a major conflict in which France could not afford to indulge. Realist and follower of a general policy of appeasement, Bonaparte defused this time bomb in a deft manner. On April 30, 1803, he sold Louisiana to President Thomas Jefferson, putting an end to a bone of Franco-American contention.

Also in the Atlantic, there remained the difficult problem of Santo Domingo, the "sugar island," a French possession avidly sought by Britain. The situation of this colony has been previously described in the section on slavery. We had left the story at the military intervention of January 1803. Commanded by Leclerc, the expeditionary force of 35,000 ended the dictatorship of Toussaint Louverture after bloody struggles. The deportation of Louverture to captivity in the Fort de Joux, where he would die in 1803, did not suffice to end the uprising. The black revolt continued, fueled in part by the fear of a reestablishment of slavery. Decimated by tropical diseases, the expeditionary corps was unable to deal with the situation. Leclerc himself found death, a victim of yellow fever. His successor Rochambeau was unable to reverse the course of events. He was forced to yield on November 19, 1803, putting a final end to the French era in Santo Domingo.

Thus, as a result of an outpouring of sixteen treaties or conventions concluded between 1800 and 1803, France was no longer at war with anyone, a situation unknown since April 20, 1792. Bonaparte, "the soldier who knows how to make war but even better how to make peace," in the words of a popular song, delivered the unexpected and priceless gift of a general foreign peace. The nation dedicated itself to him as if to a cult.

Yet, international peace, no matter how precious, was not sufficient to achieve perfect happiness in France. It was equally important to the

First Consul to bring domestic peace to the French, tragically divided since the Revolution.

The Achievement of Internal Pacification

The France that the Directory left to Bonaparte was not only distressed by war outside its borders. It suffered equally from deep internal injuries, the heritage of the violent sociological upheaval of 1789. A large number of its sons had emigrated; some had gone so far as to commit the crime of carrying arms against their country in enemy armies. In the west, the Chouan uprising went on interminably, endangering the unity of France. On the religious plane, the bitter struggle over the Civil Constitution of the Clergy continued to promote a climate of hatred between Frenchmen. Bonaparte's first duty as First Consul was thus to complete the reunification of the country.

But on what institutional basis could he accomplish this? He chose to build the new France on the values of the single, indivisible Republic.

The Republic and the Bloody Test of the Reaction

Stunted child of the Directory, the Consulate was politically fragile at birth. Emanating from the tumultuous 18 Brumaire, which many attempted to depict as a coup d'Etat, the new regime was challenged by the political minorities while lacking major public support. Many observers did not think it would survive a year.

Bonaparte's first concern was thus to assert boldly that the choice of the Republic was the new regime that would henceforth rule the country. Around this regime, and it alone, all Frenchmen must reconcile. Henceforth, the sole sovereign recognized in France would be the French people. Bonaparte soon began the habit of ending his toasts with "To the French People, our sovereign in everything!" But many people were only half listening to him.

The most violent opponents were located, as always, at the two extremities of the political continuum.

To the left, Jacobins nostalgic for the Revolution suspected Bonaparte of despotism or, to the contrary, of tepid democracy. The most enraged were labeled "Exclusives." Once the First Consul announced officially "the Revolution is fixed on the principles which began it. It is finished," the Jacobin extremists turned a hostile ear, unconvinced of the moderation declared by Bonaparte.

Fortunately isolated, these extremists plotted without success, although not without violence, to overthrow the regime. In September 1800 the police got wind of preparations for a terroristic attempt on the person of the First Consul. They discovered a barrel of gunpowder packed with large nails, the fuse already in place. A handful of "Exclusives" were rendered incapable of further injury. At the same time, one of their accomplices denounced another assassination project against Bonaparte. This had been scheduled for October 10, during a show at the Theater of the Republic in the Rue de la Loi. Well informed concerning the First Consul's schedule, the plotters intended to stab him on that occasion, hence the name "Conspiracy of the Knives." They were arrested in the corridor of the theater, in possession of the knives, condemned to death, and guillotined on January 31, 1801. A short time later, Fouché's efficient police aborted another attempt, this time with an infernal bomb instigated by a certain chevalier.

In the spring of 1802, the police discovered a shabby military putsch. Opposed to the Concordat and to pardoning the émigrés, some Jacobin generals who knew how to strike quickly prepared to march on Paris with the Army of the West, commanded by Bernadotte, to be synchronized with the assassination of the First Consul at Notre Dame Cathedral, on the occasion of an April 18 Te Deum to celebrate the Concordat. The plotters were quickly rendered incapable of damage. The soul of the plot was undoubtedly Bernadotte, but he fiercely denied the accusations of his apprehended subordinates. In the absence of proof, he could not be implicated any more than could his probable accomplices, generals Augereau, Moreau, Massena, and Macdonald.

For the moment, the radical Jacobins were neutralized. But, those Jacobin officials who had rallied to the new regime continued to fear that Bonaparte would initiate a return to monarchy, at least until the sad affair of the Duke d'Enghien cut Bonaparte off definitively from the Bourbons.

On the right, the inconsolables of the Ancien Régime would show themselves even more ferocious that the "exclusives" after Bonaparte refused to support their plans for a restoration.

From the installation of the Consulate, the Count de Provence, brother of the deceased Louis XVI and future Louis XVIII himself, had the First Consul sounded out by Hyde de Neuville, the young head of the royalist agency in Paris. In exchange for the restoration, Bonaparte would become Constable of France, invested with great powers and immense honors, including an equestrian statue on the arch of triumph of the Carrousel. This approach obviously received no response.

From his place of exile at Mitau in Courland, the Count de Provence declared himself directly in a letter in which naiveté struggled with servility:

> I have had my eye on you for a long time. For years, it seemed to me that the victor of Lodi, of Castiglione, of Arcole, the conqueror of Italy and of Egypt, would be the savior of France. A passionate lover of glory, he would wish that glory to be unalloyed. He would wish that all our descendants would bless his triumphs. Yet, despite the fact that I saw you as the greatest of generals, despite the fantasy that would increase your laurels, I have had to keep my feelings to myself. Today, when you combine power with talents, it is time that I reveal the ambitions I have cherished for you. If I were speaking to anyone other than Bonaparte, I would specify rewards. A great man may determine his own fate and that of his friends. Tell me what you desire for yourself and for them, and all your wishes will be satisfied at the moment of my restoration.

In this proposition, this claimant to the throne flattered like a servile courtesan. He was also being hypocritical. In a letter written to Cadoudal at the same time, the Count described Bonaparte as a "tyrant."

The contemptuous silence of the First Consul did not discourage the count from returning to the same theme in a letter sent by way of the Abbot de Montesquieu, his secret agent in Paris. Bonaparte's response did not permit any ambiguities:

> I have received the letters of His Royal Highness. I have always taken a lively interest in his misfortunes and those of his family. He need not give any thought to his return to France, something that could only occur over a hundred thousand dead bodies. Otherwise, I

will always be happy to do whatever is possible to soften his destiny
and to help him forget his woes.

After this irrevocable refusal, the royalist party entered into an
opposition that went as far as terrorism. A hateful campaign against the
"Corsican usurper," including even graffiti, developed in the streets of
Paris. It was conducted by those labeled as "blades," wearing blond wigs
and black collars.

But the ultra royalists did not confine themselves to verbal
opposition. Paid by the British cabinet with the approval of the Count
d'Artois, future Charles X who was exiled in London, the royalists
redoubled their attempts to assassinate the First Consul. Among these
attempts, the most famous were the attack in the Rue Saint-Nicaise and
the Cadoudal-Pichegru-Moreau conspiracy.

The barbaric attack in the Rue Saint-Nicaise occurred on the evening
of December 24, on the drive transporting the First Consul from the
Tuilleries to the Opera, where an oratorio of Haydn was to be performed.
In the Rue Saint-Nicaise, his convoy passed a stopped cart, harnessed to a
mare whose bridle was held by a little girl. An enormous explosion
occurred several seconds later. The cart burst under the effects of a large
bomb whose fuse had not functioned at the exact instant that Bonaparte
passed. There were unfortunately several victims in the convoy, but the
surrounding area was a massacre. Twenty-two dead and fifteen wounded
were carried away. They found the remains of the little girl, who had been
paid with a piece of bread to hold the cart. The material damage was
considerable and several dozen houses were destroyed. The monstrosity
of this terrorist act was unimaginable. The life of the First Consul had
dangled by a thread.

Immediately after this attack, Bonaparte suspected the "exclusives,"
while Fouché argued for a royalist plot. As a precaution while waiting for
the results of an inquiry, 130 ultra Jacobins were arrested and deported to
the Seychelles. The inquiry proved Fouché to be correct. Acting at the
instigation of Cadoudal, the principal authors of the attack were three
royalists: the Chevalier de Limoelan, Saint-Regent, and Carbon.
Limoelan succeeded in fleeing to the United States. To expiate his
abominable crime he took priestly orders. Carbon and Saint-Regent were
condemned to death, the latter asking the court to send him to the scaffold

as soon as possible. The execution took place on April 20, 1801, to the applause of the crowd.

The Cadoudal-Moreau-Pichegru conspiracy was of a completely different nature. Its failure had a considerable consequence: the advent of the Empire.

The extremely unpopular carnage of the Rue Saint-Nicaise did not deter the royalist killers from their criminal designs on Bonaparte's person. Learning a lesson from the failure, they simply modified their methods. Instead of a blind terrorist attack, they planned to substitute a spectacular military coup de main on the First Consul during his movements between the Tuileries, La Malmaison, and Saint Cloud, where he went frequently. Neutralizing the numerous and formidable escort of the First Consul was a major obstacle to overcome, requiring detailed preparation and significant resources. But that didn't stop them. The British government of Pitt generously funded the recruitment of thugs and the organization of an imposing logistical network extending from the cliffs of Biville as far as Paris. For Great Britain, the game was worth the candle, and it was eager to execute the plan. The terrible "Boney," as Bonaparte was jokingly called, was actively preparing to invade the country, and was quite capable of succeeding. The equation was simple: no more Bonaparte, no more invasion.

For the Count d'Artois and his entourage, the issue was no less clear: eliminate Bonaparte, and the door to restoration would open. Thus, hand in hand, Pitt and Artois plotted this criminal conspiracy.

The executor of black operations was already identified. Once again it was the fanatical Cadoudal, aided and informed by General Pichegru, who had gone over to the enemy, and the dubious General Moreau in Paris. Cadoudal could also count on the active complicity of the clandestine royalist circle in Paris.

Yet, Fouché's efficient police were alert for danger, notably the political branch headed by Desmarets, who detected the snake in the grass during the summer of 1802 and never lost sight of the conspiracy thereafter. Matters came to a head at the end of 1803. Two of Cadoudal's henchmen, Querelle and Sol de Grisolle, were arrested in Paris. Attempting to avoid the death penalty, Querelle did not hesitate to unburden himself. He indicated the presence in Paris of Cadoudal and Pichegru, the former since August 1803. They were in contact with Moreau.

The danger to the life of the First Consul became pressing. Yet, it was important to put Cadoudal, Pichegru, and their henchmen out of action as quickly as possible. An informal state of siege was declared in Paris. The Counselor of State Real took the entire affair in hand under the judicial direction of chief judge Regnier. Murat, military commander of Paris, and Savary, commanding the gendarmerie d'elite, were required to give Real their complete support.

Real quickly obtained decisive results. He arrested Picot, a servant of Cadoudal, and more importantly Cadoudal's right-hand man, Bouvet de Lozier, former adjutant general of the army of the princes.

Terrified by what awaited him and deceived by his partners, Lozier revealed the essentials of the plot. He confirmed Querelle's revelations. He provided details of the relations between Cadoudal, Pichegru, and Moreau, who were in disagreement, fortunately for Bonaparte's life. The ambitious Moreau was quite willing to overthrow the First Consul, but only to profit for himself rather than to benefit the Bourbons. Taking this idea very badly, Cadoudal had retorted that he "would rather have Bonaparte than Moreau," which spoke volumes for the esteem in which he held Bonaparte.

The arrest of Moreau, living quietly in his estate at Grosbois, was decided in Council on February 13, 1804. The Council intended to try him before a civilian tribunal.

During the night of February 26 to 27, 1804, the police achieved a major stroke. They accomplished the tumultuous arrest of Pichegru, of the Marquis de Ribiere et d'Armand, and of Jules de Polignac, as well as several associates. Their confessions confirmed the elements previously revealed, but carried a new piece of critical information: an unknown "prince" was part of the conspiracy. He was supposed to rally the country after the assassination of Bonaparte.

The affair's scenario was thus revealed. Cadoudal was to eliminate the First Consul, Pichegru and Moreau would rally the army, and the mysterious prince would appear to reestablish the monarchy with the assistance of the others and the blessings of Britain.

The fierce Cadoudal was captured on March 9, 1804, not without violence. In the course of his arrest, he killed one police inspector and wounded another. Remaining true to his natural arrogance, he proudly proclaimed his plan to assassinate Bonaparte. He also confirmed the involvement of a "prince" in the plot, but did not go so far as to reveal his identity.

The conspiracy collapsed after the neutralization of Cadoudal. Pichegru committed suicide in prison on April 6, 1804, thereby evading the shame of being condemned to death for treason.

In court, Cadoudal acknowledged and even emphasized his role as principal executioner in all the meanings of that term. Moreau claimed that he had known of the conspiracy but had not participated. Cadoudal, Armand de Polignac, and twenty thugs were condemned to death on June 10. Jules de Polignac, Leridant, and Moreau received only two years of prison, although they deserved death for complicity in a plot on the life of the head of state.

At their request, Bonaparte granted clemency to Armand de Polignac, the Marquis de Ribiere, and to Bouvet de Lozier.

Cadoudal ostentatiously refused to ask for mercy, not wishing to owe his life to Bonaparte. He was executed with his remaining accomplices on June 26, 1804. Upon mounting the scaffold, he exclaimed with a sense of humor tinged with grandeur: "We came to give Paris a King, but instead we have given it an emperor!" In fact, a month earlier, on May 18, Bonaparte had become the emperor Napoleon. What an extraordinary flash of lucidity at the moment of death!

The celebrated affair of the Duke d'Enghien, previously discussed, was grafted onto the Cadoudal conspiracy just before the latter's execution.

The Pardon to the Emigrés, or the Peace of the Heart

Following the revolutionary convulsions, the expatriation of a large number of Frenchmen, both noblemen and others, constituted a human hemorrhage that if left unchecked would prove as ruinous for France as that caused by the exodus of Protestants after the Revocation of the Edict of Nantes by Louis XIV. To Bonaparte, the rapid reintegration into French society of this precious human substance appeared to be a national imperative.

The emigration phenomenon had begun at the same time as the Revolution. The troubles of July 1789 prompted a number of nobles to flee the country to escape the popular anger. The Count d'Artois, youngest brother of Louis XVI, the Prince de Condé and his family, as well as a number of grand aristocrats, took refuge in Turin. With the support of numerous European monarchs, these noblemen attempted in vain to raise the south of France, which remained largely faithful to the monarchy.

The movement expanded with the growth of revolutionary violence and the decree nationalizing the property of the nobility and clergy. It redoubled with the promulgation of the Civil Constitution of the Clergy, constraining the priests to swear loyalty to the revolution.

Until 1791 Louis XVI appeared to disapprove of emigration, but his failed flight to Varennes gave a new impulse to the movement.

From Turin, the leadership of the emigration moved to Coblenz. In July 1791 the king's two brothers, the Counts de Provence and d'Artois, established themselves there and formed a sort of court, a center of various intrigues, a money pit, and even a site of corruption.

What was the estimated number of émigrés? Historians have agreed on an approximate number of 200,000 out of 30,000,000 Frenchmen. What is striking about that mass, contrary to general belief, is its diversity. Alongside great names and coats of arms were found representatives of every social layer: almost 30,000 priests who had refused to accept the Civil Constitution, plus soldiers who had followed their officers, large numbers of country squires, middle class people, and even frontier residents fleeing misery, such as the 10,000 in the Lower Rhine, etc.

Scattered to all the countries of Europe, this émigré diaspora divided into clans and coteries while remaining French to the point of insisting on national dignity, much to the irritation of their hosts.

As long as these émigrés confined themselves to political actions, nothing irreparable occurred. Matters changed completely as soon as some of them took up arms against their own country.

At first scattered and under-strength, these military formations organized themselves and regrouped into three corps by the time that France went to war in April 1792. The most important of these corps, under the orders of the two princes, grew to 10,000 men, poorly equipped, poorly fed, and without pay.

The damage was irreversible when these lost soldiers became engaged as a supplement to Brunswick's Prussian army at Valmy. The retreat of the Coalition armies was transformed for the army of the princes into a ghastly rout that ended in its dissolution. Left in reserve, the army of de Condé escaped this disaster. It continued the war against France in the pay of Austria, Britain, and Russia until 1801.

Defeated and humiliated, the émigrés also found themselves the subject of a series of revolutionary decrees that condemned them to death if they returned to France or were captured abroad. They were thus reduced to a nomadic existence, pursued across Europe by the armies of the Republic. In countries beyond the reach of the Revolution, such as the United States, Britain, or Russia, some of them made brilliant careers such as the Duke de Richelieu, founder of Odessa, or the Count de Langeron, a brilliant general in the Russian army. Others, less illustrious, continued to serve as individuals in foreign armies.

Disgusted or weary, after 1795 a large number of émigrés believed they could return to France. The movement abruptly halted in 1797 by the events of 18 Fructidor (the September 4, 1797, purge of Royalists and other conservatives from the government), which also provoked a last wave of emigration. A new decree condemned to death any émigré apprehended on French territory. A terrible special list of all émigrés was developed for this purpose at the end of 1799.

This was the situation that Bonaparte found upon his arrival in power. The question of emigration constituted one of the "great evils of the state," he remarked.

Somewhat reassured by the change in regime, a goodly number of émigrés risked the dangerous decree, returning to France with borrowed identities and false passports. The opportunity to remove names from the fatal list gave rise to a base corruption. The better-financed émigrés purchased certificates of accommodation. A traffic in false papers developed. This state of affairs had to be ended immediately.

In the higher interests of the country, it was urgent to bring the two Frances together in concord. But the First Consul soon realized that the accumulated hatreds made this operation very difficult. Some time had to pass before political leaders and public opinion would accept the idea of a pardon. He therefore needed to force the hand of some republican officials. He had to reassure those who had purchased "national property" and who feared to lose it to the original owners. Bonaparte's refusal to absolve those who had carried arms against France eventually gained the support of the majority.

After a temporary order to eliminate certain categories of émigrés from the list, a general amnesty was finally voted on April 26, 1802. As promised, it excluded those who had fought against the armies of the Republic. "National property" that had already been sold would not be returned under any circumstances, although those properties not yet sold would be restored on a case-by-case basis.

In massive numbers the children of France, briefly separated, rejoined the mother country, which in most cases they had never ceased to love. An estimated 100,000 crossed the frontiers in the first days after the amnesty. They hesitated at first upon approaching the control points, but in general all went well. Rarely spiteful, the French pardoned those who had strayed, provided that there was no French blood on their hands. Consider, for example, the testimony of one émigrée, the "former" Madame de Boigne. When she entered the French border post, she felt trapped. An employee began his routine interrogation of identity. His boss interrupted: "Forget that! Write down simply 'as beautiful as an angel.'" Madame de Boigne thus understood that she had indeed returned home.

Let us also consider the particular case of the Alsatians who had fled to the right bank of the Rhine less for political motivations than to escape the troubles. After Brumaire, they felt no need to obtain authorization before returning home. Arrested by the gendarmes, they manifested a touching patriotism, which was reported to the First Consul by the prefect concerned:

> They invoked justice and loyalty to the present government. Women, children, and old people were with them and declared that one might shoot them but not force them to leave France again. 'Take us to the great Bonaparte and you will see that we are good citizens.'

Those émigrés excluded for treason from the amnesty law reassembled in England around the future Louis XVIII and his brother the Count of Artois, waiting patiently for the hour of restoration but not without continuing to intrigue, to plot, and even to carry arms against France. They had to wait another ten years for the law known as the "émigrés billion" to be reimbursed for their losses during the revolution.

Poorly drafted, the clause concerning the restoration of unsold "national property" encountered several inextricable difficulties in implementation. Bonaparte was forced to annul it. As a result, it accomplished nothing.

The essential point was that the virulent plague of emigration could be considered at an end. Many former émigrés rallied to the new institutions, served in the army at all levels of the hierarchy, and even frequented the corridors of power. Much like those who had been called the chouans.

The Reduction of the Chouannerie, or the Peace of the Brave

This operation was conducted in parallel with the restoration of exterior peace and with the pardon of the émigrés, because the three questions were interrelated.

Since 1792 France had been prey to a true civil war at the same time as a foreign war.

The first excesses of the Revolution clashed directly with the royalist and religious beliefs of the rural regions, where the nobility and the Catholic clergy exercised great influence, especially in the west of the country but also in the center and south. The opposition aroused by the fall of the Bastille on July 14, 1789, developed in parallel with the decline of the monarchy and the policy of de-Christianization.

On November 2, 1789, the property of the clergy had been "left at the disposition of the Nation," that is, nationalized. On February 13, 1790, a decree forbad lifetime monastic vows. July 12, 1790, produced the act most hostile to the Catholic Church: the passage of the Civil Constitution of the Clergy, which literally set the powder ablaze. Priests had to take an oath of fidelity to the constitution. A large number of them refused. Having become outlaws under sentence of death, some of them emigrated as we have seen, while others joined the armed struggle alongside the peasants who were revolted.

The inevitable papal condemnation of the Civil Constitution of the Clergy encouraged the rebellion. The Constituent Assembly replied by annexing Avignon, the papal city of the Middle Ages located inside southern France. The Legislative Assembly organized the hunt for "refractory priests" by two special decrees of November 29, 1791, and

May 27, 1792. The king vetoed these decrees on June 11, 1792. Between September 2 and 6 abominable massacres occurred in the prisons of Paris, killing for the most part former noblemen and clergymen. This was the bloodiest single act of the Revolution. Two weeks later, on September 20, the government instituted the secularization of civil marriage and divorce. The next day, the newly convened Convention abolished the monarchy. The condemnation of the king and his execution on January 21, 1793, further inflamed the conflict.

The armed insurrection of rural areas in the west is generally called the "Chouannerie," coming from the nickname of Jean Cottereau, known as Jean Chouan because of his perfect imitation of the cry of a barn owl (chouette), the rallying cry of the insurgents.

The Breton royalist conspiracy of La Rouerie marked the start of the revolt during the first quarter of 1792. In coming years the revolt spread to different areas, alternating violent moments with rare periods of calm. A true civil war brought thousands of peasants into conflict with the armies of the Republic in a war without mercy.

The Chouans failed before Granville on November 13, 1793. They were crushed at Mons in a street battle on December 12. In turn, they achieved several successes in horrible ambushes. The army of the Republic replied with the mournfully famous "infernal columns." The cruelty of these conflicts was indescribable. The Representative of the Republic, Carrier, distinguished himself in horror at Nantes. His terroristic excesses offended even his most extreme friends, who condemned him to death and executed him on November 23, 1794.

The insurgents suffered a severe defeat at Savenay on December 23, 1793. This was followed by a relatively calm period. Peace appeared to be at hand with the pacification action of La Jaunaye. An amnesty with freedom of belief was accorded to the Vendéens on February 17, 1795.

Unfortunately, the Chouannerie returned in full strength as a result of the Quiberon Bay Affair. Several thousand émigrés, transported and officered by the British, disembarked on the peninsula on July 15, 1795. General Hoche threw them back into the sea or dispersed them into the countryside, where the Chouans accepted them.

After defeating the royalists, Hoche pursued an effective campaign of pacification, combining firmness with religious appeasement. The insurgent leaders were captured and shot, Stofflet at Angers on February

25, 1796, and Charrette at Nantes on March 29, 1796. By the summer of 1796 the submission was almost complete.

The anti-royalist repression of 18 Fructidor revived the rebellion once again. The ineffectual Rochecotte accomplished interregional coordination of the Chouannerie. In August 1799 came the "war of principal towns" in the Vendée, Anjou, and Normandy. Chatillon took Nantes, Bourmont Le Mans, Mercier Saint Brieuc, and de Sol seized La Roche Bernard. Frotté went as far as the suburbs of Versailles. But these locations were lost quickly. The calm along the borders after the victories of Brune and Massena over the Second Coalition permitted the Directory to regain the initiative at home.

Putting an end to this civil war was obviously a priority for the First Consul.

He began by demonstrating his clemency in goodwill gestures. He abolished the revolutionary holiday commemorating the January 21 anniversary of the execution of Louis XVI. He also abolished the law of hostages, an abolition initiated by the Directory three months earlier, and ostentatiously traveled to the Temple Prison to liberate the detainees involved. He offered a general amnesty to the Chouans and promised to reconsider the question of the Civil Constitution of the Clergy.

Convinced, the Abbot Bernier, a priest of Anjou, summoned a number of meetings throughout the west and played a considerable role in peacemaking.

Yet, the pardon and other generosity were insufficient. Regrettably, the work of pacification had to be finished by reducing the remaining pockets of resistance through the efforts of Generals Brune, Gardanne, Chabot, and d'Arnaud. The First Consul recommended that they use great firmness along with "a great tolerance for priests." He knew that those priests held the solution to the problem.

Results came quickly. The entire area south of the Loire submitted. The capture of Bourmont led to the fall of Maine and the associated territory. That unusual person would again cause great difficulty at the time of Waterloo.

The death, in conditions resembling an assassination, of Frotté after a serious misunderstanding led to the surrender of Normandy.

A general treaty of peace could finally be signed. It was in effect a pact of honor, granting pardon to insurgents in return for surrendering their arms, although that agreement was implemented very liberally.

Even the indomitable Georges Cadoudal agreed to halt hostilities, although he refused to stack arms. Bonaparte received him twice at the Tuileries in the hope of gaining his full support. Despite generous offers, he obstinately maintained his opposition. As we have already seen, he moved from guerrilla to terrorist action.

In addition to Bourmont, a number of notable Chouans rallied to the new regime, including Generals de Piré and de Scépaux.

To finish with the subject of the Chouannerie, there were later several local, short-lived uprisings with de Bar, d'Aché, Arnaud de Chateaubriand and Louis de la Rochejaquelein. These actions were connected more to clandestine operations than to armed confrontations. Thereafter the Chouan spirit continued to manifest itself in electoral opposition.

After the peace of hearts and the peace of the brave, let us turn to the peace of souls.

The Concordat, or the Peace of the Souls

We have glossed over the unusual relationship of Napoleon with religion and especially with the critical action of the Concordat, which brought religious peace to the country and put an end to the bloody trauma of the Civil Constitution of the Clergy.

On Saint Helena, Napoleon confided extensively to Las Cases about his religious beliefs. Brought up in the Catholic faith, he never completely disavowed it. The first words of his testament were to affirm this fidelity of conscience. "I die in the same apostolic and Roman Catholic faith in which I was born."

If Napoleon refrained throughout his life from assiduous religious practices, this was not due to atheism, because he affirmed, "everyone on earth proclaims the existence of God." Rather, he was influenced by the debatable rationalism of some pre-revolutionary philosophers. Undoubtedly, he felt contempt for certain clergymen whose hypocritical conduct constituted a grave offense to the faith.

Facing the difficulties of his life and in metaphysical anguish, he conceded that, for an individual, "religious sentiment is such a consolation that it is a gift from heaven to possess . . . atheism is destructive of all morale, if not in individuals, then at least in nations."

As head of state, he considered religion from an angle more political than spiritual. "It [religion] is in my eyes the support of good morale, of true principles and of good morals." He always gave religion its place in society, but no more than that, and without favoritism to any one confession.

Napoleon's experience in Egypt only served to reinforce in him this justified political conception of religion. On balance, his apparent atheism served him when he had to arbitrate between religious factions. It was impossible to be both judge and party in such a dispute.

Upon his accession to power, the religious question continued to tear France apart. The violent convulsions provoked by the Civil Constitution of the Clergy persisted, as already discussed with regard to the Chouannerie. To reconcile the French on this burning question, the pernicious religious quarrel had to be ended as quickly as possible.

Obviously, this was not the first time that France had been torn apart by religious wars, such as the Lutheran schism of the sixteenth century. The conflict between the temporal power of the king and the spiritual power of the pope traces back to the Middle Ages. This phenomenon affected all the major kingdoms. In England it carried the name of Anglicanism, in France of Gallicanism. Before proceeding, it would be useful to recall briefly the tempestuous relations between France and the Holy See.

The antagonism between royalty and papacy underwent many fluctuations in the course of the centuries. The first notable manifestation of Gallicanism brought Philip the Fair into violent opposition with Pope Boniface VIII in 1303. The "iron king" put an end to the theocratic ambitions of Rome. The papacy even passed under the influence of the French king, who installed it at Avignon.

On the occasion of the Hundred Years' War, Roman influence regained the initiative. In 1438 the king and clergy of France accepted in the "Pragmatic Sanction of Bourges" the decisions of the Council of Basel. Cathedral chapters and convents regained the right to elect their bishops and abbots.

The Concordat of 1516 marked a new victory for Gallicanism. The king's nomination of candidates to major benefices became the legal institutions. The Council of Trent in 1563 constituted a return to the domination of papal authority. Beginning in 1635 Gallicanism regained its own identity under the influence of Cardinal Richelieu, who hoped to become "the Patriarch of the Gauls and of the West."

The sovereign authority of the kings of France over the national church was reestablished under Louis XIV, who violently opposed Rome with regard to the regalian rights. This was the "right of the King to control the revenues of a vacant Episcopal seat and to name holders of benefices and of prebends relating to that seat."

The general assembly of the French clergy in 1680 sided with the king. Reproaching Rome for its interference in the affairs of the French Church in violation of the Concordat of 1516, this assembly officially proclaimed the "Liberties of the Gallican Church," drafted by Bossuet. Temporal power over the church in France belonged to the king. The pontiff retained only the spiritual power. A rupture loomed. Thereafter, the Gallican opposition declined somewhat until the Revolution. The last transformation of Gallicanism, the Civil Constitution of the Clergy of 1790, completed the rupture with the papacy.

At the start of the year 1800, total anarchy reigned in the French Church. Certainly it was no longer subject to the Revolutionary Terror, but it was still in a pitiful state. Only forty-five dioceses survived of the previous 135. Priestly vocations were very rare. A number of priests who had refused to swear loyalty to the Civil Constitution of the Clergy had been guillotined. Traditional Catholics scorned the "juring" priests, those who had taken the oath and whom Rome did not recognize. As a whole, the population no longer knew to which saint it should pray, so to speak.

In attempting to square the circle, the First Consul had to resolve the problem by achieving a triple reconciliation: the clergy with itself, the French with their religion, and the whole with Rome.

Bonaparte immediately rejected the nationalistic temptation to declare himself head of an independent Gallican Church, in the manner of Henry VIII of England in 1534. He was not afflicted with any tendency for brutal historic ruptures, all the more so because that would be contrary to his convictions and did not correspond to the dominant mind set of the French, traditionally attached to the pope.

He desperately needed to reach a general accord with Pope Pius VII, but on condition that the pope accept, as the price of reintegrating the French Catholics into the Roman Church, a renunciation of all claims to French Church properties that had become national property, as well as the complete renewal of the French bishops. In fact, this last measure implied the right of the First Consul to nominate all bishops.

To obtain such enormous concessions from the pope, negotiations would be long, bitter, and sprinkled with multiple incidents that approached rupture, in a sort of liar's poker. In addition, it was not an easy matter to convince those who were nostalgic for the Revolution of the necessity of an official return to religion. Out-of-work generals proved to be the most difficult.

To prepare the ground, Bonaparte took several measures of toleration as soon as he came to power. All holy places had to be reopened to the faithful, regardless of their religious affiliation. He restored freedom of religion by the treaty of pacification with the Vendée. He reestablished refractory priests in their functions, which provoked some friction with the Constitutional or juring priests. He also encouraged the abandonment of the tenth day cult of the Revolutionary religion in favor of the "Catholic cult." As a spectacular proof of his favorable disposition toward Rome, on January 18, 1800, he issued a decree to render military honors to the mortal remains of Pius VI, prisoner of the Directory at Valence.

Talleyrand authorized the Spanish ambassador, Labrador, to make the first overtures to Pius VII, newly elected pope. Yet, soon thereafter the war in Italy gave the First Consul an opportunity to make the contact himself.

The victory of Marengo reinforced Napoleon's authority over the atheists of Paris and placed military pressure on the Roman court. He had the opportunity to use initiative and surprise, two factors of success in politics as well as in warfare.

At Milan, the victory gave rise to a grandiose Te Deum in the Cathedral dome. All the clergy welcomed the victor upon his entry and conducted him in state to the place of honor.

At the reception of Italian priests that followed, Bonaparte spoke to them in very encouraging terms, unmistakably directed at the papal authority: "No society may exist without morals, and there are no good morals without religion. Religion must therefore provide firm and durable support to the state. A society without religion is like a ship without a compass. . . ." The message could not have been clearer.

On the road back to France, Napoleon halted at Verceil, where he had arranged a meeting with Cardinal Martiniani, who had access to the Holy

See. Knowing that he was communicating directly with the pope, Bonaparte initiated the subject of restoring Catholicism in France under the spiritual authority of Saint Peter, but also under the general conditions described above. For his part, he promised to use his power to reestablish the pope's compromised sovereignty in the Papal States.

Upon his return to Paris, the First Consul noted the first signs of internal opposition, which he had to overcome. He focused on this on August 1, 1800, before the Council of State:

> My policy is to govern men in the manner that the majority wish to be ruled. This is a means to recognize the sovereignty of the people. When I won the battle of the Vendée I was Catholic; when I took over in Egypt I was Muslim; and when I succeeded in Italy I was ultramontaine. If I governed the Jewish people, I would reestablish the Temple of Solomon.

These lines contained Napoleon's entire political philosophy. Henry IV said the same thing with his remark that "Paris is worth a mass."

A pope full of benevolence, carried more by the spiritual than by the temporal, Pius VII did not receive Bonaparte's propositions positively but instead equivocated for a long time. He had difficulty reconciling spiritual concessions in exchange for guarantees of his temporal power. In the end, however, he resigned himself to negotiating, and even accepted the choice of location for negotiations as Paris rather than Rome.

The papal negotiator, Monsignor Spina, did not reach Paris until November 6, 1800. To represent himself, the First Consul selected the Abbot Bernier, a subtle diplomat skilled in double-dealing, but very competent in the issue, having just rendered eminent services in the Vendéen question. To avoid offending the pope's sensibilities, Bernier was chosen over Talleyrand, a defrocked priest living in concubinage.

Complicated by the intrigues of Talleyrand and Fouché, the negotiations dragged on. Spina was not decisive. A diplomat of quality, Francois Cacault, was sent to the Holy See with a directive to gain the pope's signature in five days. When the pope refused to sign, the skillful Cacault persuaded him to send to Paris a proxy agent in the person of Cardinal Consalvi, received on June 22 with the greatest consideration possible.

Consalvi proved to be as difficult as Spina. Joseph Bonaparte therefore took over the negotiations, assisted by Bernier.

On July 14, 1801, the First Consul brusquely rejected a draft accord that contained too many concessions on the part of France. He therefore hurried matters to a conclusion. That same evening, he publicly addressed Consalvi at an official dinner given at the Tuileries:

> Well, Cardinal, you want negotiations to fail! Very well. I have no further need of the pope. If Henry VIII, who lacked even one-twentieth of my power, succeeded in changing the religion of his country, imagine how much more I could do. In changing the religion in France I would change it in almost all of Europe. Rome would then see the losses it suffered. It might weep, but it would have no remedy. You may leave, because that is what we will do instead. You wanted a rupture, well, then, have it your way.

Those present were shocked. Various people, notably the Austrian ambassador Cobenzl, urged Bonaparte to give negotiations one more chance. He consented, but in the form of an ultimatum: "I agree that the commissioners will meet for the last time. If they fail to reach a conclusion, we will regard the rupture as definitive, and the cardinal may depart."

This threat of a Gallican schism acted like magic to speed negotiations. The Concordat was finished on the night of July 15-16, 1801. France became again the eldest daughter of the church.

In front of a frustrated Council of State, the First Consul made only one simple comment: "The Concordat is not the triumph of any one party but the consolidation of all parties."

Without entering into details, the principal clauses of the Concordat constituted a reasonable compromise between the rights of the church, the ideas of the Revolution, and the Gallicanism of the Ancien Régime. The Catholic religion was no longer the official religion of the state but simply "the religion of the majority of Frenchmen." Bishops and priests were to be named by the government, after which the pope would grant investiture. The clergy would obey the pope's directives, but also must take an oath to the government that paid it. There would be no revision of the sale of church property. If nothing else, with the Concordat Bonaparte established the basis of laicism, a principle of all modern society.

After obtaining the approval of the College of Cardinals, the pope signed the treaty in Rome on August 15. The First Consul signed on September 8.

To render the treaty applicable as well to the two Protestant denominations, in the ensuing days it was complemented by organic articles, included in the implementing decrees. The pope was offended because this reinforced the Gallican aspect of the accord, but he did not protest.

This history of the Concordat would make a grave omission if it did not consider the Jewish question as well. Everywhere in Europe, Jews were considered pariahs, subjected to a degrading system of apartheid in the ghettos. In France, the Revolution had slightly reduced the severity of their discriminatory treatment. During the first war in Italy, however, Bonaparte truly became aware of their distress and of the need to restore their dignity. Within the limits of his power, he tried to improve their local conditions.

It is little known that, at Saint Jean d'Acre in April 1799, Bonaparte came close to creating a Jewish state in Palestine, 150 years before the foundation of the state of Israel. Only the lack of military success prevented him from implementing this plan that perhaps would have changed the face of the world.

During the Concordat negotiations, Napoleon attempted to extend to Judaism the beneficial measures of toleration and to reconcile it with the Christian religions. He encountered an insurmountable hostility both in France and abroad, however, and therefore had to delay what he considered to be the crowning achievement of his work of religious and social justice.

Once his imperial authority was asserted, in July 1806 Napoleon felt able to summon to Paris an assembly of Jews, including some of the most distinguished in France, to develop measures to assist their community.

With great solemnity, on February 9, 1807, Bonaparte brought together in Paris the Great Sanhedrin, supreme religious authority of the Hebrew people. This organization had governed Israel from 170 B.C. to A.D. 70. Since then, it had never again been assembled. Napoleon had to overcome a fierce national and international opposition, notably by the tsar of Russia and the Orthodox Church. As a sort of Jewish Concordat, the resolution of the Great Sanhedrin of 1807 made Judaism into the third official faith of France. These resolutions still constitute the foundation of French Judaism.

Unfortunately, Napoleon was forced, after Tilsit, to restrain the liberties accorded to the Jews because of the requirements of foreign and domestic politics. However, over the next several years he progressively reestablished those rights in their entirety. In 1811 Judaism was recognized as one of the three religions of France. Throughout the empire, all the Jews benefited equally from liberties granted to their French coreligionists.

Napoleon's policy of tolerance with regard to the Jews only increased the malignant hostility of Rome and the Catholic Church, with fatal political consequences. As we will see later, this opposition took a violent turn in Spain. Given Napoleon's label as "antichrist," the local clergy, who were as fanatical as they were unenlightened, preached a ghastly holy war against him.

As the first head of state to achieve a policy of integration for the Jews, Napoleon paid an exorbitant price. After his fall, the Jews returned to their humiliating conditions of life. They did not regain their rights in France until 1830, and until much later elsewhere in Europe.

Let us return to the Concordat. After its signing, the treaty still needed to be approved by the legislative chambers in order to be ratified. The opposition was in the majority at the Corps Legislatif. Bonaparte had to wait until some of the members were replaced before he could present the package of texts in the form of a Law of Religions, called the Law of Germinal of the Year X. Brilliantly presented by Portalis, the bill was adopted on April 8, 1802, by a crushing majority of 228 to 21.

As a gesture of his gratitude to the church, the First Consul decided to place under French protection the Holy Sepulcher in Jerusalem, the churches in Constantinople, and all the Christians in Syria. He signified his gratitude to Pius VII by the dispatch of two ships, the "Colibri" and the "Speedy," rechristened as "Saint Peter" and "Saint Paul."

Napoleon chose the symbolic date of Passover, feast of the resurrection of Christ, on April 18, 1802, to celebrate the promulgation of the Concordat. A grand Te Deum occurred in Notre Dame Cathedral in a great liturgical show. For the first time in ten years, amid great emotion Parisians heard the bell of Notre Dame. Moreover, by a happy coincidence, that same day they celebrated the Treaty of Amiens.

This April 18, 1802, counted among the most significant dates in the history of France. The peace of arms, the peace of hearts, the peace of the brave, and the peace of spirits reigned together in the country after a bloody eclipse of thirteen years.

But in this sky that had become so bright, one cloud troubled Bonaparte's joy. In his eager attempts to please the faithful, those who were known as the country's elite provided more passive resistance than the papacy itself. The higher military leaders described the Concordat as "monkish." The situation exhibited a disquieting political myopia, at least insofar as people placing their personal interests before the public interest.

Few political officials recognized at the time the importance of the Concordat, a sort of new Edict of Nantes. It did not, however, escape Talleyrand's notice. He later described it very favorably, contrary to his customary cynical viewpoint. "When in 1802 Napoleon reestablished religion in France, it was an act not simply of justice but of great vision. The Napoleon of the Concordat was the truly great Napoleon, guided by his genius." Later, several other lucid observers did not hesitate to describe the Concordat as a political monument and a diplomatic masterstroke.

In sum, by a religious toleration unprecedented in a head of state, Napoleon had courageously introduced religious freedom in France, ushering the country into cultural modernity. He surely did not realize that one day he would pay a high price for this.

Yet, France—finally calmed by the intelligent and generous action of Bonaparte—remained an orphan from its past, in the still-smoking ruins of the Revolution. An immense reconstruction process awaited the First Consul.

The Architect of Modern France

"I formed and implemented a law code that will cause my name to be passed to the most distant posterity."

—Memorial of Saint Helena

Napoleon is almost universally praised for the great work of reconstructing France. His quotation above refers to what many historians believe was his greatest accomplishment, namely the unified system of law that eventually became known as the Code Napoléon. Napoleon's reforms and improvements went far beyond the legal system and touched virtually all aspects of society. We will look at some of the most important of these reforms.

For the sake of clarity, this description will be organized according to function: General Administration, Law and Justice, Learning and Culture, Economy and Finances, Public Works, and Society. The essential work of reorganizing the country took place during the four years of the Consulate, from 1800 to 1804. Still, to discuss the subject completely, we will include the later work of the Empire.

General Administration

"I want to cast several granite blocks on the soil of France"

—Bonaparte, First Consul

At the moment that the Revolution exploded, Capetian France had not yet attained perfect unity. The troubles that followed revealed latent centrifugal forces, pulling the country to the brink of dissolution. The revolt of the Vendée constituted the most bloody and dangerous manifestation of these forces.

Immediately after Brumaire, the most urgent task was therefore to reinforce the unity of the country by administrative centralization. Yet, effectiveness demanded that administration be located as closely as possible to the citizenry. Thus, government had to be dispersed down to the village level. These two principles, centralization and dispersal, inspired the fundamental law of administration of the country passed in Pluviose, Year VIII (February 1800). No time had been wasted!

Locally elected representatives, too often tending to pointless chattering and inclined to demagoguery and favoritism, were relegated to the warehouse of accessories of the Revolution. The Departmental prefect became the privileged, all-powerful representative of the government in Paris, invested locally with all the government's authority and serving under the direct orders of the Minister of the Interior. Under his tutelage were the subordinate echelons, boroughs and villages, for which the mayors were appointed. The prefect took advice from a borough council, composed of prominent persons chosen by him from a list of such notables.

Short of decentralizing jurisdictions, which was inconceivable in the circumstances of the time, these dispositions contrived nothing less than an administration of proximity corresponding to the real needs of the population. The citizens were directly associated with their administration.

There was nothing of a military dictatorship, with which people tend to reproach Napoleon. On the contrary, he took great care to subordinate the army to civil authority, which earned him the description of being "the most civilian of soldiers."

Napoleon has also been criticized for putting the various branches of the state into uniform. But this he did essentially to increase their authority and prestige, and not at all to militarize them. All the corps wanted the uniforms. Originally omitted from this measure, the Institute agitated frantically to obtain the superb dress uniform that it still retains. Moreover, Napoleon did nothing more than follow an old tradition, and no one since him has renounced it.

Law and Justice

"My glory is not to have won forty battles. What will never disappear,
what will live eternally, is my Civil Code and the records
of the Council of State."

—Memorial of Saint Helena

The great master of this gigantic construction project was the
Council of State, created by Article 52 of the new constitution. It was
composed of jurists hand-picked not for their political beliefs but for their
legal abilities. The council's function was to draft the laws and codes
before presenting them to the parliamentary assemblies.

The cardinal work of the Council of State was the Civil Code. From
the formation of the council, the First Consul had instituted a special
commission that absorbed all his attention. He appointed Jean Jacques de
Cambacéres, peerless jurist, as the president of this commission, assisted
by other eminent legal authorities, including Roederer, Portalis, Bigot,
and de Préameneu.

Bonaparte participated assiduously in the discussions, and surprised
more than one by his knowledge and especially his common sense. The
former minister of Louis XVI, de Molleville, of whom Bonaparte had
asked a complex question, could not help exclaiming one day, "But
where the devil did he learn all that?"

The First Consul presided over fifty-seven of the 102 meetings
devoted to the Civil Code. Although cloaked in a certain solemnity, the
debates occurred in complete freedom of expression. Neither Royalists
nor Jacobins were prevented from speaking, and Bonaparte listened to
everyone with patience. On more than one occasion, he changed his point
of view in the face of a convincing argument to the contrary. The Count
de Plancy has left a testimony of the tolerant spirit that presided over the
work of the Council of State:

> Because the First Consul always presided over the Council of State,
> some people have attempted to infer that that assembly was
> submissive, and obeyed him in all things. I can affirm to the
> contrary that the best informed men in France, in all the specialties
> which composed the Council, deliberated in complete freedom, and

that nothing every hampered their discussions. Bonaparte was
much more interested in their ideas than in their political opinions.

All of which is perfectly true.

After four years of unremitting labor, annoyed and impeded by a
rarely constructive opposition from one part of the legislature, the Civil
Code was finally promulgated on March 2, 1804. It consisted of thirty-six
laws totaling 2,281 articles. The dispositions it established in essence
continue to regulate the lives of Frenchmen in our time. In 1807 these
laws were renamed the Napoleonic Code.

In the intervening years, the country has used and discarded many
constitutions, but the Civil Code remains. By longevity, it represents the
truly "granite" constitution of the French people.

This monument in law represented a magisterial judicial synthesis,
first between the Ancien Régime and the Revolution, and next between
the different customary rights of the various regions of the country,
melded in the same unifying crucible. There again, Napoleon continued
the history of France.

Family and property are at the center of the Civil Code. After having
denounced the administrative "Jacobinism" of Napoleon, the waiting
ideologues have confused time periods and found in the Civil Code a sort
of charter of the middle class. We will not become involved in this inept
argument, leaving the perennial nature of the Civil Code to reply to such
criticism.

Under the empire, other more limited codes followed the Civil Code:
Codes of Civil Procedure in 1806, of Commerce in 1807, of Criminal
Instruction in 1808, plus the Penal Code in 1810 and the Rural Code in
1814. These individual codes reflected a complete and total reform of
judicial organization. From the installation of Justices of the Peace to the
Supreme Court of Appeals, passing by way of the statutes of the Notary
Publics and the creation of Wise Men, an entire chain of new judiciary,
both civil and penal, saw the light of day.

Then again, the objective was to bring justice close to those under its
jurisdiction and to adapt it to the evolution of society and government at
the time.

The coincidence of administration and judicial jurisdictions was
maintained. However, because it was important for justice to become
independent, the judicial power was confided to magistrates appointed

for life, and no longer subject to election, except for justices of the peace until 1802.

In order to deal with new requirements, special tribunals could be instituted, destined notably to reestablish public order on the roads or in the countryside.

At the summit of the state, the Council of State, a sort of legal Janus, constituted the supreme court of administration, responsible simultaneously to draft the laws, ensure their application, and arbitrate as a last resort for administrative conflicts.

Learning and Culture

The reform of instruction was as broad and deep as the other changes. It was the subject of the Law of 11 Floreal, Year X (May 1, 1802).

Within this legislative framework, the creation of high schools constituted the cornerstone of the educational edifice. The new France, still convalescing from the revolutionary convulsion, needed to reconstitute its cadres and to mold them to meet the responsibilities of the new regime. The high schools were to be the crucible, thanks to an instruction without demagoguery, based on morals, discipline, civics, and merit.

Critics do not wish to see in the institution of the high schools anything except a desire to structure the population. To what absurd lengths will this obsession to condemn extend?

To facilitate access to high schools by the most modest strata of the population, numerous scholarships were offered to the most deserving students of primary schools. In a spirit of liberty, religious congregations retained their right to teach in primary schools and private secondary schools, but only in conformity with the official programs of public instruction.

Replacing the decrepit structures of the Ancien Régime, the Law of 11 Floreal Year X (May 1, 1802) founded the Special Military School, a new institute to prepare officers, with the perennial and fierce motto "They study to conquer." Established first at Fontainebleau, the school moved to Saint-Cyr in 1808. After the Second World War, it was to move to Coetquidan in Brittany. But the officers who graduate from the Special Military School still carry the prestigious designation of "Saint Cyrian."

The Foundation of the University by the Law of May 10, 1806, completed by the decree of March 17, 1808, represented the crowning achievement of the educational edifice. It took under its unifying control all the public schools, the secondary colleges, the high schools, and the faculties of the Ecolé Normale, nursery of teachers. The competitive teaching examination was reestablished in 1808.

In short, the system instituted the freedom of instruction with secularism. The proof of its soundness is that we continue today to live essentially under the same system, though obviously modified because of the evolution of society.

To demonstrate his interest in culture, the indispensable complement to instruction, Bonaparte saw to the erection of statues of illustrious men and the construction of historical monuments, such as the columns of the Chatelet and of the Place Vendome, as well as the Arches of Triumph of the Carrousel and of the Star, completed after him.

The arts were not forgotten. They were promoted by the establishment of the Musée Napoleon, which eventually became the incomparable Louvre Museum.

Even while on campaign, culture remained on the mind of the emperor. Do you know how he entertained his astonished companions in the course of a frugal meal on the eve of Austerlitz? Literature. Also, he signed the decree creating the Comedie-Francaise at Moscow on October 15, 1812, on the eve of the catastrophic retreat from Russia.

Economy and Finances

The metamorphosis of France under the Consulate and Empire was equally spectacular in the domain of economy and finances. The country attained an unprecedented prosperity despite the war. The great originality of the period was to make the economy an instrument of war by the installation of a continental blockade to force Britain to the peace table. In these conditions, the economy could not be directed in this manner without discouraging the process of free trade.

The economic and financial structures were suffocated by the creation of the Bank of France, the Stock Exchange, the Court of Accounts, the Treasury, the Direction of Imports, the General Direction of Customs, the Chambers of Commerce, the Land Registry, the Statistics Office, and the General Council of Agriculture and Commerce.

Financial policy was based on a strict ceiling for the public debt, a wise limitation on borrowing, and the systematic stimulation of all economic activity. The creation of the Franc of Germinal was an incontestable success.

Fiscal reform was again dedicated to a change in the midst of continuity. Direct taxes were reduced, alleviating the burden on farmers and industrial workers. In compensation, indirect taxes increased, the sign of a modern economy.

In this work of rehabilitating the public finances, one must render homage to two remarkable ministers in succession: Gaudin and Mollien.

Agriculture remained the foundation of the French economy and the constant object of solicitude of the head of state. It experienced a phenomenal development, favored by the acquisition of national properties.

From a subsistence agricultural economy, France shifted to a market agricultural economy. Fallow ground diminished, while cultivated surfaces and animal husbandry increased considerably. Lesser cereal crops gave way to wheat. New crops were introduced: vines, woad, and especially sugar beets, which were planted on up to 100,000 hectares.

Horse, beef, and sheep breeding also progressed in a spectacular manner in relationship with the extension of planting. To encourage merino sheep, prized for their wool, imperial sheepfolds appeared. All the animal breeds were improved by crossbreeding. Horse races were initiated to improve the horse breeds.

Manufacturing activity experienced an enormous progress, a prelude to the industrial revolution, as France began to make up its deficiencies with the rival Britain. By 1809, French industry had increased production by fifty percent in comparison to 1800.

France entered all the European markets, the continental blockade providing a major encouragement for all of its manufacturers and their products. Among these, textiles, notably cotton, took the lion's share. In Alsace, Flanders, and Normandy, workshops sprang up for spinning, weaving, and printing cotton. Textile production grew at an exponential rate. Enjoying a strong reputation, French furnishings followed the same growth pattern.

The former annual exposition of industrial products was revived in the courtyard of the Louvre. Sevres porcelain, Conté's crayon, glazed fabrics of Deharme and Duhaux, colored paper by Jacquemart and Benard, the cotton thread of Bauwens, etc.

Obviously, commerce could only profit from the development of agriculture and industry and, in addition, from the continental blockade, which closed markets to British products.

Paradoxically, trade grew the most with the United States, representing fourteen percent of imports and only six percent of exports. This imbalance was due to the facts that the United States was outside the blockade zone and above all that the majority of imports were tropical and other exotic products.

The visible growth in exports of agricultural and especially industrial products (more than twenty percent) helped visibly reduce the imbalance in French commercial trade, always hampered by heavy yet indispensable imports of raw materials and tropical commodities.

On balance, France's economic position improved in a spectacular fashion in Europe at the same time that promising commercial relations were opened with the United States.

Public Works

In support of economic development, an immense program of public works was executed. Bonaparte (as he was known during the Consulate) and then Napoleon (as he was known during the Empire) personally invested in them, not neglecting the countries attached to the Empire. Paris benefited from a special effort.

The development of lines of communication, a necessity of economic growth, took priority. Existing routes were improved and new ones built to open France to communication with the surrounding countries: routes from Bordeaux to Bayonne, from Mainz to Metz, from Amiens to Amsterdam; passes to Simplon, Montcenis, Montgenevre, and to the Mediterranean cliffs. Without counting those in Paris, numerous bridges were built almost everywhere: at Tours, Roanne, Lyons, Bordeaux, Rouen, on the Isere and Durance Rivers, but also at Turin, etc .

Canals were a matter of special attention. The idea was to develop them sufficiently to free France from the oceans, where the British fleet ruled: thus, for example, the canal that connected the Rhine to the Rhone by way of Doubs, thereby connected the Mediterranean to the North Sea, or the canal that connected Holland to the Baltic by way of the Weser, the Ems, and the Elbe. Two other projects were designed in Italy, one joining Venice to Genoa by the Po River, the other Sagone to Alexandria across the Apennines. In France itself, two important canals were dug, that of Arles and that which connects Nantes to Brest. The draining of the Pontins Marsh was also planned.

The ports were not neglected, notably those opposite Great Britain, including Amiens, Flessingue, Terneuzen on the North Sea and especially Cherbourg on the channel, which in Napoleon's mind was of primordial strategic importance.

The restoration of chateaux, palaces, and other buildings of the country was not ignored, notably at Fontainebleau, which the emperor preferred to Versailles, a structure too nonfunctional and gaudy for his taste.

We have saved the public works of the capital for last. Napoleon's ambition was to make Paris into the first capital of the universe, starting with a semi-medieval, stifling city. New arteries that were wide and airy, bordered by handsome buildings with high roofs, stone facades, supplemented by pleasant arcades, replaced the old, narrow streets with buildings that were too tall. The connection between the two banks of the Seine was improved by the construction of the footbridge of the arts and the bridges of Austerlitz, Jena, and the city, later demolished.

Concerning comfort, considerable progress was achieved: the installation of sewers and fountains, framing of palaces, markets, quays, and hills, without mentioning the public cemeteries instituted by Napoleon. With the addition of sidewalks and curbs, the streets received a numerical designation in 1805, at the same time as public lighting.

When considering Napoleon's record on public works, it can be said that never has so much been done in so short a time.

Society

The French Society of the Consulate and Empire no longer bore much resemblance to that of 1789. The gigantic split of the Revolution was naturally reflected in the fratricidal divisions that Napoleon valiantly attempted to overcome. For him, there were no longer good and bad Frenchmen. There were only citizens of a recast nation whom he wished to make one and indivisible.

One of the great unifying acts of the Consulate was the creation of the Legion of Honor on May 19, 1802 (29 Floreal, Year X in the Revolutionary Calendar). In origin, it was simply a "corps," to avoid imitating the Order of Saint Louis. Later reorganized into structures and grades, it became the National Order of the Legion of Honor that we know today. Its unifying symbolism resided in its universal character. It rewarded merit, whether military or civil, without distinction as to social class.

The First Consul had to make a significant effort to impose this order. The legislature wanted nothing to do with this "rattle." The aristocracy made ironic comments about this "knightly order of the Revolution." The military hierarchy opposed mixing military glory with civil merit, as well as sharing the decoration with the enlisted men.

Two centuries later, the institution of the Legion of Honor is going better than ever, and no one doubts its permanence. Frenchmen dream of adding that red rosette to their lapels. Nonetheless, one may deplore some abuses as to who receives the award.

The nobility of the Ancien Régime had not disappeared, and Napoleon made an effort to perpetuate that nobility. These great names belonged to the history of France, which Napoleon wished to continue. The reconstructed France could not afford to deprive itself of anyone's skills or talents. This was the meaning of the hand generously extended to the émigrés, overcoming a dangerous "Republican" opposition. A minority of aristocrats rallied to the new regime and served their country loyally in the new administration or under arms. To encourage this movement, in September 1806 Napoleon created the "Guards of Honor," a military institution opened to "those who have been estranged from their country by the circumstances of the Revolution."

On the other extreme, another tiny minority of noblemen, distressed by the disappearance of the Ancien Régime and its privileges, threw themselves into the criminal monarchist traditionalism of which we already have spoken so sadly. The great majority of noblemen remained in a sterile mode of "wait and see," focusing on the perspective of a restoration of the Bourbons. They therefore avoided any cooperation that might appear to legitimize the Consulate or the Empire. Napoleon tolerated this irritating neutrality.

It was a shortsighted calculation. As the old adage states, "The gods render blind those whom they have decided to destroy." In refusing to accept the parliamentary monarchy of the Empire as a replacement to the former absolute monarchy, the nobles were betting "double or nothing." Soon they would have an illusion of having won this gamble, an illusion that to them probably survived for some years. In fact, they had sacrificed the parliamentary monarchy about which their grandchildren could only dream.

A new nobility, founded on bravery and merit, would emerge from the Revolutionary wars and the advent of the new France. Its members came from all strata of society. Every soldier did indeed carry a marshal's baton in his knapsack.

Once the Empire had replaced the Consulate and the political regime of France became a parliamentary monarchy, the new monarchy needed to become official by founding its own nobility. On March 1, 1808, the Imperial nobility was officially created. Napoleon's objective was not simply to reward his best companions, but also to attach to the regime the great notables and even the pre-1789 nobility, those who were referred to by the label "former." It must be emphasized that the new nobility was deprived of all privileges, contrary to the old. Despite all his efforts, Napoleon never succeeded in reconciling the two nobilities. In effect, they could never see the benefit of such reconciliation.

Over time, the Empire named forty-two princes and dukes, some five hundred counts, 1,550 barons, and 1,500 knights. If the purpose was to tie these men to the emperor, many of them did not stand the test. The exhaustion of a war without end, an unavoidable tendency to become middle class in their outlook, and above all the political speculations about the future caused a large number of the Imperial nobility to drift away. Some ended by openly betraying Napoleon as well as their country.

Between these two nobilities, the two highest categories of French society, a new elite established itself and flourished, fed by economic development. Named the bourgeoisie, its sometimes-ostentatious opulence and its somewhat egotistical conduct attracted the hostility of the poor and the intellectuals alike. Marxist ideologues have tried to make this group the scapegoat for the evils of the world. Over time, the very term "bourgeoisie" has taken on a pejorative connotation. Thus, we prefer to use the term "middle class" to denote them.

The existence of a middle class in a society brings with it a certain balance as well as vitality. This class is the mark of a society's development. The France of the Consulate and Empire entered into the then-restricted circle of developed countries. To seek one's fortune is only undesirable if the society draws no benefit from that search. In a letter to Roederer, Napoleon distinguished between the sterile wealth coming from landed property and the active wealth of work: "A wealthy person is often a lazybones with no value. I want the wealthy as a means of ensuring the existence of the poor." By this, he intended to say that only the rich have the power to create employment for the poor. To penalize the rich based on ideology is thus an indirect blow against the poor. This idea has also been expressed by the eloquent metaphor: "To make the fat people thin is to kill the thin ones!" These considerations are addressed to the self-appointed moralists who, thinking to strike a low blow against Napoleon, have reproached him for favoring the "contemptible bourgeoisie."

The new French middle class included another branch, dedicated not to business but to the service of the state: the functionaries generated by the new institutions.

These two social categories supported the regime for different reasons. The businessmen were grateful to it for a return to order and for an economic climate favorable for business. The functionaries could expect to rise socially only through merit. Their zeal is thus theoretically assured. Yet, loyalty is like all other human emotions: it is inclined to opportunism.

We should not be surprised by the existence of an intellectual caste that sought to strongly influence public thought. If a simple demonstration of Napoleon's interest was sufficient to encourage artists, he had to use extreme aggressiveness to motivate many writers, whom he sometimes called "scribblers" or "advocates." Often lacking in talent, with the clear exception of Chateaubriand, these men wanted to impose their mental dictatorship on everyone. They thus invented the modern concept, if not the name, of "political correctness," which is with us today.

Napoleon always found the most generous of compensations in the unswerving fidelity of the French people, with whom he had contracted a sort of sacred pact. His infallible instinct was only dimly visible to the people, whose happiness was Napoleon's primary objective. Thus, they gave him an unconditional and solid attachment that inspired in him the highest ambition and gave him a formidable energy to follow that ambition. For his part, Napoleon loved the people as his sovereign. He only considered himself as their incarnation. Could he have achieved a higher form of true democracy? If you do not take into consideration this blended relationship between a people and its representative, you will completely misunderstand the history of Napoleon.

The invaluable progress just described only increased hostility toward the new France. From now on, above all it was important not to risk the results of this progress in the hazards of war.

The Obsession with Peace

What was the state of Napoleon's spirit at this stage in his career? Can one seriously accuse him of intending military conquest, he who had single-handedly accomplished the miracle of reestablishing general peace in Europe? He would had to have been insane to expose these achievements to the hazards of war! He was in any case so preoccupied, day and night, with his work of internal rebuilding that he had no time to spare for other things.

In reality, two nagging and complementary preoccupations occupied all his consciousness: the constant pursuit of reconstruction for France and the preservation of the country from the heavy threats imposed on her by the fatal belligerent situation that held her prisoner. If he had shown himself to be slightly naïve in signing the Treaty of Amiens, a year later Bonaparte had no more illusions concerning the hateful hostility of the European monarchies.

The principle of preventing war thus became the unchanging foundation of French foreign policy until 1815. Napoleon worked at this with an obstinacy that approached a mental fixation.

The Remorseless Race for Defensive Alliances

What could be more natural to avoid conflict than to assemble a major group of allies or at least neutrals? French diplomacy had never been as active as it was under the Consulate and Empire. There had never been so many negotiations as in this period, when France knew only four ministers of foreign affairs in sixteen years: Talleyrand (1799-1807), Champagny (1807-1811), Maret (1811-1813), and Caulaincourt (until 1815).

There had never been so many alliances, negotiations, and mutual agreements based on fluctuations in the general situation and the evolving balance of forces. An implacable diplomatic war prepared and accompanied the military campaigns and the economic war.

Napoleon's diplomatic strategy followed the same principle that ruled his military strategy: prevent the assembly of multiple enemies of France into warlike coalitions. The weaker the coalitions, the easier they would be to disperse.

The bitter diplomatic competition that occurred between 1803 and 1815 may be divided into three matches:

— 1803-1807: The first match against Britain
— 1807-1812: The diplomatic apogee of the Empire
— 1813-1815: The tragic isolation of France.

1803-1807: Britain Wins the First Match

The year 1803 was that in which danger became evident, after Britain had given the first signs of its unwillingness concerning the implementation of the Treaty of Amiens. On February 25 it openly declared its intention to retain Malta, in violation of a clause in the treaty.

The sale of Louisiana to the United States of America prepared an alliance with that state of such promising future.

On June 1 Bonaparte received an Austrian diplomat related to Chancellor Cobenzl and made overtures to him. On July 23 it was Prussia's turn. Bonaparte proposed a Franco-Prussian alliance to the private secretary of the King of Prussia, Lombard, whom he met in

Brussels. Coveting Hanover but fearing the displeasure of Britain, the Prussian king Frederick William III began a long dance of hesitation.

A defensive alliance in good and due form was signed with Sweden on September 27.

On October 19 France obtained the benevolent neutrality of Spain, which engaged through the voice of Godoy to provide France with financial aid in its struggle against Britain.

On December 19 the neutrality of Portugal, over which Britain exercised a preponderant influence, was obtained.

While 1804 witnessed domestic good fortune with the inauguration of the Empire, storms were gathering abroad. On March 24 Frederick William tilted toward the tsar of Russia, Alexander I, who promised him an alliance if the French army crossed the Weser River. On September 3 Napoleon exchanged with Cobenzl at Aachen the mutual recognition of the French and Austrian empires, an action taken very badly by the other European monarchies.

Matters worsened on October 3 with the break in diplomatic relations with Russia, while Spain, struggling with Britain over encroachments on its colonies, declared war on December 3.

Marked by the return of hostilities in Europe, the year 1805 witnessed an acceleration in the drive of the belligerents to develop alliances. On January 4 France and Spain signed a naval convention unifying their two fleets under French command. But Britain succeeded in forming the Third Coalition. On April 11 it signed with Russia the Convention of Saint Petersburg, which Austria joined on August 9. The accord fixed the objective of the Coalition as returning France to its 1789 boundaries and imposing upon it a government of the Coalition's choice. This alliance signified the rejection of the natural frontiers, which guaranteed French security, and was an intolerable interference in French domestic affairs.

France nonetheless succeeded in blocking the indecisive Frederick William from joining the Coalition. Prussia declared itself neutral but held itself ready to enter the war by a hypocritical "armed mediation," signed with Russia on November 3.

In southern Germany, by contrast, France was more successful. Bavaria declared itself in alliance with France on August 25, followed by Württemberg and Baden on October 3.

In Italy, the French negotiators obtained the neutrality of the hostile kingdom of Naples until November 19, on which date it inconveniently joined the Third Coalition, an act that was to cost it dearly.

Yet, nothing stimulates diplomacy like a good military victory. On the morrow of Austerlitz when Prussia had failed to fight, its diplomatic chief Haugwitz signed at Schonbrunn a short-lived treaty of alliance with France, an action that was poorly received by the court in Berlin.

The situation in 1806 showed a promising period of good weather, unfortunately of short duration. At Paris on February 15 the Franco-Prussian Treaty of Schonbrunn was revised at the request of Frederick William. The unreasonable demands made by the evasive Prussians rebounded upon them. Ratified on February 23, the new pact obligated Prussia to close its ports to Great Britain and to break relations with London. All that remained was for the Prussian court to launch its foolish war that ended in October with the disaster of Jena-Auerstadt.

In regards to Britain, matters had never been so favorable. The prime minister, that inveterate Francophobe Pitt, died on January 23, according to some as a collateral victim of Austerlitz. Fox, the new occupant of the Foreign Office, displayed a more favorable disposition. On March 2 Napoleon seized this opportunity to send peace overtures to London, where they were well received. Lord Yarmouth arrived for official negotiations on June 14. Peace between France and Britain has never been so close, but unfortunately Fox died on September 13 and all hopes disappeared with his successor.

The same phenomenon occurred with Russia. Negotiations began on July 6. Baron Oubril, the plenipotentiary of the tsar, came to Paris to regulate the matter of Cattaro or Kotor, an Austrian territory ceded to France by the Treaty of Pressburg on December 26, 1805, but still occupied by Russia. Favored by the good will of the two parties, negotiations soon exceeded the limits of Cattaro to extend to the resolution of all Franco-Russian issues of contention. They resulted on July 20 in a draft accord for an unhoped-for peace. France agreed to withdraw its troops from Germany in return for a Russian withdrawal from Cattaro. Yet, influenced by his court and pressured by Prussia and Britain, on September 3 Tsar Alexander refused to ratify the agreement, much to Napoleon's disappointment. The second great hope of peace had evaporated. Britain succeeded in forming the Fourth Coalition with Prussia, Russia, and Sweden.

The great diplomatic achievement of 1806 was the foundation of the Confederation of the Rhine, the details of which we will discuss below in the chapter on the "protective glacis." By placing all of southern Germany under its influence, French diplomacy achieved a resounding double stroke. Not only did it push potential battlefields far from the country's borders, but it also gained a defensive alliance with the states that composed the Confederation, states that promised to furnish a total of 63,000 soldiers to the emperor.

Matrimonial alliances helped shore up the diplomatic scaffolding. Napoleon's stepson, Eugene de Beauharnais, married the daughter of the Elector of Bavaria. The emperor's niece by marriage, Stephanie de Beauharnais, married the hereditary prince of Baden. Jerome Bonaparte prepared to ally himself with Katherine, daughter of Frederick I of Württemberg.

On the negative side, the Spanish alliance was waning. Playing a troubling game, on October 5 Godoy issued a declaration of neutrality.

The year ended with a diplomatic success against hostile Russia. The skillful French ambassador to Turkey, General Sébastiani, gained the confidence of Sultan Selim III. A personal letter from Napoleon addressed to the sultan on December 1 swung him to a French alliance. Turkey declared war on Russia on December 30. The tsar was forced to commit significant military forces to his southern frontier, which temporarily discouraged his warlike ambitions in Eastern Europe.

A few days later, the Elector of Saxony was declared king. He had joined the Confederation of the Rhine and by consequence the French alliance.

1807-1812: From the Grand Illusion to the Apogee

In 1807 French diplomacy achieved such striking successes that one could envision a lasting peace.

Spain returned to the French alliance and joined the continental blockade on February 19. On March 18, Austria proclaimed its friendly sentiments by offering its good offices to mediate between France and Russia. In fact, it was soon obvious that Vienna was playing a double game. On May 4, a Franco-Prussian alliance was signed at Finkenstein, putting another pebble in Alexander I's shoes. But what was gained on one hand was lost on another. On May 27 a coup d'etat in Constantinople overthrew Selim III. His successor would continue the war against Russia for another four years.

The most important event occurred at the start of the summer of 1807. The severe military lesson inflicted on the tsar at Friedland on June 14 resulted on July 7 in the signing of the famous Treaty of Tilsit and the miraculous Franco-Russian friendship.

The conditions leading to the conclusion of this mythic treaty merit a detailed development. They illustrate Napoleon's obsessive attachment to peace and the sacrifices he was willing to make for that purpose.

On June 19 Prince Lobanov-Rostovskii, the tsar's representative, arrived crestfallen at Tilsit to seek an armistice after the disaster of Friedland five days earlier. Napoleon received him not as a vanquished foe but rather as a partner. He put him immediately at ease and showed him every consideration. The emperor invited Lobanov to dine and paid tribute to the bravery of the Russian soldiers who had been so much more difficult to defeat than the Prussians of the previous year. He immediately indicated that the conclusion of an armistice would present no difficulty, but that in his eyes it would be more important to conclude a durable peace. He was prepared to offer conditions with which the tsar would certainly be satisfied. He even indicated the general outline of such an agreement.

This encouraging beginning immediately obtained the happiest results. The day after the signature of an armistice on June 21, Alexander again sent Lobanov to Napoleon's headquarters, carrying an equally encouraging message:

> The union between France and Russia has been the constant objective of my desires and I am convinced that only such a union could ensure happiness and tranquility for the world. An entirely new system must replace that which has existed up to now, and I flatter myself that we could easily reach agreement in a few days with the Emperor Napoleon, provided that we dealt with each other without intermediaries.

This response gratified Napoleon. An alliance with a great power in the eastern portion of Europe had been a constant goal of French diplomacy. The existence of a threat in the rear of potential enemies, currently Austria and Prussia but at some future date a unified Germany, would be a capital advantage for the security of France.

The power that could best fulfill this role was obviously Great Russia, and it was equally in Russia's highest interest to obtain a symmetrical advantage in the never-ending German-Slavic antagonism.

On June 25 the two sovereigns met in a theatrical fashion on a richly appointed raft in the middle of the Niemen River, at Tilsit. On the two opposing banks, the two Imperial Guards cheered. Napoleon assisted Alexander in boarding the raft and then embraced him. The cheers redoubled on the banks while the emperors met in private in one of the two sumptuous tents pitched on the raft.

The simplicity of their dealing was in jarring contrast to the majestic décor. Alexander declared bluntly, "Sire, I hate the English as much as you do." Napoleon replied immediately, "In that case, the peace is made." Alexander replied, "I will be your second in all that you do against them." Napoleon repeated his compliments to the Russian army, causing Alexander to blush with pleasure by remarking, "[W]e are two great nations. To make peace we can divide the globe between us." Decidedly, Russian autocrats have long been accustomed to the uncouth pattern at Yalta!

Another discussion occurred the following day at the same location, again in private, after which the negotiations continued in an enlarged fashion in the city of Tilsit, which was divided in half for this purpose. Pomp was not missing from these discussions, with cannon salutes and mutual reviews of Imperial Guards.

To please Alexander, Napoleon had agreed to the presence of the king of Prussia and of his very influential queen, Louise, whose beauty had a great effect on the tsar. She even tried to use her charm on Napoleon himself in order to obtain clemency for her country. Napoleon proved less resistant to this feminine offensive than to the assault at Friedland. But he conceded nothing to Louise, who had once styled her wig as an insult to him.

The Franco-Russian Treaty of Tilsit was signed on July 7, the Franco-Prussian agreement two days later.

The terms were astonishingly favorable to a Russia vanquished by arms. She lost only the trifles of Cattaro and the Ionian Islands. The tsar pledged to participate in the blockade against Britain, and even to declare war if the British did not accept his mediation of the Franco-British conflict. In return, he received a free hand to deal with Sweden and Finland and to act against Turkey, that is to say carte blanche to follow the expansionist policies of his grandmother Catherine II. In addition, in another exorbitant gift that spared Austria as well, Napoleon (to the great detriment of the Poles) reduced somewhat his plan to reconstitute Poland, a plan that had been close to his heart. The creation of the Grand Duchy of Warsaw under the king of Saxony affected only the Prussian portions of the former Polish state. Thus the conqueror's concessions were significant. But, what would Napoleon not have sacrificed for peace?

Arrogantly responsible for the war, Prussia paid all the costs. Berlin deserved it!

As at Amiens, Napoleon sincerely believed that he had found a lasting peace at Tilsit. Sealed by an apparently sincere friendship between the two emperors, the Russian alliance would neutralize the other European monarchies who could not risk having to fight on two fronts.

This did not make them more friendly, however, as demonstrated by the bad temper of Gustaf IV of Sweden, who on July 8 denounced the Franco-Swedish Treaty concluded in April after Mortier's victory at Anklam.

The reverberations of Tilsit contributed to a visible increase in the general system of alliances. On October 30 Denmark, violently assaulted by the British who savagely bombarded Copenhagen, aligned itself with France. The next day Spain confirmed its participation in the blockade. On November 7 Russia itself took another step by declaring war on Britain. That same day, Austria also joined the continental blockade.

The years that followed did not, unfortunately, resemble 1807. The pacifist euphoria of that year gave way to disenchantment in 1808.

After Tilsit, all of Napoleon's efforts were focused on consolidating the existing alliances. Thwarted with regard to Constantinople by the overthrow of Sultan Selim III, he gave Austria the advantage on January 22, 1808, to expand its territories with respect to Turkey, Vienna's hereditary enemy. Austria thus profited from the partition of the Ottoman Empire, which France and Russia had projected after their alliance.

Foreseeing in effect the chilling of Franco-Russian relations, Napoleon encouraged Alexander's tendency to orient on the Ottoman Empire. On February 2, 1808, the emperor proposed a plan to partition Turkey, followed by a combined military mission in the direction of India "to bring England to her knees." The tsar showed a very strong interest in the affair. Discussion began on March 2 between the representatives of the two countries, Caulaincourt and Rumyantsev. On March 31 Alexander willingly confirmed his agreement, but demanded Constantinople for Russia. Napoleon could not accept that exorbitant claim, which would have given Russia the strategic key to the Mediterranean.

Absorbed at the moment by a resurgence of the Spanish question, Napoleon waited until May 31 to propose a meeting with Alexander. Soon the unfavorable development of the Spanish situation definitively buried the project.

The fatal Spanish affair overthrew the diplomatic deal developing in the spring of 1808. The disastrous French involvement in the Spanish hornet's nest and the opening of a new British front in the French rear encouraged its enemies to raise their heads again. Profiting from the inconveniences caused by tightening the blockade, Britain opened a bridgehead in Portugal. It actively supported the ancient kingdom of Naples. London also encouraged the deterioration of relations between France and the Roman Curia.

The initial military checks suffered by France in Spain emboldened Prussia to dream of an early revenge. Austria had already begun to rattle its arms. And Russia again turned a complacent ear to British advances.

In short, the desirable French diplomatic situation had deteriorated gravely in a few months. Napoleon needed to take the situation in hand quickly. Above all, he had to save the Franco-Russian alliance, keystone of peace. This was what he attempted desperately to accomplish in organizing an imposing conference at Erfurt from September 27 to October 14, 1808.

At stake at Erfurt was the military neutrality of Prussia and above all of Austria while France was engaged in Spain. To this end, Napoleon looked to obtain a guarantee from his Russian ally to go to war in the case of aggression against France.

If he had agreed with apparent good will to participate in the conference, Alexander no longer showed Napoleon that warm friendship of Tilsit. His Francophobe court, together with British intriguers and French immigrants, had obviously taken the tsar in hand. Moreover, although he did not realize it until later, the emperor was badly betrayed by Talleyrand, whom he had been so weak as to employ after his banishment from foreign relations. In secret, this criminal unveiled a plan of French negotiations to encourage the tsar to "save Europe by standing up to Napoleon."

Under these circumstances, Napoleon could only obtain a patchwork instead of the solid renewal of the Franco-Russian alliance. In spite of important concessions and even Napoleon's request to marry the young sister of the tsar, Grand Duchess Anna, Alexander remained vague on the key point of the intervention of the Russian army in case of an attack by Austria.

With this lapse of French diplomacy, the grand illusion of the peace of Tilsit ended.

The failure of Erfurt translated in 1809 into the renewal of hostilities by Austria. Assured privately of Alexander's neutrality, stimulated by the retention in Spain of a large portion of the French army, and encouraged by British military engagement in the Iberian Peninsula, the Austrian emperor believed that the hour of revenge had come. He once again underestimated the military genius of Napoleon, who again thrashed the Austrian army in the course of a brilliant campaign from April to July 1809, crowned by the decisive victory of Wagram and concluded by the Treaty of Vienna of October 14.

This war confirmed Alexander's duplicity. He engaged his army only in a sham attack to justify his seizure of Galicia. This favor accorded to a suspect ally proves again Napoleon's obsession with peace. Without trusting too much in illusion, he still wished to give the Russian alliance one last chance, a chance that in turn produced other vicious effects. Britain profited from this by signing a peace treaty with Turkey on January 5, 1809.

Another diplomatic disappointment of that year was the grave deterioration of relations with the Roman Curia caused by the holy Spanish war. Pressured by a traditionalist entourage, Pope Pius VII encouraged Catholics to rise up against Napoleon, whom they considered to be the "antichrist." The emperor replied on May 17, 1809, by putting an end to the historic gift of Charlemagne to the pope: "The papal states are merged into the French Empire." In compensation for the resulting loss of income, the pope was recompensed with a payment of two million francs and a guarantee of his religious independence. The Curia issued a bull of excommunication against "the authors of this plundering" without citing Napoleon by name. Orders were therefore issued to "confine" the pope and his advisors. Applied with an excessive zeal, this measure was interpreted as confining the pope to a residence at Savona. The Roman crisis was only deferred.

The remarriage of Napoleon to insure the succession of the Empire gave rise to a diplomatic tournament bordering on vaudeville between the Romanovs of Russia and the Hapsburgs of Austria. Napoleon, for whom everything was political, seized the occasion to try again in the battle of alliances. He therefore excluded out of hand any French woman or princess of the second order. Lacking a princess of marriageable age, the Hohenzollerns of Prussia were out of play. The choice came down to that between a young sister of Alexander, the Grand Duchess Anna, and the daughter of Francis I of Austria, the Archduchess Maria-Louisa.

Because of the friendship, however uncertain, that already linked him to Alexander, but above all because the empire of the tsars had a superior geographic weight, Napoleon preferred the grand duchess, about whom he had already sounded Alexander at Erfurt. He charged Caulaincourt, ambassador to Russia, to negotiate. On November 4 he sent the tsar an official marriage proposal, which plunged Alexander into the greatest quandary. He was personally in favor of the match but his mother, the Tsarina Maria, widow of Paul I, would not hear of it. To strong arguments about the difference in age and religion, she added her implacable hostility to Napoleon himself.

To overcome this opposition, the emperor made a significant concession concerning his official and private ties with Poland: the recognition of the partition of 1795. Knowing the high value that Russia attached to this question, he hoped in return to get an immediate agreement with Alexander. The tsar deceived him yet again. He could not succeed in convincing his august but cantankerous mother, and was in any case advised against the alliance by all the unrepentant French émigrés at the court of Saint Petersburg. The tsar continued to equivocate.

As for the Habsburg archduchess, it was not even necessary to initiate the matter. As early as November 29, 1809, in Vienna, Metternich suggested the possibility of a "marriage by the Emperor with a princess of this family" in a meeting with the French chargé d'affaires, Count de Laborde. Obviously the Viennese cabinet wanted to preempt the negotiations with Saint Petersburg.

Seeking to beat Russia to the punch, Metternich charged his ambassador Schwarzenberg to pursue the matter actively in Paris. After beating about the bush, the Court of Vienna gave its enthusiastic agreement.

On January 29, 1810, the emperor summoned a great council to announce his decision. The options were balanced. In a minority led by Murat, the advocates of a Russian marriage pointed out the inconvenience of placing the great niece of Marie Antoinette on the throne of France. On the other side, Cardinal Fesch warned against the schismatic effect of choosing an Orthodox princess at a moment when relations with Rome were at their worst. Talleyrand, whom the emperor continued to recognize despite his disgrace, advocated an Austrian alliance to "absolve France in the eyes of Europe and of itself, of a crime that was not its own and which belonged to only one faction [of regicides]," he claimed.

Having no remaining illusions with regard to Alexander, Napoleon settled on the Austrian marriage.

It was now important to appear very prudent in the formalization of the choice. First, one must protect the feelings of Alexander, who might feel himself slighted by a decision taken without even waiting for his formal response. Moreover, it was important to anticipate the negative reaction from Saint Petersburg so that the Austrian marriage would not appear as a replacement solution. One must after all consider the dignity of France as well as of Austria!

To this end, Napoleon addressed two letters to Alexander with an interval of twenty-four hours between them. In the first, the emperor renounced the hand of the tsar's sister for the reasons he had already advanced, the age of the princess and her religion. Thus, no one could reproach him. In the second, Napoleon informed Alexander of his marriage with the Archduchess Maria-Louisa of Austria.

His haste was justified. En route to Saint Petersburg, these two missives crossed the negative response of the tsar, transmitted by Caulincourt. Alexander had not even felt it necessary to write personally.

The marriage occurred on April 2, 1810, at the Tuileries, to the great displeasure of Alexander, who had no one to blame but himself. Austria replaced Russia in the grand strategy of Napoleon.

Despite the subsequent political problems, the union of Napoleon with a descendant of the Emperor Charles V constituted a political masterstroke with two effects: it neutralized the hostility of the great powers of continental Europe and it was of a nature to calm the resentment of the monarchies. Its future failure would be a demonstration of the inevitability of wars imposed on Napoleon.

It was time for France to accept this revision of alliances. That with Russia fluttered farther and farther away since the Treaty of Vienna and the marriage negotiations. Alexander's exorbitant pretensions with regard to Poland aggravated matters. In the pure Russian tradition, the tsar dreamed of reconstituting that country under his thumb. He had the effrontery to expect a part of Austrian Poland under the Treaty of Vienna, although he had failed to fulfill his military alliance. He returned to this effort on December 26, 1809, proposing a convention in which Napoleon would engage to "prevent forever the reconstitution of Poland." Losing his head in the climate of the Court of Saint Petersburg and apparently ignorant that Poland represented a key piece in French security policy, the naïve ambassador Caulaincourt took it upon himself to sign this convention on January 4. Napoleon was constrained to disavow him on February 2. But, to prove his willingness to be accommodating, the emperor promised "never to give any assistance to any power or any interior uprising that attempted to reestablish the Kingdom of Poland." This was an enormous concession that came close to abandoning his loyal Polish friends and allies. Alexander was still not satisfied and returned to his original proposition, which obviously went nowhere. From that point on the Russian alliance existed only in Alexander's mind.

This was even more so because the tsar found another pretext for discontent in the election of Bernadotte by the Swedish diet on August 21, 1810, as hereditary prince of Sweden. Alexander knew that Napoleon had no hand in this unwanted affair, favored by the Franco-Swedish peace of January 6, 1810. He also knew that Bernadotte hated Napoleon and that he could be turned around at the first opportunity, which happened quite soon.

Meanwhile, Bernadotte succeeded in making himself the subject of much talk. This criminal in power played a disgusting game. At the same time that he was letting Alexander know of his bias in favor of Russia, on January 6, 1811, he proposed to Napoleon that the two conclude an alliance against Alexander, in return for which Bernadotte would be allowed to seize Norway from Denmark, then an ally of France.

Napoleon refused this ignoble deal coming from a prince having "so much effervescence and loose ideas in his head."

The year 1811 was very fertile with other disorderly diplomatic events.

On May 14, burned by previous disappointments and fearing to again become the bill-payer for a Franco-Russian understanding, Prussia made simultaneous overtures of alliance to both countries. It reiterated this offer to Russia on July 16. The tsar avoided the matter at first, but ended on October 17 by signing a convention that obligated Russia only to enter war to protect East Prussia. As for Napoleon, he surprised Berlin by accepting its offers on October 28. Frederick William III was very embarrassed and turned toward Francis of Austria. Reprimanded severely by France on December 24, Frederick William acquiesced on the 29th. Several days later, he discretely begged Alexander's pardon for this disloyalty.

Austria was not absent from this strange diplomatic ballet. On December 17, it accepted in principle a French alliance against Russia and rejected Prussia on the 26th.

Marked by the crystallization of Franco-Russian antagonism, the diplomatic year 1811 ended thus in success for France.

The year 1812 marked the apogee of imperial diplomacy on the eve or a renewal of hostilities against a weakened Russia, supported only by Britain and Sweden.

On July 18 at Oerebro, in Sweden, Britain signed an alliance with Russia. On April 5 at Gatchina Russia concluded a treaty of understanding with Sweden, transformed into an alliance on August 30 at Abo. Alexander suggested to a somber Bernadotte that he might replace Napoleon in France, the beneficiary of this plan having no doubt of his capacity to perform.

France brought about the two major alliances prepared the previous year. The Franco-Prussian alliance was concluded on February 28. On March 4 the Franco-Austrian alliance was signed at Paris.

Henceforth expecting nothing more from an Alexander whose country was already on a war footing, Napoleon had no further reason to give him consideration in Poland. At the end of May the emperor instructed Pradt, his representative in Warsaw, to cease blocking the meeting of a Diet that would proclaim the reestablishment of the

Kingdom of Poland. But the doubtful and incompetent Pradt bungled everything.

At the same time, Napoleon rejected with contempt the last propositions of Bernadotte, whose duplicity was now beyond doubt.

Frosting the cake of French diplomacy, the United States declared war on Britain on June 18 after various maritime incidents. But this decision was to have little practical effect for some time.

Russia did, however, have two successes. On May 28 at Bucharest it concluded a treaty of peace with Turkey, relieving pressure on its southern frontiers.

The French diplomatic dominance of the year 1812 would collapse with the disaster of the Russian campaign at the end of that year.

1813-1815: The Tragic Isolation of France

The year 1813 demonstrated that a diplomacy not supported by military power is doomed to failure. With the Grand Armeé engulfed in Russia, the supposed allies of France, who had been waiting for such an occasion, abandoned it and turned against it in the campaign of 1813.

Nonetheless, the year began with the ephemeral success of the signature of a new Concordat at Fontainebleau on January 25, resolving France's disagreements with Rome. Napoleon achieved this result by negotiating head to head with the good Pius VII, released from the pernicious influence of the traditionalist and royalist Roman Curia, which was dominated by Cardinal Capra. But this last soon took the pope in hand and persuaded him on March 24 to retract his signature.

Secretly supported by the conspiratorial attitude of Austria, Prussia reversed its alliance on February 22 with the signature of the Russo-Prussian Treaty of Kalisch. Prussia immediately prepared to enter the field against France.

On April 12 the hesitant Austria declared itself to be in a state of "armed mediation," towing in its wake a few days later the opportunistic king of Saxony.

The lightning success of Napoleon in the first part of the 1813 campaign constrained the Russo-Prussians on January 4 to conclude the false armistice of Pleiswitz. The resulting peace negotiations at Prague were intended only to gain the time necessary for the Russo-Prussians to refit militarily and for the Austrians to prepare their entry into the war

Britain manifested itself officially on June 14 by signing the Treaty of Reichenbach with Russia and Prussia, to whom it gave substantial subsidies. Austria joined in turn on June 27.

Austria declared war on France on August 12, the day after the expiration of the armistice and the end of the false Congress of Prague, which Vienna had been actively employed in undermining.

The poorly exploited French victory at Dresden on August 27 prompted the Coalition partners to tighten their alliance by the Treaty of Toeplitz, to which Britain adhered on October 30. Austria had the responsibility of rallying the south German rulers to the Coalition. Bavaria signed an armistice on September 17, followed by the Treaty of Ride on October 8.

The cruel defeat of Leipzig (October 16-19) marked the end of the French presence in Germany. The king of Württemberg rejoined the Coalition on November 3.

The brilliant campaign in France in 1814 so destabilized the Coalition that Britain had to reinforce it at Chaumont on March 8. The Coalition powers joined together for twenty years, each promising to mobilize 150,000 men. Yet, his victories did not save Napoleon, abandoned and even betrayed by the majority of his followers, from his first abdication on April 6, 1814, followed by his exile to the island of Elba.

The Treaty of Paris was signed May 30. France relinquished all of its acquisitions since the Revolution except Mulhouse, Avignon, part of Savoy and several border rectifications in the Saar and the north. Overseas, she lost the Ile de France, Saint Lucia, and Tobago.

Upon his return from Elba on March 1, 1815, amid an indescribable popular celebration, Napoleon forcefully affirmed his desire for peace, both domestically and especially abroad. Refusing any discussion, the European monarchs banned Napoleon on March 13 at Vienna. Because he was supported by almost the entirety of the French people, it was thus France that was banned by Europe. The true motive of the enemies of France was thus shown openly. Napoleon's unpardonable crime was to have restored the sovereignty of the people, after having instituted it under the Consulate.

Beginning on March 25, 1815, the Seventh Coalition formed against France, alone against everyone. At Waterloo in 1815, the monarchist reaction was the second match of its ideological confrontation against the "democratic plague." The reactionaries did not realize that in a few years absolute monarchy would lose its attraction. Even if it proved possible to defeat a genius incarnate, the reactionaries were unable to halt the march of universal aspirations.

On balance, Napoleon's unbridled pursuit of defensive alliances to prevent armed conflict proved vain because the war was tragically and inevitably inscribed in history. We will find the confirmation of this in the failure of the other defensive effort conceived by Napoleon.

A Policy Founded on the Prevention of Conflicts

Napoleon was too realistic to entrust the security of France solely to treaties of alliance. While certainly useful, these documents were still too subject to the changing spirits and fluctuating interests of the signatories to offer absolute guarantees, as we have already witnessed.

Such abstract protection obviously did not suffice to guarantee the security of France. Therefore Napoleon added a vast territorial buffer, having two purposes: to better dissuade aggression, and if that failed to allow a greater strategic depth to defeat such aggression.

It was therefore a matter of applying the principle of precaution so common in our own days.

The achievement of this defensive arrangement required a gigantic geopolitical shift, prefiguring the unity of Europe. The arrangement was constantly changing and improving up until 1814. The obligations of the continental blockade were to contribute greatly to its construction.

Determined solely by the imperative of security, this "Continental System," as it was known, owned nothing to a spirit of conquest. All the peoples involved had joined without compulsion, and those who did not belong to the French sphere of influence retained their autonomous governments.

The effectiveness of the system depended on a structure of three complementary entities, almost concentric rings arranged around a national sanctuary. We therefore find, in order from closest to farthest away: the rampart of lands integral to the Empire; the protective glacis of friendly or familial states; and the flank guard of family kingdoms.

Making the national territory into a sanctuary depended essentially on the maintenance of French sovereignty on the natural frontiers of the Rhine and the Alps, traditional routes of invasion. This old Gallic dream finally began to become reality with the Treaty of Campoformio on October 17, 1797, crowning Bonaparte's victories in Italy. Austria recognized French possession of Belgium and of the left bank of the Rhine. At the Congress of Rastadt on December 1, Bonaparte, plenipotentiary of the Directory, had watched very attentively to ensure the confirmation of this critical clause of Campoformio. When he became First Consul, he did not deviate from this imperative in the Treaties of Lunéville (February 9, 1801) and Amiens (March 25, 1802). The great powers finally recognized the Rhine as the frontier of France.

Later, Napoleon was to consolidate the Rhine frontier by the 1806 acquisition on the left bank of the fortified positions of Kehl and Wesel.

Yet, like all fortresses, the citadel of France thus achieved required the control of its surrounding areas.

The Rampart of Lands Integral to the Empire

This effort was first visible in Italy. Recognizing a situation of fact and responding to the wishes of its representatives, Piedmont joined with France by a Senatus Consultum of September 11, 1802. The island of Elba was added in August. On October 23 the Duke of Parma ceded his rights to France. At the insistent request of its senate, Genoa was incorporated into the Empire on June 30, 1805. For symbolic reasons related to the history of Corsica, Napoleon went to proclaim the event on the spot, in person. The Kingdom of Etruria and the Roman States followed in 1808-1809. The Empire received Ragusa, Fiume, Trieste, Croatia, and a portion of Carinthia. These territories joined with Dalmatia to form the Illyrian Provinces.

In Switzerland, the canton of Valais joined the Empire on November 10, 1810. In Germany, the extension of the Empire was dictated by the requirements of the blockade in order to control the North Sea coast, reaching in 1810 as far as the mouth of the Elbe River at Hamburg.

By 1811, the Empire consisted of 130 departments. This number reached its highest point (134) a few months later with the brief attachment of the four departments of Catalonia. The Empire thus included eighty-five million inhabitants, or almost three times the population of traditional France.

The Protective Glacis of Friendly Lands

Generally flanking the natural frontiers of France, the borders of the Empire were vulnerable to the recurring menace coming from the east. The Empire's security was reinforced by the creation of a protective glacis of various states, providing both a defensive alliance and a strategic buffer in case of war.

This glacis may be divided into "family" states and friendly states. Among the former, the key piece was the Kingdom of Italy, the former Cisalpine Republic whose crown the emperor assumed personally at Milan on March 17, 1805, at the request of Italian representatives. He confided effective government of this kingdom to his stepson, Eugene de Beauharnais, with the title of viceroy. Peopled with seven million inhabitants, the Kingdom of Italy bordered: on the south, the Kingdom of Naples, the Papal States, and Tuscany (these latter two later joining the Empire); to the west, Piedmont; to the northwest, Valois; to the north, Switzerland; and on the east, the Illyrian Provinces.

In Italy one must also note the designation, on June 23, 1805, of Napoleon's sister Elisa to be princess of Lucca. The following year she also received the duchies of Massa and Carrara.

The Helvetian Confederation protected the Alpine frontier. The construction of this sovereign territorial entity had been difficult. Hampered by serious internal troubles in 1801, the representatives of the Swiss canon asked for Bonaparte's arbitration. The Act of Malmaison, first outline of a federal constitution, was signed on April 29, but it satisfied no one. The Swiss deputies again requested that Bonaparte mediate. From this on January 19, 1802, came the Act of Mediation of the Helvetic Confederation, establishing for Switzerland a federal constitution of nineteen cantons, with Bonaparte reserving to himself a continuing role as mediator.

The Holy Roman Empire of Germany controlled the great traditional invasion routes to France. Therefore, it was this empire that would experience the efforts of building a shield for France.

An ancient vestige of the agitated history of Germany, the Holy Roman Empire was a curious and complex political mosaic. Under the nominal authority of the Austrian emperor, it included a loose association of many little kingdoms, duchies, principalities, and free cities. A Diet meeting periodically held them together.

Napoleon's actions were intended to simplify and restructure this puzzle in order to place it under French influence with the consent of the Diet.

This general reorganization was to occur in two phases: the Recess of 1803 and the formation of the Rhine Confederation in 1806.

The "Recess of the German Empire" took as its point of departure the Treaty of Teschen of 1779 between France and Russia. In this treaty, the two great powers asserted their role as coregents of the Empire. The tsar maintained a patronage in Germany with the princes of Hesse, Baden, and Württemberg. The Peace of Lunéville with Austria had opened the door of the Empire to France by major changes, which the peace made on both sides of the Rhine.

In the Franco-Russian peace treaty of October 10, 1801, a secret article provided for the mediation by the two powers in a sort of German reconstitution. The resulting diplomatic negotiations with a deputation of the Diet led to the "Recess" adopted by the Diet of Ratisbonne on March 24, 1803.

This "Recess" reorganized the map of Germany. One hundred twelve small states, all the ecclesiastical principalities except for Ratisbonne, and forty-five of fifty-one free cities were abolished. Overall, the Holy Roman Empire was reconfigured into three blocs: a northeastern Germany dominated by Prussia, a central portion left to the weakened influence of Austria, and a south Germany controlled by France. This last part included the principal states of Bavaria, Württemberg, and Baden.

The "Recess" pleased the great powers. Prussia received eight times more territory than it lost on the left bank of the Rhine. Austria was largely compensated for its losses in Italy: the Duke of Moderna was installed in Bresgau, while Ferdinand of Tuscany (Grand Duke Ferdinand III of Tuscany, brother of the Emperor Francis), received the territory of the archbishopric of Salzburg. Russia obtained the bishopric of Lubeck for its protégé, the duke of Oldenburg. Even Britain could be satisfied: occupied in 1801, Hanover returned to the British crown, expanded by the bishopric of Osnabruck.

As a rough sketch of the protective glacis of France in Germany, the "Recess" demonstrated its failing during the Third Coalition of 1805. In addition, Napoleon sought to consolidate his situation after Austerlitz. By the Treaty of Pressburg, he accomplished the first stage in the expansion of the Rhineland states. Baden received Ortenau and Bresgau while Württemberg obtained Constance and the Austrian possessions in Swabia. Bavaria took Vorarlberg and the Austrian Tyrol, as well as Trento and Bucine in Italy. Moreover, in his role as Holy Roman Emperor, the Austrian emperor recognized the full sovereignty of these three states. Bavaria and Württemberg became independent kingdoms and Baden became a grand duchy. Let us recall the matrimonial connections formed by Napoleon to affirm the attachment of these three states to France: the marriage of his stepson Eugene de Beauharnais with the daughter of the king of Bavaria, of his niece Stephanie de Beauharnais with the heir to Baden, and later of his brother Jerome with the daughter of the king of Württemberg.

In preparation for the constitution of the Confederation of the Rhine that was to follow, Murat was named Grand Duke of Berg on March 15, 1806.

A major supplemental step in the consolidation of the glacis was achieved with the creation on July 12, 1806, of the Confederation of the Rhine. This was an association of sixteen states in southern and southwestern Germany, including: the kingdoms of Bavaria (Maximilian Joseph) and of Württemberg (Frederick I), the grand duchies of Baden, Berg, and Hesse-Darmstadt, and various principalities of lesser importance. Monsignor Dahlberg, Prince Primate, was named arch chancellor of the new entity before becoming the Grand Duke of Frankfurt. He promptly proposed to Napoleon that the Confederation be transformed into a German empire with Napoleon assuming the crown. To indicate clearly that he was not a conqueror, Napoleon flatly refused this proposal. Preoccupied with security, he stated that he was satisfied with a military alliance with the Confederation. Threats coming from the east were thus pushed back by several hundred kilometers, but that did not prove sufficient to deter Prussia.

The Confederation of the Rhine officially separated from the Holy Roman Empire on August 1, 1806. Its Emperor Francis II relinquished the crown on August 6, becoming henceforth only Francis I, emperor of Austria.

After the 1806 war, the Confederation grew considerably to the east by the attachment of other territories, notably the Grand Duchy of Württemberg and Frederick-Augustus's Saxony transformed into a kingdom. The Grand Duchy of Warsaw was attached to the Confederation when that duchy was created on July 22, 1807.

A new federal state was founded on August 16, 1807, with a portion of Hanover, a part of the territories taken from Prussia west of the Elbe, plus Brunswick and Hesse-Cassel. It was called the Kingdom of Westphalia and given to Joseph Bonaparte.

On October 14, 1808, the Duchy of Oldenburg in turn joined the Confederation of the Rhine.

Yet, the Empire also needed to cover the wings of the rampart and the protective glacis.

The Flank Guard of Familial Kingdoms

This flank guard completed the shield, and consisted of the kingdoms of Holland, Naples, and Spain.

Under the name of the Batavian Republic, the Netherlands had occupied a key strategic position with regard to Britain. It was a potential bridgehead against public enemy number one on both the strategic and economic planes. Although preferring neutrality, by 1800 it formed part of the network of French alliances arising from the Revolution. At the conclusion of the Treaty of Amiens, by which it had recovered Flushing (Vlissingen), the Batavian Republic had shown symptoms of neutralism that were reduced to nothing by the return of war in May 1803. The French alliance was tightened, marked by a new military convention by which the Netherlands engaged to furnish a contingent of 16,000 men and to provide supplies for a corps of 18,000 French soldiers. In addition, as a maritime power the Netherlands had to prepare its fleet to play an important role in the invasion of Britain then under preparation.

On the institutional plane, the Dutch threw themselves into the arms of Revolutionary France to escape the stadholders (governors of the country.) At the time, the Netherlands had a republican regime presided by the "Grand Pensioner" Schimmelpenninck. In 1806 the Batavian authorities took advantage of their leader's illness to request of Napoleon that he give them his brother Joseph as king. Joseph had earned their respect the previous year while commanding a Franco-Dutch corps. The proclamation was issued on June 5.

This voluntary enthronement of a French king in the Netherlands in principle assured the security of France's northern frontier. Yet, the relations between Louis and the emperor quickly soured. Louis took his crown too seriously, to the point of compromising the alliance with France, especially with regard to the application of the continental blockade. The relations between the two brothers reached the stage where Napoleon issued a decree severing commercial relations between the Netherlands and the Empire and occupying Oudinot, Breda, and Bergen-Op-Zoom. Louis ordered the governor of the latter city to resist, risking an armed confrontation. Louis finally gave in, but refused to renounce his crown as Napoleon asked. After a series of unfortunate episodes, on July 3, 1810, Louis further complicated his brother's task by abdicating in favor of his son instead of simply abandoning the throne. What a low blow! Louis owed his crown to the emperor alone, and it was up to Napoleon to decide the fate of that crown. It was in this manner that the Netherlands became attached to the Empire on July 9, to the great satisfaction of the population, it must be emphasized. The country was organized into eight departments under the former consul Lebrun, who performed the functions of lieutenant-general of the emperor. Leaving the role of flank guard, the Netherlands was thus integrated into the territories of the "rampart." As for Louis, he went into exile in Austria.

In southern Italy, the Kingdom of Naples became a flank guard by military conquest. This monarchy, also known as "the Two Sicilies," extended on the southern end of the Italian boot and Sicily. The Bourbons who had reigned there had been consistently hostile to France since the first Italian war. One must note that the effervescent Queen Maria-Carolina was the sister of the unfortunate Marie Antoinette. She dominated her unfortunate king consort, Ferdinand IV, known as "Nasone."

Committing a serious error of judgment concerning the fate of the Third Coalition, on November 19, 1805, the Kingdom of Naples violated the treaty of neutrality with regard to France and declared war within a few days of Austerlitz. A corps of 20,000 British and Russian troops disembarked in the Kingdom of Naples on November 19, 1805, threatening the Kingdom of Italy and the rear of Massena's army, which at that time was fully occupied in containing the Austrian forces of Archduke Charles.

Napoleon could not tolerate for long the persistence of this danger. The disloyalty of the queen of Naples justified him in not pulling any punches with her.

Made available by the victory of Austerlitz, Massena's reinforced army crossed the Garigliano on February 8, 1806, and marched on Naples in three corps. On the right, Reynier marched on Gaeta and laid siege to it. In the center, Massena advanced to Capua, which fell on February 10, and entered Naples the 14th. On the left, Gouvion Saint-Cyr advanced toward the Gulf of Taranto. The British reembarked precipitously for Sicily, imperiling their Russian allies who in turn withdrew to Corfu. The court of Naples took refuge in Palermo. Joseph Bonaparte entered Naples with Massena's army on February 15 and was proclaimed king of Naples. The population received him favorably. On February 25 Napoleon declared the fall of the Bourbons of Naples in these terms: "the leaden scepter of this modern Athalia has been broken beyond repair."

Despite this, the conquest of the Italian boot was not yet complete. A few places resisted further, notably Gaeta, Reggio, and Scylla. The British responded offensively, taking Capri and Ponza. Landing 5,000 men near Saint Eufemia, they inflicted a severe defeat on Reynier's division at Maida on July 4. But they did not persist, and Gaeta fell again on July 18.

Massena also had to confront the endemic banditry of Culebra. Much to everyone's surprise, he brought it to an end in December 1806 by the capture and hanging of Fra Diavolo, the celebrated bandit chief who had passed into the service of Queen Maria-Carolina.

With this success in an unavoidable conflict, Napoleon pushed the specter of war a little farther back. The entire Italian boot was henceforth under his control. But, his security would never be total, because the British could not be expelled from Sicily.

With Spain, and more generally with the Iberian Peninsula, the idea of a flank security guard assumed a vital importance because of the openness of the frontiers. The question here turned into a nightmare due to a coincidence of fatal circumstances that were exploited by France's enemies.

Paradoxically, Napoleon's obsessive concern to avoid conflicts led to the most atrocious of wars. In this case, the prevention of war became intermingled with the war itself. To avoid repetition, we will develop the Spanish question below.

The Lost Dream of European Union

The construction of Napoleon's defensive shield had more than just military significance. It also reflected the overarching political idea of a unification of the European continent.

One might be surprised to find no written trace of the emperor's intent in this regard. The explanation is simple: he did not want to encourage yet another charge of conquering ambition by disclosing the project. He explained himself clearly at Saint Helena:

> To open public discussion about such higher objectives would be to open them to partisan factions, to passions, intrigue, and gossip without obtaining a result that would discredit the opposition. I therefore calculated that I would obtain this great benefit in secret.

The European Union dream held an eminent position in his thoughts:

> One of my greatest hopes was the unification, the concentration of the geographic peoples who had dissolved or broken up because of revolutions and politics. For example, in Europe there were well over 30 million Frenchmen, 15 million Spaniards, 15 million Italians, and 30 million Germans. I hoped to make of each of these peoples a single unified nation. It would have been marvelous to advance in posterity and the blessing of the centuries with such a pageant. I felt myself worthy of such glory. . . . Europe will soon be able to form a truly unified people. Each person, no matter where he travels, will always find himself in the common homeland. In such a state of affairs there would be more opportunities to provide everywhere a unit of laws, principles, opinions, feelings, and sense of self-interest. Thus, perhaps, by the light of universal ideas one

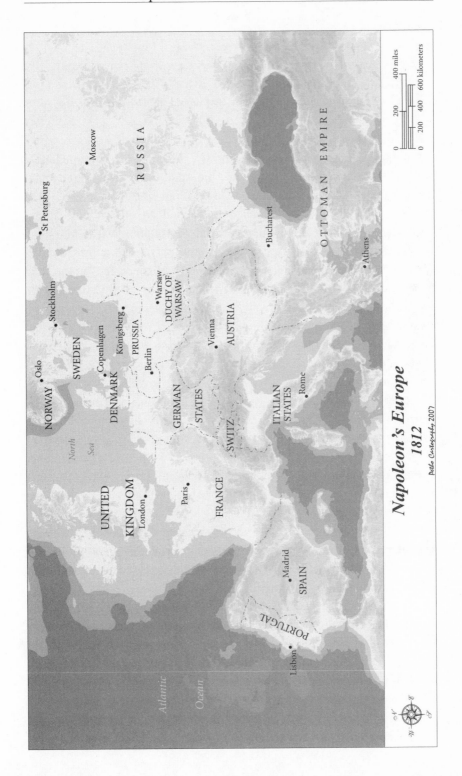

Napoleon's Europe
1812

Pete Costopoulos, 2007

might dream, for the great European family, of the application of the American Congress system, or that of the amphictyons [guardians of religion] in Greece. What a prospect of force, grandeur, delight, and prosperity that would be! What a great and magnificent spectacle!

Upon examining the map of Europe in 1812, one fact is immediately evident: the political union of the continent was practically accomplished! After Charlemagne, whose memory Napoleon often invoked, Europe now experienced its second attempt at unification. Unfortunately, like that which preceded it, this attempt was to fail.

In 1812, the organization of the empire prefigured a confederated European polity, with Paris as its capital. Economic Europe had progressed considerably, both in the enforcement of the blockade and the unification of currencies, weights and measures, and legislation. Administrative Europe was in the process of unification under the Napoleonic Code, which "might serve as the basis for a European code." As for cultural Europe, the Imperial University could provide the model for a European University. "I had in mind the creation of a European Institute and European prizes to propel, direct, and coordinate all the learned societies of Europe," Napoleon would explain on Saint Helena.

French became recognized as the common official language of Europe. On the battlefield of Waterloo, Wellington and Blücher communicated in French, as did the Austrians and Russians at Austerlitz. Had not the Grand Armeé, the "army of 20 nations," already achieved the Europe of Defense?

The conservatism of the monarchies and, above all, by the hegemonic ambition of Great Britain shattered this great European dream. Two centuries later, we have not yet rediscovered the same degree of unification achieved during the Imperial era.

On balance, the pacifist obsession of Napoleon could not succeed against the reactionary obstinacy of the irreducible enemies of the new France, which came together in a moment of implacable conflict. At a minimum, one may state that war was a hideous intrusion into the great work of that inspired builder and peace lover, Napoleon.

It remains to demonstrate that Napoleon never caused a single one of the interminable wars that rendered the history of the Consulate and Empire so bleak.

Part Three

Napoleon: Enemy of War

"An historian will prove that I have always been attacked."

*T*he extract from Napoleon's epigrams reproduced above leads us to the last part of this study. Humbly, we will assume the role of this "historian" to whom Napoleon appealed.

Pacifist Continuity from Bonaparte to Napoleon

I never vanquished nor conquered except in my own defense. That is a
fact that will become more evident as time passes. Europe
has never stopped making war on France and on
its principles. We must kill or be killed.

— Napoleon at Saint Helena

Napoleon Bonaparte exhibited his first inclination toward pacifism when he refused an order as a matter of conscience. The emaciated general, in disgrace after the 9th of Thermidor (July 27, 1794), was sacked from the Army of Italy in March 1795 and named to command an infantry brigade in the rebellious Vendée region. This reassignment mortified him. As a soldier, he thought of war as being solely against the enemies of his country and not against the inhabitants of France, even if they were royalists. He exclaimed, "I will never use my sword against the people!"

Napoleon rushed to Paris and beseeched the authorities to rescind this appointment, which was so dishonorable in the eyes of the glorious "Captain Cannon," recent liberator of Toulon. He redoubled his efforts in hopes of accelerating matters, wandering like a lost soul in the streets of the capital. His impaired health furnished him with a postponement. In August, however, he received a peremptory order to report immediately to his post in the Vendée. Persuaded by his magnetic personality, Minister of War Doucet de Pontécoulant, who had agreed to see him, rescinded the assignment and attached him to the Topographic Service.

Quickly disenchanted with such bureaucratic and sedentary activities, Napoleon sought to become the head of a mission to Constantinople to reorganize the Ottoman army. The response was slow in coming. In the meantime, the Committee of Public Safety, unaware of Pontécoulant's decision, issued a strident decree on September 15, "striking General Bonaparte from the general officer list on account of his refusal to assume the post to which he is assigned." One of the committee's members, Letoureau, even threatened Napoleon with the scaffold!

But events raced onward. The attempted royalist uprising of 13 Vendemiaire (October 5, 1795) gave a completely different direction to the career of "General Vendemiaire," savior of the republic and of the public peace.

In the course of the dazzling Italian war that followed, the irresistible General Bonaparte would confirm his pacifist disposition on two notable occasions in 1797.

In March, Napoleon confronted Archduke Charles after having routed within a single year the Austrian generals Beaulieu, Wurmser, and Alvinczy. At the end of the month, Bonaparte's offensive drove the Austrian army in disorder behind the Drove and threatened Venice. Instead of trying to conquer the capital that lay within his grasp, on March 31 Bonaparte generously offered peace to the Archduke in these terms:

To the Commander-in-Chief:

Brave soldiers make war and desire peace . . . have we not already killed sufficient people and inflicted sufficient damage on suffering humanity? The Europe that took up arms against the French Republic has stacked those arms. Only your nation remains in the field, and yet more blood flows than ever before. The executive Directory of the French Republic has communicated to H. M. the Emperor its desire to put an end to the war that devastated our two peoples. The Court of London is opposed to this. Is there no hope of our reaching agreement? Must we continue to slaughter in the interests or passions of a nation uninvolved in the ills of war? You, Commander-in-Chief, who by your birth are so close to the throne and are above the petty concerns that frequently animate ministers and governments, have you decided to earn the title of benefactor of all humanity and true savior of Germany? . . . As for me, sir, if the opportunity which I have the honor to offer you could save the life of even one man, I would be more proud of that than of the civic crown which I have earned, than of all the sad glory which can come from military successes. . . .

The Austrian chancellery lacked the wisdom to seize this hand extended to it and instead yielded to armed force three weeks later at Leoben, where the preliminaries of peace were signed.

But the moderation of the conqueror did not satisfy the bellicose Directory. Bonaparte therefore offered his resignation: "I wish to return to the population, to take up Cincinnatus' plow while setting the example of respect for the magistrates and of distaste for the type of military regime which has destroyed so many republics and lost so many states." The Directory hastened to reaffirm its confidence, "believing in the virtue of General Bonaparte."

The conclusion of the Treaty of Campoformio on October 17, 1797, signed by Bonaparte, again earned him the serious disapproval of the government, which considered the provisions too weak. The Directory sought nothing less than the overthrow of the Hapsburgs and the institution of an Austrian Republic. Under these circumstances, Bonaparte's moderation had avoided a new military campaign of uncertain outcome.

Public opinion was not deceived. The return of Bonaparte to Paris on December 5 represented nothing short of a veritable triumph. Crowds assembled spontaneously with cries of "Long live Bonaparte the peacemaker!" The Rue Chantereine where he lived was renamed the Rue de la Victoire (Victory Street). A song was composed in his honor:

"Henceforth no glory will escape you, because you know how to make peace as well as you make war."

As another sign of his peaceful intentions, Bonaparte, upon acceding to power in 1799, had inscribed in the Constitution the surprising provision forbidding the First Consul from commanding the armies of the field in person.

Thus, one must avoid the facile temptation to confuse Napoleon's military genius with his alleged love for war. In reality, he did not love war, and that is without doubt the most paradoxical trait of his personality, as if he were an artist who didn't love his art.

Contrary to a widely held belief, Napoleon was not a conqueror, in contrast to the two monsters of history to whom he is frequently compared, Alexander the Great and Julius Caesar. He never aimed at the conquest of land or the domination of peoples. His goal in war was always limited to overpowering the enemy with the sole object of opening negotiations for peace. Even his expedition to Egypt can only be understood as an operation of indirect grand strategy, in place of an invasion of Britain, which was considered impossible. Had he not said under those circumstances, "the true conquests are those made over ignorance?"

As has already been shown, Napoleon's obsession with protecting the national sanctuary dictated his hold on the territories of the "shield." It never took the form of a territorial conquest with an enforced change in sovereignty. Inclusion in the empire was always preceded by a voluntary request from the representatives of the country in question, with the justifiable exception of Naples. Popular consent was never lacking, even at the outset in Spain. A clear sign of this was that most of the countries involved voluntarily adopted the Civil Code and many other Napoleonic institutions.

In truth, the conquests of Napoleon, an authentic man of talent, were situated on the philosophical field of the Rights of Man.

Another observation of simple common sense is that war could only be an intrusion on Napoleon's demanding work schedule. The immense and urgent task of reconstructing France on the smoking ruins of the Revolution monopolized his time, day and night. We possess convincing testimony of his great reluctance each time he was forced to leave his desk to go on campaign.

Therefore, it is appropriate to make a semantic point of some importance, even if it may seem insignificant. The wars of the empire are often labeled as the Napoleonic Wars. For the general reader, this term conveys the message that Napoleon was responsible for initiating these wars. In the interest of precision and objectivity, it is preferable to substitute the expression, "Wars of the Consulate and Empire."

We will now sift through all of these wars to determine their origin, in the process confirming Napoleon's assertion that he was always attacked.

At the outset, one must recognize a crucial distinction. The true warmonger is not necessarily the person who opens hostilities. That decision relates primarily to operational strategy, i.e., to give battle under the best possible conditions. In addition, in Napoleon's case one must add his constant concern to spare France from the violence of the battlefield by conducting the war outside the national frontiers.

The source of initiative for war is on the field of national politics. Too many superficial observers are confused by these two ideas and commit a grave error of judgment in defining responsibility.

As our purpose here is to identify those responsible for launching these wars, their subsequent conduct will be reduced to a general outline of events. We will not enlarge upon the military genius of Napoleon, another subject of passionate debate.

Out of concern for simplicity and continuity, we will proceed in chronological order, beginning with the early efforts of First Consul Bonaparte to adjust the war economy to the Treaties of Lunéville and Amiens that had brought the return of peace.

The Dissolution of the Second Coalition

Recall first that the Second Coalition formed while Bonaparte was in Egypt. Britain, Austria, Russia, Sweden, the Kingdom of Naples, Portugal, and the Holy Roman Empire all joined this coalition. Prussia remained neutral.

When he returned from his campaign in Egypt, Bonaparte discovered a compromised—albeit temporarily stable—military situation.

As previously shown, despite the best intentions of the First Consul, a general peace could only be obtained at the price of reopening hostilities in Italy and in Germany. We will now review the efforts Napoleon expended in those circumstances to avoid war.

Napoleon's first act as head of state was to take the initiative for a broad effort to make peace with the belligerents. He attempted to work both through diplomatic channels and in personal contacts with other heads of state.

He first attempted to bring Prussia out of its neutrality to enlist on the side of France, or at least to act as mediator. Sent to Berlin for this purpose, Duroc, though received politely, did not succeed in convincing Frederick William to abandon his wary neutrality.

Another diplomatic effort obtained better results from Russia. Embittered by the defeat of his armies in Switzerland, a defeat he blamed on Austria, Paul I left the Coalition and even announced himself willing to take concerted action against Britain. This reversal of alliances would prove fatal to him.

As soon as he entered into office, the First Consul extended diplomatic actions by personal letters addressed to the two principal monarchs who were at war with France. To the Emperor Francis of Austria, he wrote, "rejecting any sentiment of vain glory, my first desire is to halt the effusion of blood that is flowing. . . . The well-known character of Your Majesty leaves me in no doubt of the peaceful desire of your heart. . . ." This bordered on the obsequious, but in his eyes peace was well worth the small concession of his own dignity.

It was on this occasion that Napoleon expressed to George III of Great Britain his famous maxim, quoted at the front of this study:

> Peace is the first necessity and the first of glories. Must this war, which has ravaged the four corners of the earth over the past eight years, be internal? Is there no means to reach an agreement? By abusing their forces, France and England might continue this consumption for many years, to the distress of all peoples. Yet, I venture to say that the future of all civilized nations depends upon the end of a war that has engulfed the entire world. . . . I assure Your Majesty of my sincere desire to contribute for the second time to a general pacification, by a prompt attempt completely in confidence and unencumbered by the formalities which can only support the mutual desire to deceive ourselves . . .

These offers of peace were rejected with disdain. The two monarchs did not even take the basic courtesy to reply in person. They rejected anything not received through diplomatic channels. Britain pushed its contempt so far as to demand the restoration of the Bourbons and a return to the borders of 1789. We thus again see the unchanging objective of the European monarchies: return to the Ancien Régime and weaken France.

The purpose was clear. Britain and Austria wished to fight it out. This was the first of the wars imposed on Napoleon.

Hostilities recommenced in Italy on April 5, 1800. The Austrian General Melas forced the pass of Cadibone and pushed Massena into Genoa, to which he laid siege. Suchet was forced back on the Var. The Army of the Rhine, under Moreau's command, attacked that of General Kray, replacement for Archduke Charles, who had been relieved of command for having recommended a sensible negotiation with the French.

The outcome of the war would be determined in northern Italy. While the Army of the Rhine successfully contained the Austrians in Germany, on May 13 the First Consul took the leadership of the Reserve Army that was located in the Alps and held back for decisive action. He had to give nominal command of the army to Berthier, thereby respecting the letter of the provision in the Constitution forbidding the First Consul to take direct command of field armies.

Like Hannibal more than 20 centuries earlier, on May 20 Bonaparte with difficulty crossed the Great Saint Bernard Pass and fell on Melas' petrified rear elements. He entered Milan on June 2 but was not in time to deliver Massena in Genoa, which capitulated on June 4. On the 9th, Lannes achieved the well-executed victory of Montebello. The war culminated with the celebrated victory of Marengo, at first undecided but finally decisive.

The Convention of Alexandria that a desperate Melas signed on June 15 gave France northern Italy as far as Mincio.

If hostilities had ceased in Italy, they continued on the Rhine. In a letter written at Marengo on June 16, the First Consul again proposed negotiations with the Austrian emperor, but in vain.

Because the irresolute Moreau was too gentle with the Austrian army, Vienna believed that it had lost a battle in Italy but not the war in Germany. Stimulated by British subsidies, it continued to fight for eight

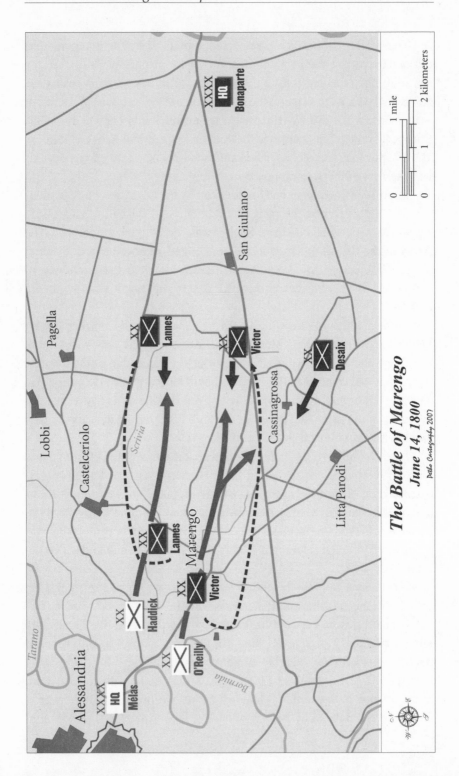

The Battle of Marengo
June 14, 1800
Pete Cartography 2007

months before concluding a peace treaty. Matters were resolved only when Austria suffered another defeat.

Five months after Marengo, the interminable Austrian evasions exhausted the patience of the First Consul. Hostilities recommenced in Germany on November 22, 1800. Opposed by the insignificant Archduke Johann, on December 3 Moreau won a decisive victory at Hohenlinden and exploited his success in the direction of Vienna. He was only 65 kilometers from the capital when he reached Steyr on December 25. The Austrians finally felt compelled to sign an armistice.

In Italy, Brune, reinforced by Macdonald's troops from Switzerland, imposed the Armistice of Treviso upon Archduke Charles on January 15, 1801. Murat hounded the Neapolitan Army out of Tuscany and Rome and invaded the bellicose Kingdom of Naples, which was saved from occupation only by the diplomatic intervention of the tsar. Signed on February 18, the Armistice of Folgano only imposed the closure of Neapolitan ports to the British. As we have already seen, this act of clemency by the victor had no effect on the rancorous aggressiveness of the Kingdom of Naples.

Beaten on all fronts, Austria finally consented to abandon its British ally and, on February 19, 1801, signed the Treaty of Lunéville, whose provisions have already been discussed.

Lunéville only went halfway toward a general peace. Britain remained at war, and it was against it that peace efforts would now focus.

At the outset, the situation appeared favorable. Britain was isolated, having lost its principal ally at Lunéville. The Russia of Paul I had become friendly with France. He had organized a League of Neutrals along with Sweden, Denmark, and Prussia. Britain thus lost the major markets of Germany and the Baltic.

The British were losing heart. The implacable enemy of France, Prime Minister William Pitt, was forced to resign on March 14, 1801. His successor, Addington, appeared more conciliatory. Bonaparte sent him a permanent representative in the person of Otto. At first, Britain offered Egypt in exchange for recognition of all of its recent colonial conquests. Seeking a world peace and not an arrangement of details, the First Consul refused this partial accord.

At this moment, an important event occurred that had considerable consequences for the present and future: the assassination of Tsar Paul I on March 23, 1801. The conspirators took three-quarters of an hour to kill the tsar in his bedroom, suffocating him in his sash and bludgeoning him with a sword pommel. Officially, he died of apoplexy. Though suspected of complicity, his son Alexander assumed the throne.

For the British, the implications of this elimination of a pro-French monarch were clear. Paul I had been a great admirer of Bonaparte. He had installed a bust of the First Consul at the Hermitage, and according to rumor he tipped his hat each time he passed the statue. Paul considered Bonaparte to be, in his words, "the greatest general of modern times."

Paul I's assassination upset the French diplomatic plan. Let us repeat that the Russian alliance had been a trump card for France, leaving Paris a free hand against the main enemy, Britain.

London was well aware of the importance of Russia, and would stop at nothing to obtain an alliance with (or at least the neutrality of) the empire of the tsars. Britain made this the priority of its diplomacy, not counting any cost. The years to come would be dominated by a bitter Franco-British diplomatic struggle to gain the good graces of Russia.

In the short run, Britain took heart again. On April 2, 1801, Nelson's ships savagely bombarded Copenhagen. There is no better message of peace! The neutrals dissolved their league and submitted their navigation (excluding Russia) to English law. In October 1801, Turkey concluded an accord with London, confirming British supremacy in the Mediterranean.

In this conjunction of events so favorable to it, Britain did not hesitate to raise the stakes, which explains the length of peace negotiations.

For his part, Bonaparte did not remain inactive. He ostentatiously assembled troops and ships in the Channel ports, flourishing the threat of invasion. He knew that the British people were very attached to peace. This military demonstration had some effect, since ultimately it was an economic crisis in the markets that convinced the government of George III to give up war temporarily. The immediate concern of the British business oligarchy was for peace. It was thus that Otto and Lord Hawkesbury concluded on October 1, 1801, what became known as the Preliminaries of London, to the general satisfaction and even celebration of the British and French populace.

In Amiens, negotiations followed between Joseph Bonaparte and Cornwallis, in the presence of representatives of Spain and the Netherlands. It took another six months of bitter discussions to arrive at the acclaimed Treaty of Amiens of March 25, 1802, received with general revelry throughout Europe. For the first time in a decade, there was no fighting on the continent.

For a moment at Amiens, Bonaparte believed that he had found a Holy Grail of peace. He would be quickly disenchanted. This promising treaty soon proved to be a false truce of three years. At least it permitted the accomplishment of the great works of the Consulate.

The Lightning Destruction of the Third Coalition

This peace could not be definitive for the simple reason that it had not reduced the hostility of the monarchies toward the new France. Quite the contrary. Austria and Britain had only agreed to peace because they were forced to do so by circumstances. It was obvious that both awaited better days to take their revenge, killing the revolutionary hydra incarnated in that devil, Napoleon Bonaparte.

Britain Relights the Fires of War

The frequently advanced thesis of a shared responsibility for the failure of the Treaty of Amiens will not stand up to serious examination. The resumption of war resulted solely from the deliberate will of the British government. One has only to consider the comment made in person by Prime Minister Addington on the day after the signing of the peace. In front of Parliament, he felt the need to excuse the treaty in these terms: "For the moment, our duty is to preserve our forces. We will conserve them for future occasions, when it will be possible to resume the offensive with hopes of success." These few words summarize the entire warlike philosophy of Britain. Everything else was part of a deceptive rhetoric.

In a confidential discussion with his Russian colleague, the British Ambassador to Paris, Lord Wittworth, admitted, "my heart would like to take advantage of my current position, which enables me to strike serious blows against France without fear of retaliation."

In the archives of the Prussian and Russian courts one may find interesting indications of British guilt. The king of Prussia wrote, "I am far from excusing the British actions." The Russian tsar was even more blunt: "the British conduct appears to be contrary to the letter of the Treaty of Amiens. What could have motivated them to retain Malta in contravention of solemnly-contracted agreements?"

Britain agitated constantly with its collaborators. The most anti-French of Russian diplomats, Morkoff, admitted that "right is more on the side of Bonaparte [sic] than of Britain. The First Consul seems willing to provide anything that might reassure not only Britain but all of Europe."

For his part, the most anti-Napoleonic of Prussian ministers, Karl August von Hardenberg, affirmed in his memoirs that "it would have been desirable if England had demonstrated as much goodwill for peace as did Napoleon."

Having said that, one needs look no farther to determine responsibility. Nevertheless, let us examine matters further, because the British cabinet attempted in Machiavellian fashion to attribute the rupture to the First Consul.

The maintenance of peace depended essentially on respecting the clauses of the Treaty of Amiens, whose signature engaged the honor of all parties. Yet, the British government found all manner of pretexts to avoid fulfilling its obligations.

The most important of these concerned the evacuation of Malta that was to have occurred in September 1802. At the beginning of 1803, there was no sign of departure. Yet, France had evacuated the Neapolitan ports ahead of schedule, which was the provision connected to the British withdrawal from Malta. On February 15, Britain instead announced its intention to retain the island.

When the First Consul expressed his "chagrin" about Malta, the British cabinet attempted to justify itself by citing the annexation of Piedmont to France and the presence of French troops in the Netherlands. Pitiful arguments! Piedmont had become French at the request of its representatives, to the general satisfaction of the population. No clause of the Treaty of Amiens had dealt with that question. And, how did a French Piedmont present a threat of invasion to Britain?

As for the French military presence in the Netherlands, it was completely normal for a territory ceded under the Treaty of Lunéville, which was independent of the Treaty of Amiens.

Accustomed to dominating, Britain sought nothing less than to dictate French foreign policy by such demands. If even then Britain had demonstrated a minimum of courtesy! Instead, the government encouraged a low press campaign to drag Bonaparte through the mud. In London, the new France was openly humiliated, the Consulate's power flouted. The Count d'Artois received the honor of reviewing an English regiment, an intolerable interference in the internal affairs of France. Open provocations were made. When offering a dinner to the French ambassador, General Andreossy, the Prince of Wales also invited the Duke of Orléans, the future King Louis-Philippe, who wore the royal blue ribbon. Was this the conduct of a government aspiring to peace?

It was too much! On February 18, 1803, the First Consul summoned the British ambassador, Lord Whitworth, for a showdown. For some time, he had burned to speak plainly to this diplomat who made no effort to conceal his contempt for France. His designation as ambassador was an unfriendly act in itself. Bonaparte firmly called upon Britain to fulfill its obligations and to put an end to the ignoble attacks against his person.

In response, the British cabinet on March 8 asked Parliament for supplementary military funds "to reply to France's preparations for war," if one can imagine the nerve! This measure certainly was not dictated by a passion to preserve the peace! In reality, Britain had already decided to relight the fires of war.

On March 13, Bonaparte replied with a new rebuke to Lord Whitworth: "Thus, the English want war! . . . woe to those who do not respect their treaties! They will be responsible in the eyes of all Europe!"

On April 26, the British ambassador had the effrontery to propose to Talleyrand an incredible deal, obviously intended to provoke rejection and thus cast responsibility for the rupture on France. The proposition was even more unacceptable because it was presented in the form of an ultimatum expiring only seven days later. Britain offered to hold Malta for ten years and the neighboring island of Lampedusa permanently, provided that France evacuated the Netherlands and Belgium. In other words, Britain was to hold what she should have given up, while France had to surrender something that was not subject to their treaty with each other. Nothing could be more contemptible.

More patient than is usually admitted, because he desired to preserve the peace at any price, Bonaparte resisted the temptation to break relations immediately. He directed Talleyrand to continue with the negotiations. The failure was total, however. The British cabinet was unwilling to change any of its exorbitant demands. Talleyrand reported to the First Consul that Britain was already virtually in a state of war and that there was nothing more to be tried.

Despite this, Bonaparte did not give up. To permit one more chance for peace, on June 12 he suggested to the Russian ambassador, Markov, that his country should mediate the dispute. He proposed to neutralize Malta, giving it in pledge to Russia, as a means by which France would renounce definitively this very important strategic position. Even this enormous concession obtained no response. Britain returned a disdainful reply. Peace had failed. On May 11, Bonaparte rejected the British ultimatum after taking the advice of his council.

The die was cast. On May 12, 1803, the British ambassador returned home. The next day, the British cabinet confirmed its intention to hold Malta for ten years, in open violation of the Treaty of Amiens. To signify his determination, Bonaparte ordered Gouvion Saint-Cyr to occupy the ports of Otranto, Brindisi, and Taranto in Italy.

On May 17, without a declaration of war, the British government of the ultra-warmonger Pitt (who had returned to office a few days before) seized all French and Dutch ships in British waters. Britain thus took over 1,200 ships and 200 million in merchandise by an act of state piracy on a grand scale. It was a case of open aggression; the mask was off!

The First Consul replied on May 22 by arresting all British subjects in France and its possessions. The next day, Pitt officially declared war on France, a total war that did not reach its conclusion until June 18, 1815, at Waterloo.

Britain took advantage of its maritime superiority to strike the first blows in the French colonies. Saint Lucia and Tobago, Saint Pierre and Miquelon, and the India trading stations were occupied immediately.

France responded on May 27 by occupying Hannover, the personal property of the king of Great Britain. In thus taking control of the estuaries of the Weser and the Elbe Rivers, France struck a serious blow to British commerce in Germany, a sensitive point for London.

This latent state of war continued for two-and-a-half years, not without Bonaparte making one last attempt at peace by a personal letter to the king of Great Britain, in which one may read: "I attach no dishonor to making the first move. I believe that I have sufficiently proved to the world that I have no fear of the fortunes of war. The world is large enough for our two nations to live in peace." This renewed gesture of good will was another sword stroke into the water.

Thus, all the fallacious quibbles cannot excuse Great Britain from its total responsibility for shattering the Peace of Amiens.

As demonstrated by the remarkable progress under the Consulate, peace was so profitable to the new France that Britain dreaded the resulting threat to its own imperialist and economic hegemony. Pitt's political opponent, the honest Fox, made an interesting observation to the House of Commons on May 24, 1803, once peace had been sacrificed: "Thus, any progress France may make in its interior, commerce, manufacturing, etc., etc., is to be a cause for war, an injury to us?" We return again and again to the irreducible belligerent situation of the moment. Britain could not stand any competition to its supremacy. It chose to settle its differences by force of arms. Had she not already founded the Third Coalition on April 11?

Britain Saved by its Navy at Trafalgar

With due allowance for the differences, the Franco-British confrontation may be compared to that between Rome and Carthage during the Punic Wars, with the leading land power opposed to the leading maritime power. Napoleon found himself in some ways in the situation of Scipio, forced to defeat Hannibal at Zama in 202 B.C., with the slogan "delenda Carthago"—Carthage must be destroyed.

Yet, the first important difference was that Napoleon's war aim was not to annihilate and conquer the new Carthage and its allies, but solely to destroy their armed forces, in order to dissuade them from recommencing the war. One cannot over-emphasize the limited character of Napoleonic geo-strategy, laid down as a fundamental principle.

The second difference from Scipio was that Napoleon suffered from a crushing naval inferiority. The British army could only be defeated in England itself. This required a crossing of the channel by an expeditionary corps that the emperor estimated at 150,000 men, 450 guns, and 11,000 horses. This gigantic force assembled around Boulogne, from whence came the label "Boulogne Camp."

The crossing depended on two requirements: an appropriate transport fleet and the neutralization of the Royal Navy in the channel during the crossing. The first presented no insurmountable obstacles. A flotilla of 2,000 flat-bottomed, armed boats was constructed in all the neighboring ports, including river basins. The second requirement was a completely different matter. The assistance obtained from the Spanish fleet could not compensate for French maritime weakness. As was his habit, Napoleon sought by a strategic maneuver to obtain the local naval superiority he needed during the period of time necessary for his army to cross.

The emperor's plan depended on a naval diversion on a grand scale. It consisted of luring Nelson's fleet to the Antilles by a threat against the British colonies caused by the concentration of the French squadrons of Toulon, La Rochelle, and Brest. Once that was accomplished, the combined fleet must return with all sails set to the Channel, stripped of British ships. Unfortunately, the execution of this plan was to lead to the greatest catastrophe in the maritime history of France.

Since Aboukir Bay in 1798, the relationships between Napoleon and his admirals were persistently fatal. As commander-designate of a naval operation, the brave Admiral Latouche-Tréville died suddenly on August 19, 1804. The same fate struck Admiral Bruix, commander of the invasion fleet, in March 1805. Their successors, Villeneuve and Ganteaume, were not of the same stature. Villeneuve (from Toulon) and Missiessy (from La Rochelle) missed their rendezvous in the Antilles first in February 1805 and then in June of the same year. Reinforced by the Spanish squadron of Admiral Gravina, Villeneuve could find nothing better to do in August than to take refuge at Cadiz, where Nelson mounted guard.

After all these delays, the invasion plan for Britain had become precarious. The Third Coalition had had sufficient time to form. Napoleon thus had to abandon the invasion of Great Britain to deal with aggression coming from the east. Without even having been in action, its fleet already had saved Britain.

In order to get some use out of the French fleet, on September 15 Napoleon ordered Villeneuve to make a demonstration in force in the Mediterranean, off the coast of the Kingdom of Naples, which was being tempted to join the Coalition. Before his successor, Rosily, could arrive from the emperor, Villeneuve abruptly decided to set sail on October 20, 1805. Nelson intercepted him the next morning at dawn off Cape Trafalgar. The slight numerical superiority of the Franco-Spanish fleet and the incontestable bravery of its sailors could accomplish nothing against the experienced professionalism of the British crews and the superior tactics of Nelson. The desperate conflict led by the end of the day to the total annihilation of the Franco-Spanish fleet.

Thereafter, it was never possible for Napoleon to exorcise the demon of war in its own den. In fact, Trafalgar had already sealed the fate of the empire. At the moment, however, Napoleon needed to face the renewed menace coming from the east.

The Sunshine of Austerlitz

The campaign crowned by triumph at Austerlitz foreshadowed a pattern that would be repeated five times before Waterloo in an invariable sequence: violation of an existing peace treaty under a false pretext; victorious military campaign by Napoleon; conclusion of a new peace treaty, usually generous to the vanquished; and recommencement of war for another fallacious reason . . . and so on, until 1815.

With General Mack commanding in the principal theater of Germany, on September 13, 1805, the Austrian army invaded France's ally, Bavaria. Committing the fatal error of not waiting for Kutusov's Russian army, Mack fell upon Munich and pursued the Bavarians to Ulm.

After a lightning reorientation of his dispositions at Boulogne and on the Danube, Napoleon executed one of his most dazzling strategic combinations. Cut off and encircled, the Austrian army shut itself up in Ulm. Only a few thousand men succeeded in fleeing under the command of Archduke Ferdinand. Without hope of aid from Kutusov, who fell back toward Moravia, or from the army of his compatriot Buxhowden, Mack capitulated October 20. There was virtually no Austrian army remaining in Germany. That of Archduke Charles, operating in northern Italy against Massena, belatedly fell back with the intention of going to the defense of Vienna.

After the capitulation of Ulm, Napoleon granted to General Mack, his unfortunate opponent, a compassionate interview at the Abbey of Elchingen. Mack recounted the meeting thusly, as recorded in the Austrian national archives:

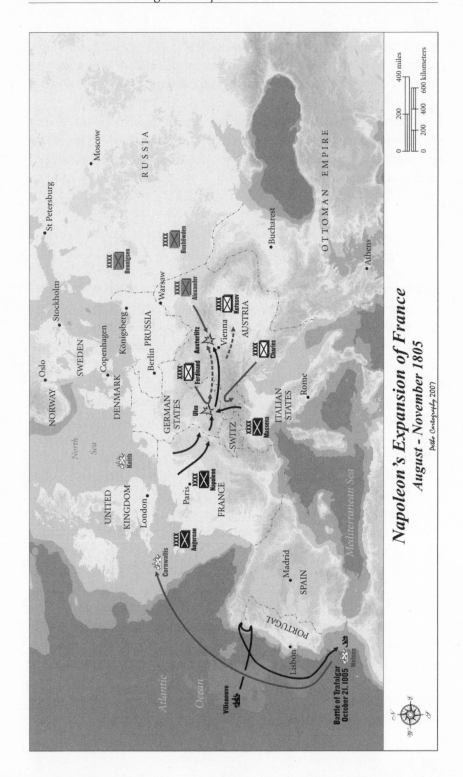

Napoleon's Expansion of France
August – November 1805

Pete Cestopody 2007

Go to Vienna. I authorize you to say to the Emperor Francis that all I desire is peace and that I am quite irritated that peace has been interrupted. I am willing to reach a very equitable agreement with him, and I will deal equally with Russia if you wish. Let someone tell me the propositions of the two powers—I am quite anxious to hear them. I am willing to make sacrifices, even great sacrifices. I tell you yet again, and authorize you to say to your sovereign, that (he repeated again, very distinctly, what I have just quoted) he has only to send to me you or the Count of Cobentzel or whomever, together with a Russian plenipotentiary, to negotiate with me. [And General Mack added] Everything that I have written above I attest to on my word of honor.

Once again, this generous extended hand would be spurned with contempt.

The Grand Armeé entered Munich on October 24. Vienna fell without resistance on November 12. The Grand Armeé pursued the Russians as far as Brünn and the town of Austerlitz, near which on December 2 Napoleon achieved a victory that has entered into legend. Let us expand somewhat on this mythic event.

The situation of the Grand Armeé on November 20 was not good. It sat exposed in Moravia. At Brünn (100 kilometers from Vienna), Lannes and Murat barred the route to Olmutz (50 kilometers to the northeast), where 85,000 Austro-Russians (including about 15,000 Austrians), in the presence of both the Austrian and the Russian emperors, prepared to attack. Napoleon had directed Soult's corps to occupy the town of Austerlitz.

Napoleon left significant troops in Vienna as a covering force against a possible reaction by the forces of Archdukes Charles and Johann, who between them controlled another 85,000 men. The Grand Armeé thus risked being defeated in detail.

The emperor had not yet achieved the concentration of all the units needed for the great battle that loomed. Bernadotte's and Davout's corps were still several days' march away. Until these troops rejoined him, he had only 70,000 troops available.

Another sword of Damocles was suspended over him. On November 3, the King of Prussia signed a treaty with the Russian tsar, under which the Prussian army (150,000 men) was to move from a posture of armed mediation to membership in the Coalition if France did not accept the conditions specified by the Coalition. Fortunately, the Prussian king's prudent minister of foreign affairs, the Count von Haugwitz, engaged in delaying tactics with Talleyrand in Vienna. The Kingdom of Naples, whose attitude was menacing, threatened Northern Italy, almost undefended.

Alone against the world, Napoleon had to crush the Coalition or go under. He had ten days to prepare for battle. He decided first to await the shock of arms with Kutusov on ground he had chosen between Brünn and Austerlitz. For several days he surveyed the terrain to familiarize himself with every detail.

Two routes led out of the crossroads of Brünn. One extended due east toward Olmutz, and formed the enemy axis of advance. Fifteen kilometers east of Brünn, this road branched toward Austerlitz, five kilometers to the south. The second route led directly south to Vienna, 100 kilometers away. This represented the vital communications line of the Grand Armeé.

Ten kilometers east of Brünn and perpendicular to the Brünn-Olmutz road, the Goldbach River flowed from north to south. Immediately south of the road, the Pratzen Heights stretched north-south on the eastern bank of the river. The heights measured five kilometers east to west and twice that distance north to south. Two hills crowned this plateau: on the north, the Stary-Vinohrady, with a modest height of 298 meters; on the south, the Pratzberg of 324 meters. The river flowed 90 meters below, while to the south of the heights ran the Satchen Pool. A route stretched between the heights and the pool, connecting Austerlitz to the road between Brünn and Vienna and passing through the village of Telnitz. Finally, at a distance of ten kilometers from Brünn in the direction of Olmutz, the Zuran Knoll provided an excellent observation point 197 meters high.

This was the battlefield chosen by Napoleon to gain one of the greatest victories in military history. All the place names above would enter into legend, especially the Pratzen Heights, which logically should have lent the battle its name. It is called Austerlitz simply because this was where the emperor wrote his famous proclamation after the battle.

The enemy's intent was to cut the road to Vienna south of Brünn. To that end, the Austerlitz-Telnitz axis would constitute the natural direction

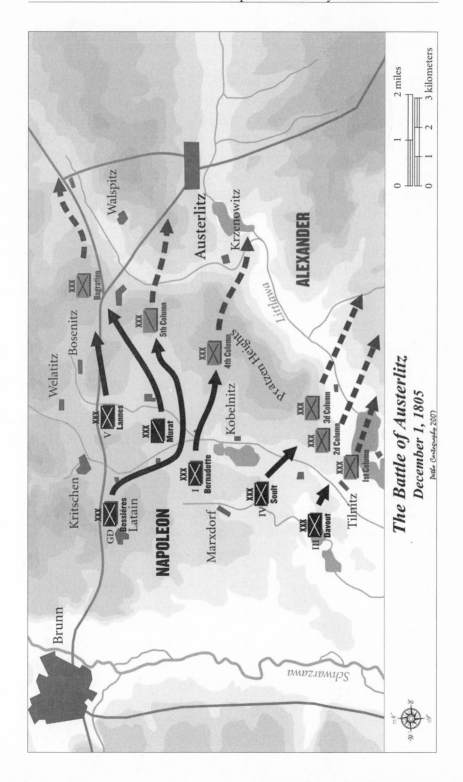

Brunn

Schwarzawa

Kritschen

Welatitz

Bosenitz

Walspitz

Austerlitz

Krzenowitz

XXX Bessières Latain GD

NAPOLEON

XXX V Lannes

XXX Murat

XXX I Bernadotte

XXX 5th Column

Marxdorf

Kobelnitz

XXX 4th Column

Pratzen Heights

Littlawa

ALEXANDER

XXX IV Soult

XXX 2d Column

XXX 3d Column

XXX III Davout

Tilnitz

XXX 1st Column

The Battle of Austerlitz, December 1, 1805

Dale Costerworth, 2007

0   1   2 miles
0   1   2   3 kilometers

of the enemy's main effort. In turn, to disrupt the French dispositions he must first control the Pratzen Heights.

To encourage his opponent in this tactic, Napoleon baited the trap by leaving the heights unoccupied. Once the enemy moved from the heights toward Telnitz, so as to break the French defenses, the emperor would penetrate the enemy's weakened dispositions on the heights itself. After that, the French would envelop their opponents to the south, using the terrain as an anvil to destroy them.

On the tactical level, Napoleon added a legitimate psychological deception. To encourage the presumptuous Alexander to abandon his caution, Napoleon would ostentatiously suggest that he dreaded the coming battle, an action that protected him from the accusation of warmongering. In truth, Napoleon wished sincerely for peace as the only reasonable solution. On November 28, he had Savary carry to the tsar a letter of friendship in which he asserted that "all [Napoleon's] desire and hope is to find opportunities to prove to [Alexander] that he hoped to make himself agreeable to [the tsar.]"

Too sure of himself, Alexander took a high tone, omitting in his belligerent response even the courtesy of addressing Napoleon as "Sire." Instead, he addressed the letter to the "head of the French government." The tsar obviously believed that Napoleon was afraid of him.

To reinforce this sentiment, Napoleon ordered his first response measures by troops near the Pratzen Heights. To help convince Alexander of his defeatism, he again sent Savery to the tsar on the 19th to propose an interview for the next day. The tsar sent Savery back in the company of his senior aide de camp, the arrogant and scatterbrained Prince Dolgorouki. Napoleon went to meet the prince so as not to give him freedom to spy on French positions. This pretentious amateur disdainfully announced the conditions set by his master: a return to the boundaries of 1789 and the immediate surrender of Vienna and its hereditary lands. In other words, a capitulation so humiliating that it could not be accepted. Highly irritated by the contemptuous attitude of this nonentity, the emperor ordered him to leave immediately. This display of temper would undoubtedly be interpreted by the tsar as an additional indication of Napoleon's anxiety. All of Napoleon's peace overtures had been repulsed.

By December 1, the French army had become a coiled spring. It was disposed as follows: On the north, blocking the route from Olmutz to

Brünn, were Lannes' corps (17,000 men) and Murat's cavalry (7,000). Their defense was anchored on the fortified knoll known as Santon Hill, because of its resemblance to Egyptian topography. In the center opposite the Pratzen Heights and behind the Goldbach, sat Soult's corps (22,000) and the two divisions of Vandamme and Saint-Hilaire. Behind Soult and slightly to the left, Bernadotte's corps (9,000) was still assembling. The Imperial Guard (5,000), under the command of Bessieres, was located close to the Imperial bivouac, near the observation point on the Zuran Knoll. On the southern wing, deliberately left exposed, Davout's corps (10,000) had hurried by forced marches to cover Telnitz and Sokolnitz (two kilometers to the north). This corps had traveled 130 kilometers in 48 hours, losing only a few stragglers. In all, some 70,000 Frenchmen.

On the opposing side, the Austro-Russians were arrayed as Napoleon had anticipated, as confirmed by his informants and reconnaissance: In the north, opposite Lannes and Murat, lay Peter Bagration's corps (15,000) supported by Liechtenstein's cavalry (5,000). In the center, was Kollowrath's corps (15,000). Behind him, near the headquarters of the two emperors at Austerlitz, was the Russian Imperial Guard, commanded by Grand Duke Constantine, in reserve. In the south, as Napoleon had expected, was the principal mass of the enemy (40,000 men), commanded by Buxhowden and including the corps of Doktorov, Kienmayer, Kangeron, and Przhebishevsky.

One circumstance favoring the French was that Mikhail Kutuzov had only a nominal command. The tsar, inspired by his presumptuous chief of staff Weyrother, reserved important decisions to himself. Weyrother's amateurism would cost Alexander a great deal.

Napoleon decided about 10:00 p.m. to make a last-minute inspection of the troops, escorted by several mounted Chasseurs of the Guard. Traveling along the Goldbach, the detachment came face-to-face with a patrol of Cossacks that charged, and for an instant put the French in a dangerous position. Leaving his escort to deal with this skirmish, the emperor returned to his bivouac. Dismounting, he stumbled over the trunk of a tree. The noise alerted a grenadier who, to determine what was going on, improvised a torch to illuminate the area. Imagine his astonishment at discovering the emperor covered with mud! It took him several seconds to react, after which he shouted at the top of his lungs, "Vive l'Empereur!" The entire camp was awakened. Cries of "Vive l'Empereur" were everywhere. Someone remarked that it was the anniversary of Napoleon's coronation, a coincidence that he had not even considered. Everyone lit torches. Unit bivouacs lit up one after the other along the entire front line. His soldiers thus presented him with an improvised "sound and light" spectacle and danced the farandole. Bands struck up to accompany the cheering. Drums were beating on the field. The uproar was deafening, and Napoleon's emotions were at their peak. He remarked, "This is the best day of my life, and you are all my children!" He could not have helped by think how he would lose some of them in a few hours.

This unexpected interlude provided an unforeseen tactical effect. The Russians concluded that the French were burning their camps in preparation for a retreat, hoping to accelerate their movements and leave the Coalition forces behind. The Russians therefore moved even faster toward their own destruction!

As a result, Davout would receive the attack earlier than expected, especially considering that he was far from having finished the assembly of his units. The emperor immediately reinforced him with Legrand de Soult's division. The resistance of this force made the victory possible.

By dawn on that memorable December 2, 1805, the marshals and generals had assembled around Napoleon on the Zuran Knoll. They received their final instructions and hurried back to their units. It was cold, and a thick fog covered the ground, permitting the movement of units to their starting points out of sight of the enemy.

The battlefield quickly flared up. In the north, Lannes and Murat easily contained Bagration and Liechtenstein, whose static mission corresponded to that of Davout. He in turn received a terrible attack but held on stoically. In the center, Soult fidgeted with impatience to throw himself into the assault on the Pratzen Heights. The emperor made him wait a while. The idea was to emerge on top of the plateau at the exact moment it was exposed by the Russian movement to the south.

At 9:00 a.m. the legendary sun of Austerlitz rose blood red above the Pratzen heights, revealing the Russian silhouettes. The fog dissipated, as if by magic.

Napoleon finally released Soult's corps like a pack of hounds. Vandamme and Saint-Hilaire's divisions assaulted the slopes of the Pratzen Hieghts, each one headed for a hilltop. The spectacle was grand. With shouldered arms, the men moved calmly forward, singing "On va leur percer le flank, rantanplan, tirelire en plan" (we'll pierce their flank, they'll leave their money boxes behind). They had well understood their leader's concept of maneuver, expressed in a harangue the night before. The bands accompanied the march with patriotic airs. Then the drums beat the charge. A witness said that the impetus would have been enough to carry a paralytic forward.

The plateau was conquered fairly easily by 11:00 a.m. The Russians were surprised by this attack, which forced them to return to the Telnitz, relieving the pressure on Davout when he had been hard pressed. Telnitz and Sokolnitz changed possession several times in hand-to-hand fighting. Outnumbered three to one, the intrepid Davout had stoically accomplished his mission. Napoleon reinforced him with four of Oudinot's battalions and, as soon as the heights were conquered, he moved his command post to the Stary-Vinobrady hill, where Kutuzov had been located a few moments before. Napoleon issued new orders, carried instantly to their destinations by willing aides de camp.

In the north, Lannes and Murat attacked Bagration and Liechtenstein in force. Nansouty's cavalry performed well. Kellerman, the son of the Duke of Valmy, covered himself with glory, as he had done at Marengo. The Russians fell back in disorder behind the Holubitz ravine.

In the center, Soult received the order to shift Saint-Hilaire and Vandamme's divisions to the south, in order to take Buxhowden in reverse. Bernadotte had to relieve them on the plateau.

It was now about noon, when the inevitable Russian counterattack occurred. Grand Duke Constantine's ten battalions and six squadrons of the Russian Imperial Guard surged suddenly onto the plateau and fell brutally on Vandamme's division. Bernadotte missed the opportunity to take the Russians in flank. Prominent in their white and green uniforms, the famous Knight Guards, gigantic men, as well as the Preobrajenski and Seminovski Guards Regiments, crushed everything in their path, cutting into the squares of French infantry.

Symptoms of panic appeared in the ranks. The 4th Line Regiment dissolved under the charge and fugitives got as far as headquarters. The regimental eagle was captured. The emperor called upon the Guard, which he had held in reserve nearby. He sent Rapp to Bessieres to organize the counterattack. A clash of titans loomed, the meeting of the two Imperial Guards, with the elite of the Russian army against the elite of the French army. Morland's mounted chasseurs and Ordener's mounted grenadiers charged side by side. This first assault failed to halt the Knight Guards, and Morland fell dead. His replacement, Dahlmann, regrouped three squadrons. For his part, Rapp reassembled two squadrons, the Mameluke cavalry and the mounted grenadiers. In concert, they again launched an assault. "Let's make the ladies of Saint Petersburg weep," rang from the ranks of the mounted chasseurs.

This fantastic charge overwhelmed everything in its way. The Mamelukes performed miracles, as one witness recounted: "They cut the reins of a soldier with their curved sabers. One of them went three different times to carry a Russian standard to the Emperor. After the third occasion, the Emperor tried to hold him back, but he attacked again and did not return. He remained on the battlefield."

After having passed the heights, Rapp regrouped his horsemen and launched a second charge to complete the effects of the first. The Russian Guard was cut to pieces or dissolved. The Coalition center was broken, and the Grand Armeé had succeeded in "piercing their flank."

Rapp came to the command post, wounded but triumphant. He brought as his prisoner Prince Repnine, colonel of the Russian Guard. Napoleon congratulated Rapp warmly for his exploits, which he had observed by field glasses. His bleeding wound concerned him, but Rapp replied, "It's nothing but a scratch."

It was now 1:00 p.m. The emperor moved his command post to the Saint Antoine Chapel, south of the plateau. He was presented with a key prisoner, the Baron de Wimpffen, a French officer in Russian service. Wimpffen's bearing was pitiful, but Napoleon offered him a class of wine "from France," he specified.

Relieved of all concern for his rear, Soult pushed his troops toward Telnitz, where Davout continued to hold Buxhowden firmly. The two French jaws closed on him. Buxhowden's troops sought an escape route by way of the frozen lakes of the Satchen. Cannon balls broke the ice. Those Russians who did not drown were incapacitated by hypothermia, and surrendered in mass. Their artillery pieces and caissons sank.

At 4:00 p.m., as darkness fell, the battle ended. The remnants of the Austro-Russian army fled eastward. The pursuit was interrupted by darkness. The Grand Armeé suffered 1,500 killed and 6,000 wounded. The enemy lost twice that number, and left behind large numbers of prisoners, cannon, and regimental colors.

Believing that the punishment was sufficient, the emperor did not attempt to pursue the debris of the Russian army. On December 4, he received the Austrian emperor in an improvised bivouac near Austerlitz, in order to discuss the basis for a peace treaty. Put at ease by the courtesy and good humor of his conqueror, the Emperor Francis let fall several confidences. He admitted to having been duped by the British: "The English trade in human flesh. There is no doubt that France was correct in its quarrel with England." Conscious of having violated the Treaty of Lunéville, Francis agreed to all of Napoleon's proposals. "Well, then, the affair is arranged. I haven't been free until this morning," he exclaimed.

The emperor of the French admonished him gently: "Your Majesty promises not to recommence the war?" Francis' response was categorical: "I swear it, and I will keep my word!" If only that word had been kept!

By the Treaty of Pressburg, signed on December 26, 1805, Austria accepted a substantial reduction in its territorial possessions beyond its borders. The Hapsburgs were considerably weakened in Germany. They ceded Ortenau and Brisgau to the Duchy of Baden, Constance and their dispersed Swabian possessions to Württemberg, and Vorarlberg, the Tyrol, Trient, and Brixen to Bavaria. In addition, as Holy Roman Emperor Francis recognized the full sovereignty of the Kingdoms of Bavaria and Württemberg and the Grand Duchy of Baden. In return, Austria received the trifling compensation of the Archbishoprics of Salzburg and Wurzburg.

In Italy, Austria renounced all its possessions except Trieste. Venetia was attached to the Kingdom of Italy, which also received the protectorate of Dalmatia and Cattaro. Finally, the Austrian Empire had to pay an indemnity of 40 million francs to defray the costs of the war.

Austerlitz also had another notable victim, let us remember—William Pitt, who never recovered from the news of the defeat and died soon thereafter.

We have now seen how, after Austerlitz, Napoleon's generous diplomacy was thwarted. The question is to determine who took the initiative to make war. For the second time it would not be the emperor.

Prussia Ignites the Fourth Coalition

Prussia sat out the war of 1805 in the ambiguous position of armed mediation. It had been on the verge of entering the Third Coalition on the eve of Austerlitz. Napoleon's victory constrained Berlin to choose the French alliance. This action had been humiliating, earning Prussia the contempt of the other European monarchies.

Developments in 1806 appeared auspicious for Prussia to act as a great power by leading a crusade against France. Prussia's disproportionate hatred of Napoleon caused the court of Berlin to lose its head. In a few months, its position with regard to France passed from restrained hostility to warlike furor.

It must be said that, yet again, Great Britain was not blameless. In the course of "negotiations" for a Franco-British peace, the question had arisen of the return to Britain of Hannover, held by Prussia in compensation for its neutrality. The faithless British negotiator passed this information to the Prussian ambassador to France, Lucchesini, depicting the transfer of Hannover as disloyalty by Napoleon. This was the drop that caused the cup of Prussian hostility to overflow.

The French explanation and justifications did not receive a fair hearing, as if Prussia had been waiting for a pretext to settle matters once and for all. To calm Berlin, Napoleon proposed to cede to the king of Prussia that slice of the Holy Roman Empire that lay outside the Confederation of the Rhine. This was a wasted effort, as the weak Frederick William abandoned himself fully to the war party, which had been champing at the bit for a long time.

The result was an outburst of hatred and contempt for France and its army. The emperor's admiration for Frederick the Great was misinterpreted as being a fear of offending the invincible army that the king had left to Prussia.

These sad distortions caused the war party to lose all reason and press for an unbridled provocation. General Blücher wanted to "prepare the tomb of all the Frenchmen along the length of the Rhine." He claimed to be able to conquer Paris with his cavalry alone. Prussian officers sharpened their swords on the steps of the French embassy in Berlin. Their colonel was heard to announce that "to defeat these French dogs, swords are unnecessary—all we need are clubs."

The pale and indecisive Frederick William also became involved in this bloodthirsty folly. The head of the war party at the court of Berlin was none other than Queen Louise, supported by the king's nephew, Prince Ludwig (Friedrich Ludwig Christian). Magnificent in her haughty beauty, she was the actual sovereign of Prussia. She dedicated an implacable hatred to Napoleon, insulting him publicly. The favorite pastime of this Germanic Valkyrie was to encourage the soldiers while parading, mounted and in uniform, at the head of the regiment of queen's dragoon guards.

Laforest, the French ambassador to Berlin, dispatched reports that were increasingly alarmist. Recognizing that a passing fury was responsible for the excesses of the Prussian conduct, the emperor still dared to hope that the worst was not inevitable.

A general mobilization of the Prussian army on August 9, 1806, forced Napoleon to accept the evidence. Yet, one more time, he wished to exhaust all chances for peace. On September 12, he addressed the following personal plea to Frederick William:

> If I am forced to take up arms in my defense, it would be with the greatest regret that I would employ them against Your Majesty's troops. I would consider such a war to be a civil war, because the interests of our two states are so closely tied. I want nothing of this; I have not asked for it in any way!

Nothing availed. Prussia broke diplomatic relations with France. Napoleon therefore halted the ongoing redeployment of troops from Germany so as to confront this new challenge. He had begun this redeployment to prove his good and peaceful intentions; now he was forced into war, contrary to clumsy allegations of aggression.

The Collapse of Prussia at Jena-Auerstadt

Prussia's entry into war marked the formation of the Fourth Coalition, which included Prussia, Russia, Sweden, and of course, Britain.

Manifesting a remarkable desire to thrash the presumptuous French all by itself, the Prussian army commenced hostilities without waiting for the Russian army. It thus committed the same mistake that the Austrian army made the previous year. Prussia thrust deeply into Thuringia and Franconia, forcibly dragging Saxony and its allies of Brunswick, Hesse-Cassel, and Saxe Weimar along.

Once again, Napoleon was constrained to leave pressing civil matters in abeyance while he took his headquarters to the field. At Bamberg on October 7, he received a Prussian ultimatum demanding that all French troops immediately retreat behind the Rhine and that France promise not to put "any obstacle to the formation by Prussia of a Northern League that will include all the states not already part of the Confederation of the Rhine." Nothing less! Prussia thus openly expressed its ambitions for German leadership.

The same causes had the same effects. On a military plane, Prussia was about to experience the same fate as Austria in the previous year, only more serious.

The two armies made contact on October 10 at Sallfeld. In a few hours, Lannes overwhelmed the Prussian advance guard commanded by Prince Ludwig, who found death in his first combat.

This first reverse brutally chilled the aggressiveness of the old Duke of Brunswick, the commander-in-chief. But it was too late. Napoleon had already enveloped the entire Prussian army on its southern flank, forcing it to fight on a reversed front in the vicinity of Jena.

On October 12, the Prussian army found itself in such a position that it could not escape disaster. Davout wrote, "this campaign promises to be more miraculous than those of Ulm and Marengo." Nonetheless, despite the certainty of a brilliant victory, Napoleon persisted in preferring to make an honorable peace. Consider carefully these informative extracts from a long letter to the king of Prussia, a letter written on that same October 12, 1806, which Napoleon sent by way of his aide de camp, Montesquiou:

> I am in the midst of Saxony. I ask Your Majesty to believe that I have sufficient forces to achieve a quick victory. Yet why spill so much blood? To what end? I offer to Your Majesty the same language that I offered to the Emperor Alexander two days before the battle of Austerlitz. . . . But why permit our subjects to be slaughtered? I have no desire for a victory that would be purchased with the lives of a good number of my children. If I were at the start

of my military career and if I feared the hazards of combat, this language would be completely misplaced. Sire, Your Majesty will be defeated! You have disturbed the calm of your days without the shadow of a pretext. Today you are still intact and able to deal with me in a manner befitting your rank, but in less than a month you will be in a very different situation.

You have the ability to spare your subjects from the ravages of war. Having just begun the war, you can easily halt it and make something that Europe will know is better. Sire, I have nothing to gain against Your Majesty. I want nothing and have never wanted anything from You. The current war is an impolitic war. I pray Your Majesty to see in this letter only my desire to save the blood of men and to help a nation, which geographically could never be a threat to mine, from having to repent of having listened too much to the ephemeral emotions that rise and fall so easily among peoples.

Thus, the "Attila" who held his implacable enemy at his mercy and yet implored him to make peace! Could one imagine a better profession of pacifism?

Montesquiou encountered a Prussian officer so hidebound that he held the envoy prisoner for a long time "because he was not accompanied by a trumpeter as specified in regulations." The letter did not reach Frederick William until the day after the disaster. Would it have changed anything if it had arrived on time? Given the circumstances, this seems doubtful. Yet what counts for the memory of Napoleon is that he tried yet another time, risking the impossible to seize the elusive prize of peace.

On October 14, the double battle of Jena-Auerstadt unfolded.

While Napoleon pushed Hohenlohe's forces back from Jena toward Weimar, at Austerlitz the intrepid Davout defeated the bulk of the Prussian army, which was attempting to escape the encirclement. Brunswick was mortally wounded, and Prince William was also hit. Queen Louise barely escaped capture. Decapitated, the Prussian army dissolved quickly, prey to an uncontrollable panic. It was a general rout to avoid capture.

Napoleon did not allow the Grand Armeé to rest on its laurels for a moment. To ensure that the enemy would be incapable of waging war against France for a long time, the retreat must be converted into an

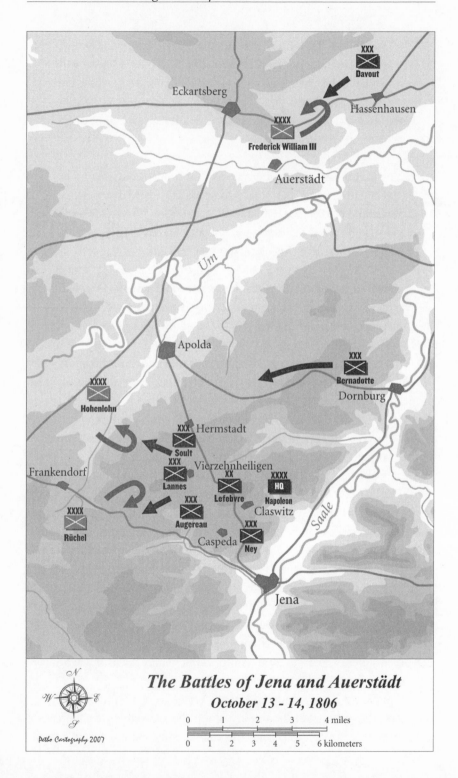

The Battles of Jena and Auerstädt
October 13 - 14, 1806

0   1   2   3   4 miles

0 1 2 3 4 5 6 kilometers

Petho Cartography 2007

exemplary punishment, in proportion to the contempt that the Prussians had shown to France. There followed a general pursuit of the Prussians that lasted almost a month, ending at the Baltic coast and the Russian frontier.

Nansouty's and Hartpoul's cuirassiers, as well as Lasalle's hussars, raided everywhere. The foot soldiers had difficulty keeping up with the cavalry's pace. Yet, behind the horsemen, the infantry captured the bypassed garrisons one after another. The Prussians threw down their arms and surrendered without resistance.

On October 15, Murat took Erfurt and 6,000 prisoners. On the 18th, Bernadotte secured Halle, taking 5,000 prisoners, four colors, and 30 guns. He was better at pursuing fugitives than at fighting. On the 19th, Soult captured 1,600 prisoners and 30 cannon. On the 18th, at Prenzlau, Prince von Hohenlohe surrendered with 20,000 men. On the 29th, Lasalle made 6,000 prisoners and captured 2,000 horses. On the 30th, he took over the fortified position of Stettin, seizing 5,500 prisoners and 500 cannon. On November 6, having taken refuge in the free city of Lubeck, Blücher capitulated with 27 battalions of infantry and 52 squadrons of cavalry. On the 9th, Murat captured another 16,000 men at Schwartau. On the 11th, the garrison of Magdeburg surrendered with 22,000 prisoners and 700 cannon.

Thereafter, as Murat told the emperor, "combat ended for lack of combatants." This was not completely accurate, since the fortified port of Danzig continued to resist.

The Prussian army no longer existed, with the exception of Lestocq's corps of 9,000 men, which succeeded in reaching East Prussia with the king and queen. By mid-November, the total of Prussian prisoners had reached 110,000, and the number of captured flags was 250, practically all that remained. To these losses must be added 15,000 killed or wounded at Jena and 10,000 at Auerstadt. For its part, the Grand Armeé lost 6,000 killed and wounded at Jena and 7,000 at Auerstadt. Not until the French campaign of 1940 would history know a military disaster of similar magnitude.

On October 24, the emperor occupied the chateau of Frederick II, the "Sans Souci," at Potsdam. It was not without emotion that he meditated at the tomb of this great captain whom he admired.

Rendering honor where honor is due, Napoleon reserved for Davout the privilege of being the first to enter Berlin, the capital of Prussia, on

October 26. The next day, the emperor presided over a grand military parade. The most astonishing aspect of the capture of Berlin was the enthusiastic welcome of the population. The crowd filled Unter den Linden and wildly applauded the parade of French troops. The Prussian populace thereby disassociated itself from its arrogant aristocracy.

The lack of combativeness of the Prussian soldier can be explained in the same manner. As in Italy and Central Europe, Berlin confirmed the fact that the Grand Armeé, heir of the Revolutionary armies, was still the bearer of emancipation hopes for the peoples of Europe.

Prussia was defeated, but the war was not yet over. The Russian army had not yet been engaged. It was stationed on the far bank of the Vistula in East Prussia under the command of the presumptuous Bennigsen. At Konigsberg, the Russians had taken under their protection the Prussian king and queen, who waited for Tsar Alexander to reconquer their lost kingdom.

In early November 1806 the weather did not favor military maneuvers in that frigid and muddy terrain. Napoleon decided to wait for spring in security behind the Vistula, with his forces deployed from besieged Danzig to Warsaw.

Russia Tested at Eylau and Subjugated at Friedland

Bennigsen made an ally of "General Winter." Because his troops were well acclimated, he showed himself to be very active in the area of Pulstusk, threatening Warsaw. He suffered a serious reverse on December 28, however. Other minor actions also turned to his disadvantage at Soldau and Golymin.

At the end of January 1807, Bennigsen resumed the offensive. Napoleon's counterattack halted abruptly after Cossacks captured a copy of his operations order. Warned at the last minute, the Russian general withdrew precipitately toward Eylau, where on February 8 an appalling frontal battle occurred in the midst of a snowstorm.

Murat's fantastic cavalry charge permitted the emperor to remain master of the field. Yet, it was a pyrrhic victory, very costly in human life. It proved a pointless exercise in any case. With the valiant Davout threatening to envelop his left, Bennigsen was again saved in extremis by the arrival of Lestocq's Prussian corps, just as later Wellington would be

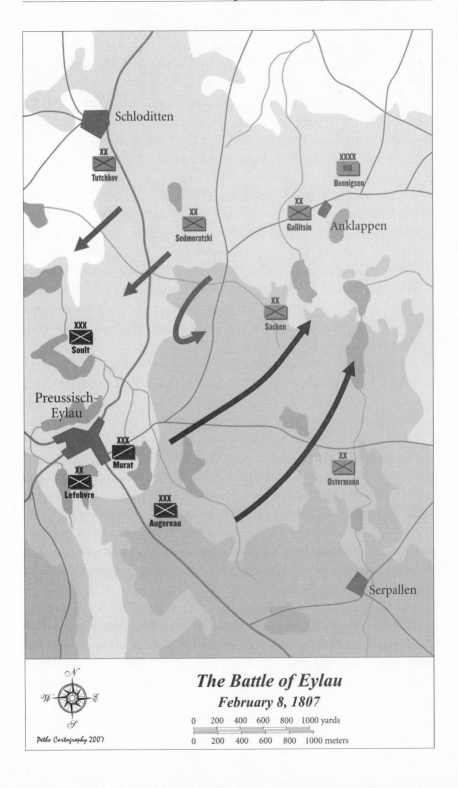

The Battle of Eylau
February 8, 1807

0   200   400   600   800   1000 yards

0   200   400   600   800   1000 meters

Petho Cartography 2007

saved by the appearance of Blücher at Waterloo. Assigned to hold Lestocq in check, Ney had been unable to accomplish his mission, and thus may be compared to Grouchy in 1815.

The fury of combat resulted in grievous losses on both sides. For the Russians, 20,000 were killed or wounded, with the loss of 3,000 prisoners, 23 cannon, and 16 colors. For the French, 14,000 were killed or wounded, including eight generals killed and 14 wounded, with five eagles lost. Surveying the battlefield the next day, the emperor was overcome by the horrible spectacle.

The exhaustion of the two armies after Eylau prevented them from conducting large-scale operations for several months. At that point, the next battle would of necessity be decisive.

Forced to remain on location, Napoleon established his headquarters first at Osterode, then after April 1 at Finkenstein. For more than five months he was constrained to administer France at a distance of 2,000 kilometers, while at the same time preparing for the coming confrontation.

How did the diplomatic situation evolve during this period? Although beaten to a pulp, Prussia remained in a state of war. Moreover, Danzig, its sole remaining garrison, continued to resist, and did not fall until May 24, yielding 14,000 prisoners.

The emperor's principal apprehension concerned the attitude of Austria, whose entry into the war could be fatal by threatening the rear of the Grand Armeé. Having been burned at Austerlitz, however, the Austrian emperor resisted the insistent entreaties of the Coalition. On that side, at least, diplomatic arguments were for the moment effective.

At Osterode, Napoleon met with Colonel Kleist, the special envoy of the king of Prussia, who had come to determine his intentions. The response was the same as always: "I want peace, because I would be horrified if I were the cause of more bloodshed."

As on the eve of Austerlitz and again before Jena, the Coalition members took this affirmation of good will as a sign of apprehension that encouraged them to resume hostilities. "Errare humanum est, perseverare diabolicum" (To err is human, to persist in error is satanic). At Bamberg on April 26, Frederick William and Alexander reasserted their alliance. They were greatly encouraged by Britain, where the Duke of Portland had formed a new cabinet consisting of men who had been devoted to

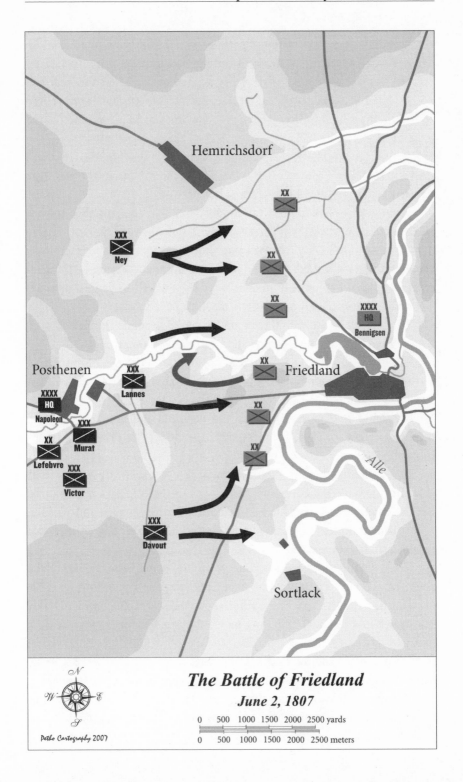

The Battle of Friedland
June 2, 1807

Pitt, including the warmongers Castlereagh, Hawkesbury, and Canning. The renewal of hostilities was now only a matter of opportunity.

The two armies were of roughly equivalent size, on the order of 150,000 combatants and 250 cannon each. The Russian army could receive additional reinforcements, whereas the Grand Armeé was at the peak of its strength.

Bennigsen's units were deployed to cover Konigsberg, the capital of East Prussia. The French forces were on the other bank of the Passarge River, with an advanced guard corps on the Alle.

Bennigsen attacked first on June 5, but had to withdraw toward Heilsberg on June 10. Napoleon thrust his units toward Konigsberg by the left bank of the Alle. Bennigsen replied by launching a counterattack on the French right flank at Friedland. In the process, he made the fatal error of enclosing himself in that bend of the Alle where Napoleon isolated and destroyed the Russians on June 14, 1807.

The Russians lost 30,000 men, including 25 generals, and 80 cannon. On the French side, 1,500 were killed and 8,500 wounded.

Napoleon's new and brilliant victory reverberated throughout Europe like a thunderclap. Konigsberg fell like a ripe fruit. The Grand Armeé closed up on the Niemen River, the border of Russia.

Friedland put an end to both the war and the Fourth Coalition. Napoleon went to Tilsit in an attempt to collect the dividends of his triumph.

Yet, on September 2, vexed by Denmark's refusal to come over to its side, Britain had its fleet bombard Copenhagen savagely for five days. Let us remember that Britain had acted in a similar manner on April 2, 1801. Thus did this monarchy, so willing to lecture others, conceive of international relations!

We have already seen that the enormous concessions given to the enemy at Tilsit to guarantee the peace had accomplished nothing. This great surge in the history of the Empire carried with it the hope of a new era in the international relations of France. In fact, it proved to be a mirage.

Despite the patchwork tinkering at Erfurt, in October 1808 the providential Franco-Russian alignment would wilt, much to Napoleon's chagrin, and turn back against him. Less than two years after Tilsit, war would resume in Germany, as if playing some sort of military tag team against France. After the Austro-Russians at Austerlitz, the Prussians at

Jena, and the Russians again at Friedland, it would once again be Austria's turn to take up the cudgel, profiting from France's difficulties with Spain.

Spain: The Lightning Rod that Attracted the Thunderbolt

What a somber and tortuous affair was Spain! Napoleon's detractors present it, along with the coming war with Russia, as the incontestable proof of his megalomania. One must be cautious about such simplistic judgments. This extremely complex question merits further study.

At the outset, the war in Spain reflected underlying tensions that were awaiting the right moment to erupt.

After Tilsit, Napoleon waited for the next action of Britain, pushed out of Northern Europe, rejected by Portugal, and contained in Italy. London fell back on the "soft underbelly" of Spain to relight the fire. It was vital for France to prevent the opening of a new front at its rear.

In 1808, Spain was allied with France, with whom it had shared the disaster of Trafalgar. It had just expelled the British from Buenos Aires and had provided a military contingent, under the command of General La Romana, to support the French army in Germany. Quite recently, Spain had cooperated loyally with France in the military expedition to Portugal intended to expel the first British bridgehead there. In theory, therefore, everything was well in the best of all possible worlds. All that should have been necessary to ensure the Spanish flank guard would be to maintain the alliance.

In reality, the situation was far different. The Spanish alliance presented all the signs of a disquieting fragility.

First, there was proof that the court of Madrid delighted in duplicity and double-dealing. During his visit to Potsdam in 1806, Napoleon happened by chance upon correspondence between King Charles IV of Spain and the king of Prussia, correspondence that had been forgotten when Frederick William fled in haste. In his letter, the king of Spain offered to attack Napoleon in the back while he was involved with Prussia. Crown Prince Ferdinand, for his part, pretended to be a Francophile while his correspondence overflowed with hatred for France and the French. His entourage included a large number of anti-French aristocrats and clergymen, in particular his tutor, Canon Escoïquiz.

In addition, these Bourbons of Spain, descendants of Louis XIV, exhibited the signs of advanced degeneracy, of which nothing was said for the sake of Christian charity. The painter Goya had no such scruples in his portraits of them.

The members of the royal family were on poor terms with each other. The king was a vaudeville character, Queen Maria-Louisa was a shrew subject to excessive mood swings, and the queen's favorite and prime minister, Godoy, christened the "Prince of Peace," formed a ménage a trois. The eldest son Ferdinand, Prince of the Asturias, was as aware of this situation as the rest of the country. Ferdinand could not tolerate the situation, feeling contempt for his parents and hatred for Godoy, who more than reciprocated the sentiment.

The family quarrel became more venomous in the fall of 1807, and the protagonists appealed to the emperor to arbitrate their differences. The king accused his son of plotting to overthrow him and to murder his mother. He asked that Napoleon should "Aid me with his wisdom and counsel." The crown prince, the personification of drabness, implored the emperor to take him under his wing and protect him from Godoy, whom he suspected of wishing to dispossess him. He went so far as to seek a marriage with a Bonaparte princess. Napoleon apparently made no reply to this repugnant offer. But he sent his chamberlain, de Tournon, to the Spanish court to calm things down and report on the situation.

The Franco-Spanish alliance of October 1807 and the conquest of Portugal muted the family quarrel for a time.

What was the attitude of the Spanish population? The presence of the French army in transit to Portugal was very well received. The Spanish people, principal actor in the play that was about to unfold, were less evolved than other European peoples. They had remained under the stifling influence of a clergy not yet completely freed of the "Torquemadian" fundamentalism of the Inquisition. In the short term, the Spanish opinion wanted France to put an end to the unacceptable situation of the royal family. It pitied the king and hated the queen and Godoy. For want of anyone better, it tended to the side of the Prince of the Asturias.

Meanwhile, Napoleon learned that Britain was preparing for a military return to the Iberian Peninsula. London hurried, believing that it could seize the occasion of a palace revolution that seemed imminent in

Madrid. This information was no surprise, but it did confirm the necessity to find a quick solution to the imbroglio of the Spanish dynasty.

At this point in the matter, the question was not whether to act in Spain but rather how to act, in accordance with the evolving situation but without waiting too long.

Talleyrand proved to be a very radical advisor. Arguing for a sort of right of national preemption, he urged Napoleon to dethrone these pitiful Bourbons of Spain, orphan descendants of the great Louis XIV. In his eyes, their replacement by a new dynasty stemming from the Imperial family was the sole solution to keep Spain securely. This expedient advice, coming from a usually moderate expert, astonished Napoleon and aroused a horrible suspicion. Having been replaced as foreign minister by Champagny, was Talleyrand seeking revenge by advocating the worst possible policy?

Meanwhile, Napoleon took a preventive military measure. He named Murat his lieutenant general in Spain, at the head of an army corps located north of the capital, Madrid. It is noteworthy that the French Army was welcomed by a population not yet angry against it. At the same time, Admiral Rosily's squadron anchored at Cadiz. Permitted under the Franco-Spanish accords of October with regard to Portugal, this decision offered the advantage of locating combat power to be deployed rapidly in the country, because the British were clearly up to something.

But events came to a crisis. On March 18 and 19, supporters of Ferdinand fomented riots in Aranjuez. Godoy was imprisoned, and owed his life to the personal intervention of Ferdinand. Charles IV abdicated "in favor of my well-beloved son, the Prince of the Asturias." This prince was proclaimed king of Spain with the title Ferdinand VII. Without the least modesty, the dethroned queen wrote to Murat to ask "that he obtain from the Emperor sufficient so that the king my husband, the Prince of Peace, and I should live all three together in a place suitable for our health, without authority or intrigues."

At this critical juncture, a political head was needed on the scene, capable of making the appropriate decisions immediately. Murat took it upon himself to occupy Madrid on March 23, 1808, and prepared to put the former king back on his throne. What a farce! Charles IV wrote to Napoleon,

I was forced to abdicate. However, I am so full of confidence in the genius of the great man who has always shown himself to be my friend that I have decided to conform completely to whatever this great man may decide about my fate and that of the queen and the Prince of Peace. I protest to Your Majesty against the events of Aranjuez and against my abdication. I place myself with complete confidence at the heart and friendship of Your Majesty.

It is unclear whether he was completely sincere, but one thing is apparent: Charles IV reneged on his abdication, obtained by constraint, and he left it entirely up to Napoleon to resolve the Spanish problem.

At this stage, the emperor really did not see how he should proceed. Had Murat not interfered, there would not now be two kings in Spain, and he would have been able to arrange matters with the new one. He was tempted simply to abandon Charles IV, but Talleyrand's advice continued to trouble him. To achieve his objectives, he considered transferring the throne to a Bonaparte. He thought first of Louis, who arrogantly refused. Joseph showed himself more cooperative, however. In addition, the report of the investigation Napoleon had ordered demonstrated the confirmed Francophobia of the new king and especially of his entourage.

Napoleon needed more time to consider the problem. Just as in preparing for a battle, he decided to inform himself more by arranging a confrontation between the protagonists at Bayonne. He directed Savary to persuade Ferdinand VII to cooperate. That should not have been difficult, considering the prince had recently requested the emperor's assistance.

Before his departure from Paris, Napoleon wrote a letter to Murat, whom he reproached and gave instructions to avoid aggravating the situation by further intemperate initiatives. He began to doubt the loyalty of the Grand Duke of Berg, who was married to his sister Caroline.

Many mistakes could have been avoided if Murat had taken the time to read this letter carefully. Let us consider these extracts that show the foresight and the wait-and-see policy of Napoleon at that date:

I fear that you have deceived me and perhaps yourself about the situation in Spain. The actions of March 23 have greatly complicated matters. I am greatly perplexed. Do not believe that you are attacking a disarmed nation or that you have only to parade your troops to force Spain to submit. . . . The Spaniards are full of energy. You are dealing with a new people who have all the courage and enthusiasm of men who have never experienced political passions before. The aristocracy and the clergy are the masters in Spain. If they fear the loss of their privileges and their existence, they may raise up the masses against us and prolong the war eternally. At the moment, I have Spanish supporters, but if I appear as a conqueror I will have none. . . .

It is never useful to render oneself odious or to arouse hatred. Spain has more than 100,000 men under arms, which is more than enough to support a war in the interior. . . . England will not miss this opportunity to multiply our difficulties. It is sending daily instructions to the forces it maintains off the coasts of Portugal and the Mediterranean. Britain is recruiting Sicilians and Portuguese . . .

What are the best measures to take? Should I come to Madrid? Should I exercise a great protectorate and choose between father and son? It appears difficult to put Charles IV back into power: his government and his favorite are so unpopular that they would not last three months. Ferdinand is an enemy of France, and that is why he was made king. Placing him on the throne serves the factions that for 25 years have sought the destruction of France. A family alliance would be a weak reed. . . .

I think that we must not do anything rash. . . . I do not approve of the party that urged Your Imperial Highness to act precipitately in Madrid. The army must remain at least ten leagues from the capital. By disturbing the Spanish, your entry into Madrid had greatly aided Ferdinand. I have sent Savary to visit the new king and determine the situation. . . . I will eventually advise you as to which party to support. In the meanwhile, this is what I judge appropriate to prescribe to you. You will commit me to meet Ferdinand only if you judge that the situation is such that I must recognize him as King of Spain. . . . You will act in such a way that the Spaniards will have no idea which party I will support. That should not be difficult for you, because I don't know myself. You will let the nobility and the clergy understand that, if France must intervene in Spanish affairs, their privileges and immunities will be respected. . . .

You will demonstrate to them the advantages they would gain from a political regeneration. . . . Do not take any abrupt actions. . . . I will bear your personal interests in mind, so you need not do so. . . . Let no personal project occupy you or control your conduct: that would be prejudicial to me and even more so to you. . . . I order that the most severe discipline must be maintained: no leniency even for the smallest faults. We must show the greatest respect for the inhabitants, and especially for the churches and convents. The army will avoid all contact with Spanish Army units. . . . Not a shot must be fired on either side. . . . If war commences, you will be lost. The destiny of Spain must be decided by politics and negotiation. . . ."

This letter perfectly summarized Napoleon's uncertainty when he left for Bayonne:

(1) He had not yet decided anything because he did not yet see his way clear in the Spanish imbroglio. He had not prepared a trap, as is often (and foolishly) alleged. The two sides had solicited his arbitration—the dethroned king to obtain revenge and the new one to be recognized. Why would he have rejected all possibility of arranging the matter?

(2) He sought a compromise that would satisfy both French national security and the Spanish royal quarrel, with the approval of the Spanish population. He wished above all to avoid war. In any case, he had no intention of conquest.

(3) He did not conceal from Murat that the latter's conduct had already compromised the possibility of a solution and that he was not deceived by the marshal's tricks. Murat was not to dream of the Spanish throne for himself!

Napoleon left Paris on April 2, 1808, and arrived at the chateau of Marracq, in Bayonne, on April 20. There he received Ferdinand and his reduced court. Upon approaching France, the pseudo-king had become reluctant to enter that country. At Vitoria, his two principal counselors,

Canon Escoïquez (who was also his confessor) and his First Gentleman, Cevallos, advised him not to go any farther, despite the assurances of Savary, who quickly reported to Bayonne. Savary returned to Ferdinand with the following letter from the emperor, which convinced the young king to complete his journey: "I say to Your Highness, to the Spanish people, and to the entire world, that if the abdication of King Charles was a voluntary act, if he was not forced to it by the insurrection and riots of Aranjuez, he will make no difficulty in accepting it, and I will recognize Your Royal Highness as King of Spain. I therefore wish to discuss this topic with you. . . ." Napoleon's position had not changed: he wished to arbitrate the Spanish royal conflict that had been submitted to him by the interested parties.

At their first meeting, Ferdinand made a terrible impression on the emperor. The man inspired revulsion. The security of France and the well-being of Spain could not be based on such a man. He was obviously a puppet in the hands of a faction of the nobility and the clergy. As the future would confirm, his only influence lay in the disgust inspired in the Spanish nation by his parents. Was Napoleon condemned to choose between cholera and the plague?

That same evening, Napoleon had Savary deliver a deliberately provocative proposal to Ferdinand, a proposal whose purpose was to place a very high bar for the coming negotiations: the renunciation of his crown in favor of his father, in exchange for the modest crown of Etruria. Ferdinand and his counselors loudly expressed their indignation. This was the starting point for substantive discussions.

Negotiations opened under these conditions while waiting for the other party. Escoïquez ardently defended his master's position. In return for his recognition as king, Ferdinand promised a government "completely devoted to Napoleon." That would be the best solution. But what assurance did Napoleon have that Ferdinand would fulfill his promises, knowing the hostile sentiments of the prince and his advisors toward France in general and the emperor in particular? When Napoleon did not respond, Escoïquez went so far as to promise that Spain would place one of its northern provinces in French hands as a guarantee of its loyalty.

In order to decide, Napoleon next had to learn the attitude of the other protagonist, Charles IV.

The family reunion that took place on April 30 avoided becoming a fistfight. It was difficult to decide which spectacle was more painful: that of the father hugging his son while calling him by all his names, or his mother outbidding the king. And all this in the presence of Godoy, her paralyzed lover.

Charles IV's purpose and attitude convinced Napoleon that the only thing that really mattered to the king was to deny the Spanish throne to his son. Charles formalized that position in a letter to the Prince of the Asturias on May 2, in which he stated that Ferdinand's crimes would disqualify him from succeeding to the throne and that "Spain may no longer be saved except by the Emperor."

Determined in his mind but continuing to negotiate with Escoïquez, the emperor inclined somewhat toward the replacement of Ferdinand by Joseph Bonaparte, recalled from Naples where Murat had replaced him. Yet, nothing was officially decided. Something still held him back. The affair would come to a brutal crisis on May 5.

The Madrid Trap

That day, news reached Bayonne of a bloody riot on May 2 in Madrid, the famous "Dos de Mayo" made notorious by Goya. Napoleon's critics characterize his interview with the Spanish royal family as "the Bayonne Trap." What a false judgment! In reality, the trap was for Napoleon in Madrid.

Agitators had presented the announcement of the departure of the princes from the capital, summoned to their father, as if it were a kidnapping by the French army. Madrid became inflamed by the news. Those French soldiers who were caught off guard were massacred with stupefying savagery. The Spanish army joined the rioters. The next day, Murat struck back hard at the insurrection. Thousands of deaths occurred.

This bloody event caused Napoleon to commit the greatest error of judgment of his entire reign. Everything suggested that Ferdinand's partisans had organized the uprising. Brought into the emperor's presence, the queen went so far as to strike her son in the face, daring to call him a bastard and to speak of sending him to the scaffold.

In this tragic setting, Napoleon also lost his temper. He sternly ordered Ferdinand to recognize his father as the legitimate king by midnight and to let this recognition be known in Madrid. If not, he would be treated as a rebel. Ferdinand did not resist, but accepted the proposition and agreed to retreat in comfort to the chateau of Valencay, offered by Talleyrand.

That same day, Charles IV formally fulfilled his promise to cede to the emperor all his rights to the throne of Spain, in exchange for the chateaux of Compiegne and Chambord and a very comfortable stipend. Thus, on May 5, 1808, the Bourbons of Spain voluntarily renounced their throne.

When Joseph succeeded him a few days later, Ferdinand found everything acceptable and promised "the allegiance that I owe to you, just as do all the Spaniards who are with me." This was the individual to whom Napoleon was supposed to entrust the security of France!

Instead of calming the situation, Ferdinand's impulsive decision actually aggravated matters. Neither his proclamation to the Spaniards nor Joseph's recognition by a committee of Spanish notables changed the spreading agitation. Soon, with the support of the Spanish army, this agitation became a general partisan war, from which the term "guerrilla" took its name.

A spiral of failure began. On June 14, Admiral Rosily surrendered to the Spanish at Cadiz. Two days after Joseph's entry into Madrid, on July 22, General Dupont surrendered in open country at Bailen. Almost 20,000 French soldiers capitulated to General Castanos without a fight. Joseph had to flee ignominiously from his capital.

The dishonorable surrender at Bailen resounded across Europe. It struck a serious blow to the Grand Armeé's reputation of invincibility, thereby encouraging France's enemies who were lying in wait.

Obviously, the British did not delay in sticking their noses in. On August 30, the mediocre Junot capitulated at Cintra to Arthur Wellesley, the future Duke of Wellington, quickly exploiting France's difficulties. The fatal war in Spain had begun.

One cannot ignore Napoleon's own responsibility in the Spanish affair. The considerations discussed here are intended only to clarify certain matters.

On that fateful May 5, Napoleon had committed the capital mistake of demanding that Ferdinand renounce the Spanish throne so as to pass it to a member of the Bonaparte house. The thirst for vengeance for the French blood shed on May 2 and the absolute lack of confidence that the Bourbons of Madrid inspired in him might explain a human reaction, but not justify the decision of a head of state, who must never give way to anger.

If the riots of May 2 had not occurred, would matters have turned out differently? It was not impossible that Escoïquiz could be brought to offer convincing guarantees. The negotiations were moving in that direct prior to May 5. Would such guarantees have been reliable? That is impossible to determine, but the outcome could hardly have been worse than the revolt of all of Spain.

The riot of May 2 had become the detonator of the Spanish tragedy. Who had instigated it? The rioters of Madrid had attacked the French soldiers while shouting "death to the infidels!" The monks and priests had preached revolt against Napoleon, "the antichrist." The soldiers were called "servants of the devil" or "troops of Voltaire." At Oviedo, the furor of Canon Llano Ponte was striking. At the head of a mob that slaughtered 38 soldiers of the garrison of Valencia was the Canon Calvo, etc.

Those notables who favored France, and there were many such, were not spared. At Badajoz, the Count of Torre was torn to pieces. At Seville, the Count of Aguila was shot while hanging from a balcony. At Cadiz, General Solano was stabbed and decapitated. At Malaga, General Trujillo was burned alive.

Everything pointed to a fanatical local clergy, opposed to progress and leading the people under their influence in a vengeful crusade against the anti-clericism of the Revolution. The hypersensitive Spanish nationalism provided fertile ground for—but not the cause of—this uprising. To give an example, here is an extract from a Spanish catechism of that era:

> From whence did Napoleon come? From the inferno and from sin! What are his principal methods? To deceive, to steal, to assassinate, and to oppress. Is it a sin to kill Frenchmen? On the contrary, that action is worthy of merit from the country if, by this means, we are delivered from insults, from theft, and from trickery!

This was a true incitement to murder, a blend of religious fundamentalism and nationalistic fanaticism.

Yet, the local clergy would not have acted in such an extreme manner if they had not been encouraged to do so by the Roman Curia. Certain high prelates had never accepted the Concordat that had trimmed the power of the Church in France. In their eyes, Napoleon's greatest crime was to have established the principle of laicism. His recent quarrels with the Pope had not improved his image among Catholics. On May 12, Pius VII decided to refuse investiture to bishops nominated by the emperor, contrary to what had been agreed. Ten days later, he forbad his subjects to swear allegiance to the French government. To top it off, the Pope asked all Spanish bishops not to recognize Joseph, "this freemason king, heretic and Lutheran as are all the Bonapartes and the French nation."

In reality, Napoleon had accorded great religious tolerance to Spain, especially with regard to the status of Jews, to whom he had just granted freedom of religion in France. In attempting to avoid the English plague and the Bourbon cholera, Napoleon had contracted the Roman rabies. He would now deal with a holy war as well as a nationalist uprising. If one concedes that this war of atrocities was the grave of the Empire, it is no exaggeration to assert that the papacy had dug that grave.

As for military operations, under the circumstances Napoleon had no choice. He had to reestablish order in Spain as quickly as possible.

Ephemeral Reestablishment of the Situation

For Napoleon, the ideal would have been to intervene immediately and in person. A fire is most easily brought under control if it is dealt with quickly. But the emperor's first duty was to prevent the opening of a second front in Germany. That was the purpose of the Congress of Erfurt in September-October 1808. While this was going on, Napoleon used the time to bring the army in Spain up to a strength of 150,000 excellent soldiers, many of them veterans of Austerlitz, Jena, and Friedland.

As usual, Napoleon's campaign plan was simple. Starting from the northern bank of the Ebro River, he would defeat the Spanish army then reinstall King Joseph on his throne in Madrid. This first action should entice Moore's 40,000 British troops from Portugal to the interior of Spain so as to assist the Spanish army. The French army would then attack by surprise, annihilating the British before they had time to react.

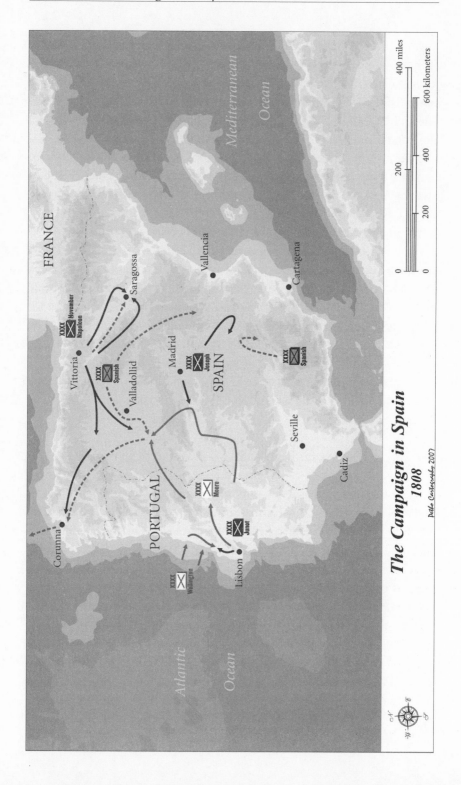

The Campaign in Spain
1808
Peter Cartensdale 2007

Napoleon as Consul (Painting by Jean Auguste Dominique Ingres)

Emperor Napoleon

Giraudon

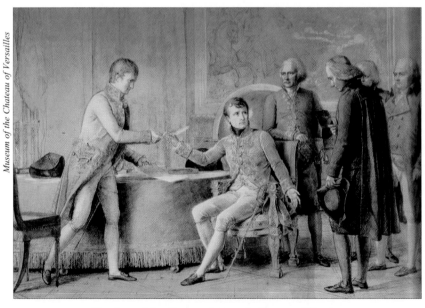

The Reforging of France: Installation of the Council of State.

(Painting by Auguste Couder)

Signing of the Concordat, or the Peace of Souls.

(Drawing by Francois Gérard)

The Great Hope of the Peace of Amiens. (Painting by Anatole Devosge)

The Capitulation of Ulm, October 20, 1805.

(Painting by Charles Théverin)

The Victory of Austerlitz, December 2, 1805. (Workshop of Carle Vernet)

The Day after Austerlitz: The Victor offers his hand to the Emperor Francis II.
(Painting by Antoine Gros)

Battle of Jena, October 14, 1806. (Painting by Charles Théverin)

Napoleon's Entry into Berlin, October 25, 1806.
(Painting by Charles Meynier)

The Victory of Friedland, June 14, 1807 (Painting by Horace Vernet)

Meeting of Napoleon I and Alexander I on the raft at Tilsit, after Friedland.
There is no distinction between victor and vanquished.

(Painting by Adolphe Roehn)

Napoleon decorates a Russian soldier with the cross of the Legion of Honor.
(Painting by Jean-Baptiste Debret)

"The Second of May" – The Madrid Uprising of May 2, 1808. (Painting by Goya)

The Congress of Erfurt, September-October, 1808. (Painting by Nicolas Gosse)

The Fantastic Charges of Somosierra, November 30, 1808.
(Painting by Louis-Francois Lejeune)

Bavarian and Württemberger Soldiers of the Grand Army, April 20,
1809, at Abensberg. (Painting by Jean-Baptiste Debret)

The Crossing of the Danube before the Battle of Wagram, July 5, 1809.
(Painting by Jacques Swebach)

The Battle of Borodino (or of the Moskova), September 7, 1812.
(Painting by Lejeune)

Crossing of the Berezina River, 26-29 November, 1812.
(Attributed to Francois Fournier-Sarloveze)

The Dazzling Victory of Hanau, October 30, 1813.

(Painting by Horace Vernet)

Napoleon during the fabulous French Campaign of 1814.

(Painting by Ernest Meissonier)

Invasion of 1814 – The Population Fights Alongside the Army.
(Painting by Edouard Detaille)

Victory of Montereau, February 18, 1814.
(Painting by Jean-Charles Langlois)

The Defense of Paris at the Clichy Gate, March 30, 1814.

(Painting by Horace Vernet)

Napoleon's Farewell to his Guard, April 20, 1814, at Fontainebleau

(Painting by Horace Vernet)

The Return from Elbe: The Joyful Rally of the Army.

(Painting by Wilhelm Sternberg)

The Population of Grenoble tearing down the gates to
admit Napoleon, March 7, 1815. (Engraving of the French School)

The Battle of Waterloo, June 18, 1815.

Napoleon on his Deathbed. (Painting by Charles Steuben)

This plan would be executed almost perfectly. Only appalling weather conditions enabled the British to avoid total destruction.

Napoleon began the campaign on November 4. He struck first at the Anglo-Spanish left under Blake, destroyed the right under Palafox, and then dashed in the center toward Burgos. Fine victories were won by Soult at Reinosa, Victor at Espinoza, and Lannes at Tudela over Castanos. Saragossa was besieged.

At Burgos, the emperor witnessed dreadful excesses of this atrocious war. Although unbearable, these practices of incredible cruelty illustrate the fanatical brutality of the war in Spain. Let us consider a few horrible scenes extracted from an official report:

> Captured soldiers were tortured and emasculated, with their private parts placed in their mouths . . . others were sawn in half between two boards . . . still others were buried alive or hung by their feet in lit fireplaces. . . . This unfortunate hussar captain was crucified on a door with his head down over a fire . . . and again the brave General René, captured with his wife and child, cut in half before his wife after watching her be dishonored . . . then the child was cut in half in front of the mother who in turn was also cut in half. . . . At Manzanares the inhabitants cut the throats of 1,200 sick or wounded soldiers in a hospital. A captain was cut up into little pieces and fed to the pigs. . . .

In reprisal, the French army indulged in horrible excesses and had to be taken firmly in hand.

After the capture of Burgos and Santander, Napoleon pursued the enemy toward Madrid. On November 30, the Polish lancers seized the pass of Somosierra after a memorably heroic charge. Madrid capitulated on December 3. Joseph resumed his throne and Napoleon gave Spain a liberal constitution.

As expected, Moore moved from Portugal into Spain with 35,000 men who came to reinforce 5,000 others who had been disembarked at Coruña. Moore linked up with La Romana's Spanish army. Napoleon's apprehension of a British intervention in force in Spain was well founded, justifying his preventive action in the peninsula.

The emperor next put the second phase of his plan into operation. On December 22, 1808, he marched north. He planned to destroy Moore in the region of Valladolid.

However, the cold, the snow, and the mud slowed him down considerably, giving him a foretaste of the retreat from Moscow. Moore thus escaped destruction. In his headlong retreat, the British general abandoned to this "henchman of the devil," Napoleon, a thousand British women and children, found on January 2, 1809, in a large shed at Astorga. They were starving, shivering with cold, and trembling with fear. The mothers threw themselves at the emperor's feet and begged him to preserve the lives of their children. He made all arrangements to reassure, lodge, warm, and feed these unfortunates before returning them in good health to the British army several days later.

At Astorga, Napoleon received alarming dispatches concerning the situation inside and outside of France. He decided on January 17 to return to Paris at full speed, assigning Soult the task of completing the campaign. Too slow, Soult allowed a major portion of the British forces to reembark at Corona on the 19th. Moore, however, found his death in this affair.

The military situation in Spain was temporarily reestablished. Yet, this was only a remission of the cancer in Spain, a cancer that would never heal. Napoleon never again commanded personally in Spain, an error for which some have criticized him. Too absorbed in other, more menacing wars, he had to dedicate his remaining time to the government of France. In any event, the nature of the war in Spain, which was more a matter of guerrillas than of great battles, demanded decentralization of command. Moreover, how can those who criticize Napoleon for being bellicose also censure him for "deserting" this war?

The Spanish Cancer

After the emperor's departure, mopping-up operations continued. On March 28, Victor and Sébastiani defeated the Spaniards at Medellin and Ciudad Real, respectively. Soult seized Porto in northern Portugal but did not exploit his success toward Lisbon.

After the indecisive battle of Talavera on July 28, 1809, Arthur Wellesley, the new commander of the British expeditionary force, was

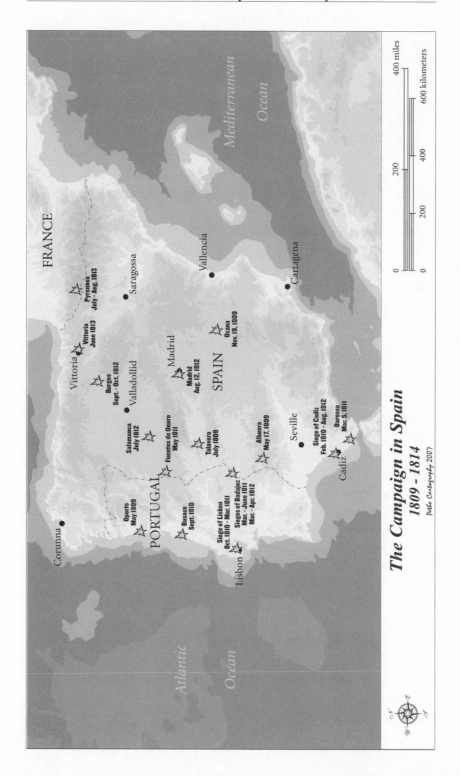

FRANCE

Corunna

Oporto
May 1809

PORTUGAL

Busaco
Sept. 1810

Siege of Lisbon
Oct. 1810 - Mar. 1811

Lisbon

Sieges of Badajoz
Mar. - June 1811
Mar. - Apr. 1812

Fuentes de Onoro
May 1811

Salamanca
July 1812

Vittoria
June 1813

Vittoria

Burgos
Sept. - Oct. 1812

Valladollid

Pyrennes
July - Aug. 1813

Saragossa

Madrid

Madrid
Aug. 12, 1812

SPAIN

Talavera
July 1809

Albuera
May 17, 1809

Ocana
Nov. 19, 1809

Vallencia

Seville

Siege of Cadiz
Feb. 1810 - Aug. 1812

Cadiz

Barossa
Mar. 5, 1811

Cartagena

Mediterranean

Ocean

Atlantic

Ocean

The Campaign in Spain
1809 - 1814

Peter Cartography 2007

0   200   400 miles

0   200   400   600 kilometers

made Viscount Wellington and retired toward Portugal. This permitted several French successes. On November 19, Soult won a victory at Ocana and opened Andalusia. In December, Gouvion Saint-Cyr took Gerone in Catalonia while Soult pacified Aragon. In January 1810, Soult and Victor launched an offensive toward Seville and retook control of the south. Yet, they failed before Cadiz.

In May 1810, Suchet seized Lerida and Soult took Badajoz while Massena was the victor at Ciudad Rodrigo in June and at Almeida in August. On September 27, Massena missed a good opportunity to finish Wellington at Busaco.

The victim of misunderstandings with the other generals and of difficulties in resupply, Massena abandoned Portugal in March 1811. For this entire year, the fighting would focus around the fortresses on the Spanish-Portuguese border at Almeida, Ciudad Rodrigo, and Badajoz.

On May 3, 1811, Massena inflicted a serious reverse on Wellington at Fuentes de Onoro. Bessieres' indiscipline hampered the effort to crush the British. A decisive victory faded away. On May 10, Marmont assumed command of the army in Spain from Massena, who was at the end of his tether.

On the 16th, Soult achieved a significant victory at Albuféra, but again he failed to pursue, instead retiring on Seville. In Catalonia, Suchet took Tarragon by surprise.

Throughout the remainder of 1811, Wellington tried in vain to seize Badajoz and Ciudad Rodrigo. As winter approached, he again retreated on Portugal, waiting for a shift in the balance of forces.

This shift occurred at the beginning of 1812, when Napoleon was constrained to withdraw some units from Spain to deal with threats from the east. Wellington profited immediately. On January 18, he inflicted a major reverse on poor Marmont before Ciudad Rodrigo. The city suffered unparalleled atrocities. At the same time, the brave Suchet occupied Valencia, permitting the annexation of Catalonia to the Empire on January 26. On April 6, 1812, Badajoz suffered the same fate as Ciudad Rodrigo. Portugal was definitively lost.

In June, battles occurred around Salamanca. Despite a numerical equality of forces, on July 22, 1812, Marmont was severely defeated at Salamanca in the Arapiles Mountains, losing 14,000 out of 50,000 engaged. Wellington entered Madrid on August 1 after it was again abandoned by King Joseph. Clausel replaced Marmont, who had been wounded.

Between September 9 and October 18, Wellington failed to take Burgos, heroically defended by General Dubreton. Threatened by a French counter-attack, the British commander prudently avoided a major battle. Lifting the siege of Burgos and abandoning Madrid, he took up winter quarters in the shelter of the ramparts of Ciudad Rodrigo. In the course of a second retreat, he was severely handled by Soult in a second battle of the Arapiles. Yet again, Soult did not exploit his success.

Still, the prize was already, definitively, lost. The disastrous defeat of the campaign in Russia that had just occurred obliged Napoleon to progressively withdraw more and more forces from Spain, whereas on his side Wellington received a steady stream of reinforcements.

The exiled government of Spain put 21,000 soldiers at the disposition of Wellington, who was named commander-in-chief after his victory at Salamanca. Henceforth, he was able to coordinate the activities of guerrilla bands with his conventional offensive. In addition, he established a new base for maritime resupply at Santander.

Regrettably, the French army could no longer hold Spain, but had to focus on defending the frontier of the Pyrenees.

The emperor instructed Joseph to regroup his reduced armies on a defensive line anchored by the Ebro. Wellington did not allow Joseph time to do this. Overcome by superior numbers on June 21, 1813, after a spirited defense Joseph was knocked flat at Vittoria. The remnants of his army withdrew in disorder toward the frontier.

Soult assumed command of what remained of the French army, with the exception of Suchet's force in Aragon and Catalonia. After regrouping his meager forces behind the frontier, Soult attempted to relieve the besieged garrisons of Pamplona and San Sebastian. He was able to delay the capitulation of San Sebastian until August 31, after 69 days of siege, and that of Pamplona until the end of October.

On November 8, 1813, Wellington crossed the Bidossa and attacked Soult's positions behind the Nivelle. Condemned to a hopeless delaying defensive, Soult conducted the retreat brilliantly. His resistance was only part of the general rush to French collapse. The last position in Spain, Lerida, fell on January 25, 1814. On the 17th, Soult was defeated at Orthez. The British entered Bordeaux on March 12. The final battle between Soult and Wellington took place before Toulouse on April 10, 1814.

On December 11, 1813, a treaty signed at Valencay had reestablished Ferdinand VII on his throne, for which the Spaniards would have little to congratulate themselves.

What overall judgment can be made on the conclusion of the disastrous war in Spain? To sum it up in a single word, the most appropriate would be fate. In Spain, Napoleon suffered the longest and most murderous of wars, the war he had intervened in order to avoid. Paradoxically, the lightning rod had brought down the thunderbolt.

The Fifth Coalition

After Tilsit, the general situation of France progressively deteriorated under the combined effect of the Spanish war, the continental blockade, and the emergence of German national identity, without counting the decline in relations with Rome.

At the start of 1809, Austria believed that its hour of revenge had come, in violation of its emperor's oath after Austerlitz, let us recall. Under the impulse of the warmongering minister Stadion, Austria had become the center of German opposition to the French empire. The Hapsburgs had just completed a major reorganization of their army, causing that army to regain a confidence that bordered on arrogance.

Austria would not have dared to assume such a bellicose attitude if it had not had secret assurances that Russia was not disposed to honor its alliance with France in regard to offensive warfare. The situation that the Treaty of Erfurt's ambiguity suggested had come to pass. Fortunately, the Franco-Turkish alliance prevented Russia from doing more against France.

If Prussia, still traumatized by the disaster of Jena, remained quiet, Britain was more active than ever. In signing a new alliance with Austria at Vienna on April 20, 1809, London was not stingy about subsidies. In addition, it promised diversions in the west. Over and above its force engaged in Spain, Britain prepared a landing in Italy, based on Sicily, to attack the rear of the army of Prince Eugene. The British also envisioned several other landings in north Germany. Masters of subversion, they also had in their files a utopian plan for a mutiny of the French army in

Spain, coordinated with a resumption of the uprising in the Vendée. Their excessive confidence in these schemes suggested that Vienna had only to take the first step. This was only the fifth time in ten years that Austria would face post-revolutionary France.

The Lightning Campaign of Five Days (APRIL 19-24, 1809)

Without a formal declaration of war, the Austrian army opened hostilities on April 8, 1808, by invading Bavaria.

Yet again, Napoleon had to leave his desk to take command of the army, once more leaving important matters in suspense. His strong sense of annoyance was reflected in his traditional proclamation to the troops, in which he clearly denounced the warmonger:

> Soldiers: The territory of the Confederation has been violated. The Austrian general wants us to flee at the sight of his arms and to abandon our allies. I will be with you at the speed of light. Soldiers, you surrounded me when the Austrian sovereign came to my bivouac in Moravia. You heard him ask for my clemency and swear eternal friendship. Defeated in three wars, Austria owes everything to my generosity: three times it has perjured itself. Our past successes are a certain talisman of victory that awaits us. Let us march, and at sight of us the enemy will recognize their conquerors!

Commanded by Archduke Charles, the Austrian army was a family affair. Composed of 320,000 active soldiers and 200,000 Landwehr (the recently created territorial militia), this army was divided into three groups: (1) Opposite the Rhine, a striking force of 220,000 combatants under the direct orders of Archduke Charles. Archduke Ludwig commanded a corps; (2) In Italy, 60,000 soldiers commanded by Archduke Johann; (3) Opposite Poland, Archduke Ferdinand had 20,000 men. In the capital, Vienna, a garrison of 20,000 remained under the authority of Archduke Maximilian.

A European force of more than 270,000 men, Napoleon's army was not composed of his best troops, who were engaged in Spain. The emergency mobilization of this army was barely completed in time. It was deployed in four theaters: in Germany, the Army of the Rhine, with

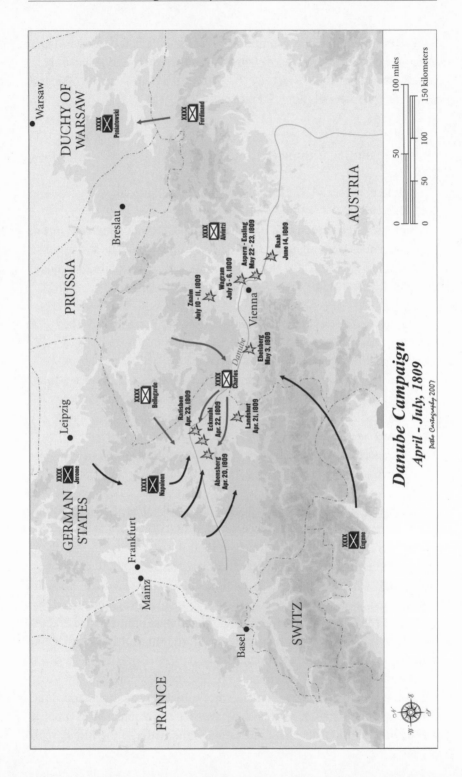

Danube Campaign
April - July, 1809

Pete Cartography 2007

180,000 combatants under the direct control of the emperor; in Italy, 60,000 soldiers commanded by Prince Eugene; in Dalmatia, 15,000 men with Marmont at their head; and in Poland, a corps of 15,000 Poles commanded by Poniatowski.

Once again, Napoleon's military genius achieved miracles. In only five days, and despite his great inferiority of numbers, he overthrew and routed the army of Archduke Charles, who barely escaped in Bohemia. Each of these days was marked by a stunning victory: the 19th at Tengen, the 20th at Abenberg, the 21st at Landshut, the 22nd at Eckmuhl, and the 23rd at Ratisbon. In his victory proclamation, Napoleon boasted of "50,000 prisoners, 100 cannon, 40 colors, 3,000 harnessed wagons, and all the regimental strongboxes."

The cost to the enemy would have been much heavier if Napoleon had possessed sufficient cavalry, much of which had been left behind in Spain, for the pursuit. Vienna capitulated on May 13. In Italy, Archduke Johann retreated to Hungary, where he suffered defeat at Raab on June 14.

The conquest of Vienna did not end the war, however. The Austrian army had suffered very heavy losses but was not completely out of action. Its remnants regrouped and reorganized east of the capital, sheltered by the Danube. There would be no peace without a decisive victory on the far bank of that river.

The emperor would have to reengage the Austrians twice more: at Essling (also known as Aspern) on May 21-22 and at Wagram on July 5-6.

The Lost Victory of Aspern-Essling

In the aftermath of capturing Vienna, the emperor decided to pursue Archduke Charles. He crossed the Danube some ten kilometers south of Vienna, opposite the island of Lobau, using it as a platform from which to launch a bridgehead. For this purpose, he had a great bridge constructed across the wider arm of the river, on the friendly side, as well as a shorter bridge on the enemy side.

The French established a bridgehead on May 21, including the villages of Aspern and Essling. The bridgehead successfully withstood the Austrian counterattack and continued to expand. The next day, Napoleon personally commanded a general offensive. Beaten, the

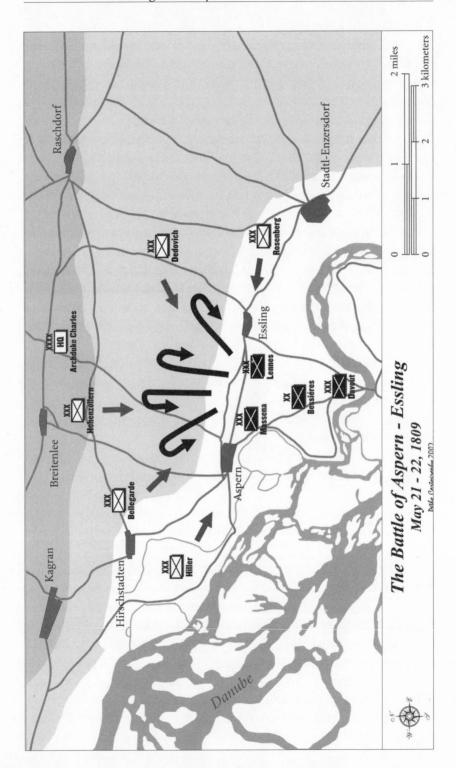

The Battle of Aspern - Essling
May 21 - 22, 1809

Austrians retreated in disorder. Lannes was on the verge of penetrating the Austrian line when the news arrived that the great bridge had been destroyed by fire rafts that the enemy had launched from upstream in the Danube. The flooded Danube made this particularly destructive. Davout's corps, which was supposed to exploit the breach, was unable to reach the battlefield. The victory was lost!

The archduke immediately exploited this gift from heaven. With a numerical superiority of four to one, he counterattacked with all his forces, aiming to destroy the bridgehead that suddenly had been deprived of all hope of support.

A nameless butchery ensued, impossible to avoid for lack of any room to maneuver. Aspern and especially Essling were taken and retaken repeatedly. The slaughter was equal on both sides. Lannes, the "Roland" of the army, was mortally wounded. Gazing helplessly at this carnage, Napoleon barely escaped himself on several occasions.

The bridgehead resisted all day. Yet, its survival depended on withdrawing to the other bank of the river. During the night, Massena performed a masterwork in the delicate task of disengagement.

Because of this bridge, the emperor lost a decisive victory while mourning the cost of 18,000 killed and wounded, slightly less than the Austrian casualties. The decisive battle remained to be fought.

The Expensive Peace of Wagram

After the butchery of Aspern-Essling, the two belligerents had to lick their wounds and reorganize, which explains the forced 43-day truce that followed the battle.

Encouraged by his partial success at Essling, the Archduke decided to give battle on the Marschfeld between the Danube and Wagram. He had reorganized his forces, bringing them up to 180,000 men and more than 400 cannon.

Napoleon transformed the island of Lobau into a gigantic operational base crowded with a strike force of 150,000 men and 450 guns.

All Europe held its breath. On a field measuring 15 by 10 kilometers, more than 300,000 men confronted each other in a sort of judgment of God, to the deafening sound of 800 artillery pieces. No one had ever seen a battle of such scope.

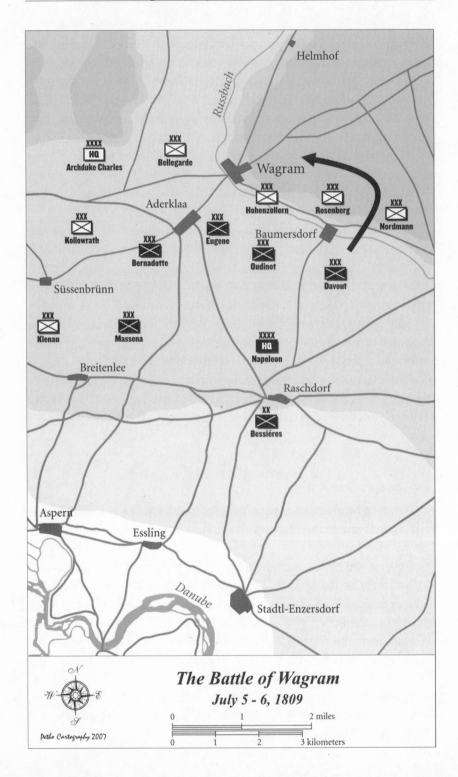

Helmhof

Russbach

XXXX
HQ
Archduke Charles

XXX
Bellegarde

Wagram

XXX
Hohenzöllern

XXX
Rosenberg

XXX
Nordmann

Aderklaa

XXX
Kollowrath

XXX
Eugene

XXX
Bernadotte

Baumersdorf

XXX
Oudinot

XXX
Davout

Süssenbrünn

XXX
Klenau

XXX
Massena

XXXX
HQ
Napoleon

Breitenlee

Raschdorf

XX
Bessiéres

Aspern

Essling

Danube

Stadtl-Enzersdorf

N
W · E
S

The Battle of Wagram
July 5 - 6, 1809

0   1   2 miles

0   1   2   3 kilometers

Petho Cartography 2007

Napoleon opened hostilities on July 4. While making a diversion toward Aspern, he launched a surprise crossing of the Danube during the night of the 4th to the 5th under cover of the sound of the river, and three kilometers away from the diversion. Without pausing, he attacked the Austrian positions all along the line.

The archduke expected an envelopment, especially on his left so as to cut the natural line of communication with Bohemia, from which must come any reinforcement from Archduke Johann. This was the type of maneuver that any good tactician might undertake and that the emperor had taught the Austrian army to expect during the past 13 years. Yet, Napoleon again deceived his adversary. His secret thrust was to strike where he was not expected, at the vulnerable point in the enemy's dispositions. Reinforcing the wings of the Austrian line out of fear of an envelopment had of necessity weakened the center. It was there that Napoleon would apply his offensive effort. And at that point stood Wagram.

After several hours of relentless combat, Wagram was on the point of being taken and the Austrian line broken. At that moment, a foolish event occurred that put everything at risk. Reaching the Wagram plateau, two of Bernadotte's Saxon battalions were attacked by Macdonald's Italians, who mistook them for Austrians because of similarities of uniform. This produced a rout in Bernadotte's corps, a rout that the Imperial Guard had enormous difficulty in containing. Oudinot's neighboring corps was constrained to pull back to protect its flank, and the Austrians profited by sealing the breach in their lines.

An imminent victory dissipated in a few seconds. Night approached, forcing the opponents to recommence on the next day, July 6.

But this time it was the Archduke who took the initiative, undoubtedly emboldened by the French disappointment of the previous day. Beginning at 4:00 a.m., he launched a violent attack on the French right, held by Davout, as much to preempt any attempt at envelopment as to make a diversion. Soon thereafter he attacked Massena on the left wing, along the Danube, with the evident intention of cutting Napoleon's communications with the island of Lobau and seizing its bridges. The archduke attempted to strike a blow similar to that of Napoleon at Friedland.

Napoleon was on the point of succeeding when Bernadotte's Saxons again routed, dangerously exposing the right wing of Massena, who already had all he could handle. Under fire, the emperor moved quickly to Massena. With one accord, the two organized a defensive block to halt the Austrian envelopment.

Napoleon did not forget his own plan, which the archduke's dangerous offensive had indirectly favored. Charles' pronounced effort on his right had of necessity denuded his center, in the area of Aderklaa-Wagram. In that region, the emperor rapidly reassembled a striking force destined to slice open the Austrian line.

At 9:00 a.m., the emperor ordered a general counter-attack. All units advanced at the same time. In the center, on which everything depended, the artillery concentration would enter history under the name of the "Battery of Wagram." Concentrated on a one-kilometer front before the assault troops, more than 100 cannon fired simultaneously, pulverizing everything with their shot and shell. Continuing to fire, they advanced in good order for two kilometers, always in the lead. After having thus opened the breach, the artillery gave way to Macdonald's infantry as well as the cavalry and the Grenadier Guards.

At 2:00 p.m., Archduke Charles recognized his defeat and ordered a timely general withdrawal toward Bohemia, thereby permitting a large portion of his forces to escape Davout's pincer movement. Disheartened, the Landwehr recruits threw down their arms and went home. The exhaustion of the French troops prevented an immediate pursuit.

Despite this delay, the Austrian rear guard was defeated at Znaim on July 11. Fearing total destruction, the archduke requested an armistice, which Napoleon authorized against the advice of his marshals. "Enough blood has been shed!" he told them in the episode already recounted.

At Wagram, the Austrians lost 44,000 killed, wounded, and captured, as well as 20 cannon and ten regimental colors. The French suffered 30,000 killed and wounded. Among the dead was the legendary light cavalryman General Charles Lasalle. The 1809 campaign in Germany was finished, giving way to peace negotiations.

Speculating on the results of the British landing in the Netherlands, the Machiavellian Klemens von Metternich, who had replaced Stadion as Austria's foreign minister, temporized for three months. The disastrous outcome of the British expedition at Walcheren on September 30 convinced him to sign the Treaty of Vienna on October 14, 1809.

Napoleon permitted Francis to retain his crown, but severely punished his perjury by reducing the Habsburg possessions. Bavaria, an active and courageous ally of France, received the Austrian region of the Inn. Russia, surprisingly, gained a portion of Galicia (Ternopol). This gift to a fainthearted ally illustrated Napoleon's obsession with peace in the east. He would be poorly repaid for it! The Grand Duchy of Warsaw received the other part of Galicia (Cracow). The remaining Austrian possessions on the Adriatic, including Trieste, Fiume, some remnants of Carnolia, and Croatia, were transferred to France for their strategic importance and as a portal to the east. They became the Illyrian provinces. In addition to these lost territories, Austria was to pay an indemnity of 85 million francs.

To demonstrate yet again that he cherished no territorial ambitions in Germany, Napoleon immediately abandoned his military positions, with the exception of Westphalia and the Prussian fortresses, which were indispensable pledges for the security of France.

But, like its predecessors, the Treaty of Vienna was considered by France's enemies to be nothing but a new and temporary ceasefire. Two-and-a-half years later, it would again be Russia's turn in the tag team of war.

Russia's War-like Relapse

After the war in Spain, the 1812 campaign in Russia is the military enterprise that most appears to justify the accusation that Napoleon waged wars of conquest. Throughout the necessarily long discussion of this question, we will see yet again that Napoleon bore no responsibility for this conflict that, in fact, he had done everything to avoid.

Here is where our preliminary remark concerning the true responsibility for war is most important. The initiation of hostilities relates solely to operational strategy. The true warmonger often finds it advantageous to be the one attacked. The war in Russia constitutes an excellent example of this. To believe that Napoleon, buried up to his neck in the Spanish hornet's nest, would open a second front out of a desire for conquest is quite simply an insult to common sense.

Since Erfurt, and especially since the Franco-Austrian War of 1809, Napoleon knew that one day or another a war would occur with Russia. Everything pressed Tsar Alexander in that direction.

As we have seen, overcome by the possibility of continental peace, at Tilsit Napoleon manifested an excessive patience with the defeated

Russian tsar. One would almost ask who really was defeated at Friedland, France or Russia? The tsar himself had not concealed his surprise at receiving conditions so favorable to his country. To please Alexander, Napoleon even had renounced the reconstruction of a strong Poland that would have represented the ideas of the Revolution and served the strategic interests of France. He had contented himself with the poorly tailored rump state that was the Grand Duchy of Warsaw, consisting of the Austrian and Prussian portions of the former Poland, while the tsar kept his portion.

Russia had been able to annex the Danube provinces and take over Finland, two longtime dreams of the Romanovs. Bordering on the decrepit Ottoman Empire, Russia nourished ambitions of conquest, ambitions that a complacent France had encouraged.

At Tilsit, Alexander and Napoleon had sealed an almost fraternal friendship, a gage of the enduring Franco-Russian alliance. At that moment, Alexander appeared to be sincere. Yet, upon his return to Saint Petersburg, he did not resist the anti-French forces of his court and of Britain. He became again what he had always been in reality: the incarnation of duplicity. He profited from the benefits of the alliance without honoring its obligations. He did not lift his little finger during the war against Austria, contrary to the Erfurt accord. If he had honored his alliance, Austria would not have dared attack France.

At that moment, Napoleon realized how naïve he had been at Tilsit. He might have done better if he had acted implacably to the vanquished. Yet what sacrifice was he unwilling to make to obtain a durable peace?

In 1810, a realistic analysis of the situation would lead to the conclusion that everything impelled the tsar toward war against France. The only remaining unknown factor was the exact date of the conflict. The motive, however, was established.

For Alexander, all the requirements had been met to continue the expansionist policies of Peter the Great and of his grandmother, Catherine II. Above all, he coveted Poland. The unexpected satisfactions that Napoleon had offered at Tilsit had put the tsar's boot in the stirrup. Militarily flattened, Prussia and Austria were neutralized for some time to come, but he could not wait too long. Strangled by the blockade, a Britain at bay constituted an unconditional, but not necessarily long-lasting, ally.

France was ensnared by the fatal trap of the war in Spain. The necessity to maintain major forces there correspondingly decreased the power of the French army on the Niemen. For Russia, this was an historic and unprecedented opportunity to realize its worldly ambitions.

The tsar's only concern in waiting for the appropriate hour to strike was to avoid appearing as the aggressor. With a perfectly bad faith, he multiplied his declarations of friendship while surreptitiously preparing for war. He assembled a litany of complaints against France, transforming easily rectified differences into insoluble issues. With complete hypocrisy, he invented whatever was necessary in order to foist responsibility for the coming war upon Napoleon.

It was thus that he pretended to feel bitterness concerning the emperor's marriage with Maria-Louisa of Austria, despite the fact that Alexander had officially refused an offer for the hand of his sister, a refusal that was a clear indication of rejecting French friendship overall. He knew with certainty that Napoleon did not approve of the designation of Bernadotte as heir to the Swedish throne. He knew also that this new monarch was an enemy of Napoleon and therefore an additional ally for Russia, as would soon be demonstrated. Nevertheless, he presented the matter as if Bernadotte were a French threat against Russia.

The French occupation of Oldenbourg was spotlighted beyond measure. Although it was held by Alexander's brother-in-law, this minuscule territory was of no consequence to the power and security of Russia. Napoleon offered very advantageous territorial compensation, such as Erfurt. Alexander preferred a portion of Poland, which would have transformed the disappointment of the Poles into outright hostility. The tsar knew perfectly well that Napoleon could not accord such an exorbitant concession.

The Polish concession had rightly contributed to the growing discontent of the Poles. Alexander forgot that at Tilsit Napoleon had made him the undreamt-of gift of allowing Russia to keep its slice of the Polish pie. By this, the emperor had profoundly disappointed the Polish patriots solely to please the tsar. But Alexander aspired to much more. Preoccupied with Poland in the purest Russian tradition, he dreamed of reconstituting the country under his control, and was influenced in this by his friend, Prince Adam Czartoryski. He was therefore distressed when, by the Treaty of Vienna with Austria in 1809, a part of Austrian Poland, Cracow, was reattached to the Grand Duchy of Warsaw. He had hoped that this would return to him, he who had failed to fulfill his obligations under the alliance! The tsar nonetheless proposed a convention by which Napoleon promised "to prevent forever the reconstitution of Poland." Overcome by the climate of the court of Saint Petersburg, the extremely naïve French ambassador, Caulaincourt, thoughtlessly signed this unworthy promise. Of course, Napoleon refused to ratify it. He proposed in its place a text promising "never to give any assistance to any power or any interior uprising that attempted to reestablish the Kingdom of Poland." This was an enormous concession that risked abandoning his Polish friends and allies. Nonetheless, Alexander was not satisfied, and returned to his initial proposition. He wanted to portray Napoleon as having refused his offers. The matter rested there.

Napoleon expressed his distress in a letter to Alexander:

> My feelings for Your Majesty will not change, although I cannot conceal the sense that Your Majesty no longer has any friendship for me. Already our alliance does not exist in the eyes of Britain and of Europe. Regardless of what is in Your Majesty's heart or in mine, this general belief is still a great evil. I remain the same for You, but I am struck by the evidence of the facts and by the thought that Your Majesty is already disposed, as soon as circumstances permit, to make a deal with England, which is the same thing as to ignite a war between our two empires.

An incident that spoke volumes about Alexander's duplicity succeeded in opening Napoleon's eyes. As a token of friendship, in 1809 the tsar had assigned an aide de camp named Count Alexandr Chernishev to Napoleon. A search of Chernishev's quarters revealed several secret documents of the War Ministry, delivered by the traitor, a certain Michel.

The continental blockade was the seed of discord that completed the rupture of the Franco-Russian alliance. The obligation to enforce blockade regulations against British commerce constituted a major clause of the treaty of alliance. To violate this promise was to act as an enemy of France, since such an action was equivalent to turning against France the economic weapon of the blockade.

Conscious of the negative effects of the blockade, Napoleon closed his eyes to certain discrepancies in the contract. He knew that the Russian economy, like that of all his allies, suffered by certain aspects of the commercial restrictions imposed. It was for this reason that he tried to alleviate matters. He was prepared to go farther, provided that the matter was carefully discussed. But the scheming aristocracy of Russia saw in the difficulties caused by the blockade the ideal pretext to break with France, which also threatened their antiquated social privileges, in particular serfdom. In this we find the major cause of opposition to France, the emancipator of peoples.

In the fall of 1810, the blockade functioned virtually everywhere in Europe, except in Russia. The emperor received information that 700 Russian wagons transported British merchandise to Leipzig. An enormous convoy of 1,200 ships, flying the Swedish, Portuguese, Spanish, or American flags, had sailed in the North Sea under the escort of 20 British warships. Filled with British products, they had been denied port calls by all of France's allies, in conformance with their promises. Now, however, these ships were bound for Russian waters.

Warning in time, on October 23, 1810, Napoleon asked the tsar not to admit these vessels: "If Your Majesty admits them, the war will continue. If You sequester them and confiscate their cargoes, you will have struck a major blow against England. Your Majesty can thus determine whether we have peace or continued war."

In response, Alexander not only admitted this convoy but, effective December 31, 1810, he opened his ports to all neutrals and doubled his defiance by strongly taxing French goods. All illusions were dissipated. By breaking the blockade and violating the principal clause of his treaty of alliance with France, the tsar had openly tilted toward the British camp. War between France and Russia had practically been declared.

A long eighteen-month period of preparations preceded the official commencement of hostilities. Russia had already made preparations for war, proof that its declarations of good will were nothing but a smokescreen. Napoleon's intelligence agents regularly informed him of the mobilization and reinforcement of the Russian army and of the displacement of its units to the frontiers.

Germany was dangerously denuded of French troops at this time. Napoleon had only limited effectives in the Grand Duchy of Warsaw plus a few thousand men at Danzig, under Davout's command. As quickly as possible, the emperor increased these troops while also forming a new army of Germany, all without reducing the troops in Spain too greatly. All the allies were levied to furnish large military contingents.

During this time, diplomatic relations continued as if nothing were amiss. Jacques Lauriston became ambassador to Saint Petersburg as replacement for Caulaincourt, who would have made an excellent Russian ambassador to France. That individual, Prince Alexandr Kurakin, passed his time deceiving people, affirming that "the tsar is the most loyal friend of France, the person most devoted to the Emperor." On August 15, 1811, Napoleon rudely interrupted the prince in public, as he had done previously with the British ambassador, to demonstrate that he was not deceived and to warn his master.

The bitter diplomatic competition that accompanied the military preparations has already been described. Let us add a few details.

In the face of British hostility, France could expect nothing. However, to avoid the reproach that he did not do everything possible for peace, Napoleon made a final overture on April 18, 1812, received with arrogance. Britain was already negotiating with Russia for an alliance that was concluded on July 18. Britain promised to finance the Russian war effort.

For France, it was essential to reinforce its alliances with Prussia, Austria, and Sweden in central Europe. It was inconceivable to have to confront the Russian bear with a hostile great power at the French back.

Despite the efforts of the tsar, the king of Prussia resisted Russian advances. In March 1812, he agreed that Prussia would become an operational base for the French army to which, in addition, he would add a contingent of 20,000 men. It was true that the ultra-Francophobe Queen Louise had been dead for two years. Immediately, the principal military advisors of the king—Scharnhorst, Gneisenau, Boyen, and Clausewitz—defected to Saint Petersburg to demonstrate their opposition. The deceitful Frederick William privately informed the tsar that "if war comes, we will do only what is strictly necessary. We will always bear in mind that we are united, and that one day we will be allies again."

The Austrian emperor revealed the same duplicity, even though Napoleon was now his son-in-law. Metternich agreed to furnish a contingent of 34,000 men, but hastened to inform the tsar secretly of the "auxiliary" nature of these troops. Not without irony, Alexander replied that he would return them "without a scratch."

The prize for double-dealing went to Bernadotte. Approached concerning the solidarity of the Swedish-French alliance concluded in 1810, Bernadotte took exception to any doubts about his triple loyalty to

Napoleon, to his native country, and to his signed agreements. He would rather "straddle a barrel of gunpowder and blow himself up" than act otherwise, he claimed.

As the price of its alliance, Sweden had received Pomerania as a gift. After Bernadotte's accession to the rank of crown prince, Sweden continued to ignore the blockade in that province, even though enforcement was a sine qua non of the acquisition. In January 1812, France installed customs officials in Pomerania under the protection of Davout's troops.

Bernadotte found in this a pretext to tilt toward the camp of his country's enemies. The mask fell! Dragging the reluctant sovereign with him, Bernadotte acted as if he were more Swedish than the Swedes, even though he had only been prince for a short while. He entered into negotiations with the court of Saint Petersburg, and passed to the Russian side.

In doing so, Bernadotte betrayed not only France but also his newly adopted country, recently amputated of its Finnish province by the Russian enemy. This former marshal of France pushed his abasement so far as to give tactical advice to Alexander:

> Avoid major battles, work on the enemy's flanks, force him to make detachments which you then harass by marches and counter-marches. All this is distressing to the French soldier and will have the greatest effect. Ensure that there are numerous Cossacks everywhere!

Alexander would soon apply this advice almost to the letter. Such personal hatred on Bernadotte's part did not become a man who could have been greater. It was disgusting.

The declaration of war by the United States against Britain was not of a nature to affect the correlation of forces in Eastern Europe. America was too far away, unfortunately.

On May 28, 1812, Russia concluded a peace accord with the Ottoman Empire. At the price of its Danubian conquests, Russia secured its southern flank. Held there for the previous two years by a war against Turkey, two Russian armies thus became available on the Niemen. This was very bad news for peace. Turkey should have played the role for Russia that Spain was playing for France.

In the spring of 1812, the diplomatic and military preparations were completed on both sides. In his tireless quest for an arrangement with the tsar, in February Napoleon sent him a secret letter by means of his "official" spy in France, Count Chernishev, just before the latter was unmasked by French police. The tsar made no response.

Sure of himself, the tsar took the initiative in the rupture and thus the war. On April 8, he dared to send France an ultimatum devoid of the least diplomatic nicety. In this message, Alexander demanded the immediate withdrawal of all French forces behind the Elbe.

Did the tsar really believe that France could abase itself by such a humiliation even to save the peace? Napoleon implied this to Ambassador Kurakin, who carried Alexander's message to him. The emperor offered a final proposal of understanding: the neutralization of the entire territory between the Nieman and the Passarge (now the Pasleka.) As a gage of good intentions, no one could ask for more. Kurakin manifested a very great interest. Napoleon sent his aide de camp, Count Louis de Narbonne, a former minister of Louis XVI, to Alexander to plead for this final attempt at an agreement. On May 26, Narbonne reported to Napoleon at Dresden that Alexander had categorically rejected the idea. Moreover, Narbonne informed him, the tsar had deliberately given great publicity to his ultimatum to be doubly sure that Napoleon could not accept it. More than an ultimatum, this was a provocation. To indicate clearly that diplomatic relations were de facto broken, Alexander refused to receive the French ambassador, General Lauriston.

War was practically declared, but Napoleon still did not want to precipitate matters. He waited another month before departing on May 9, 1812, to rejoin the armies in the field. For the thousandth time, he was forced to suspend his civil function as head of state and builder, the sole function that he really valued. On the way, he organized an assembly of all the allied sovereigns at Dresden. Accompanied by the empress, solemnly welcomed by the king and queen of Saxony, he made an imposing entrance to the illuminated city on the evening of May 16. He spent several days there reconnecting the links with a crop of kings, princes, and dukes who eagerly surrounded him in an imperial festival.

Napoleon did not hesitate to leave this glittering society in the lurch on May 29, traveling to rejoin his veterans on the frontier. He felt best when he was among them!

The Russian Campaign: Ultimate Chance for Peace

"Global peace was in Russia,
and its success could not be in doubt."

War having been declared on him, in fact if not in law, could Napoleon have avoided the invasion of Russia? Briefly, he considered waiting in Poland for Alexander to attack him. He quickly perceived that the tsar had no such intention. Alexander feared a new Friedland that would not, this time, lead to a new Tilsit. Time was on Alexander's side. He had a sufficient period to complete the mobilization of the most powerful army ever possessed by Russia. He had all the time he needed.

From Napoleon's perspective, the situation was completely different. It was obviously not in his interest to await the completion of Russian military preparations. He could only maintain for a short time the enforced allied mobilization that provided his new Grand Armeé. Above all, he needed to act prior to the opening of a British front in Western Europe. The war in Spain gave him enough concerns by itself! He regretted even having waited until summer. A spring offensive would probably have permitted him to avoid the coming catastrophe.

Napoleon issued his traditional order of the day to the Grand Armeé on June 21:

> Soldiers: The second Polish war has begun. The first ended at Friedland and Tilsit. At Tilsit, Russia swore eternal alliance with France and war against England. Today Russia violates its oaths. Does it believe that we are degenerate? Are we not still the soldiers of Austerlitz? Russia has placed us between war and dishonor. There can be no doubt as to which we will choose.

Beginning on June 24 with a spectacular yet unopposed crossing of the Niemen in the Kovno area, the war with Russia ended in tragedy in December. This war consisted of two very distinct phases: first, a diabolic pursuit of the Russian army to Moscow, marked by the indecisive victory of Borodino or the Moskva; next, a catastrophic retreat back to Poland from October to December.

The Diabolical Pursuit

Once again, no desire for territorial conquest underpinned the Russian campaign. The goal of Napoleon's campaign was to destroy the enemy army, thereby forcing Russia to make peace.

The army operating in Russia approached a total of 600,000 men. Half were assigned to hold occupied territories and provide logistical support, while the other half were first-line combat troops.

The invading force consisted only of the attack echelon of the Grand Armeé, whose unprecedented strength of more than half-a-million men stretched from the Rhine to the Niemen. Its international composition was one of the more original aspects of this gigantic military amalgam. Frenchmen represented only a third of the total force and half of the attack echelon. It was a true European army, an army of "twenty nations" as it was labeled at the time.

The largest foreign contingent, 100,000 men, came from the Confederation of the Rhine (Bavaria, Westphalia, Württemberg, Baden, Saxony, and several duchies and principalities). Next in descending order were Poland (50,000), Austria (32,000), Italy (30,000), Prussia (20,000), and Switzerland (10,000). The Netherlands, Denmark, Naples, Spain, and Croatia also provided contingents of several thousand soldiers each.

Such a disparate and uneven ensemble could not go far without experiencing problems of cohesion and logistics. It was a long way from the minuscule and uncouth Army of Italy of 1796!

Barclay de Tolly, Peter Bagration, and Alexander Tormasov commanded the Russian armies, more than 300,000 men with some 900 guns. The Russians deployed thusly: (1) Barclay de Tolly's main body of 140,000 blocked the axis from Vilna to Saint Petersburg; (2) a secondary body of 60,000 men, commanded by Bagration, operated on Barclay de Tolly's left on the axis of Moscow; and (3) and Tormasov's reserve army was being formed south of the Pripiat Marshes.

Napoleon operated on four axes: (1) in the north, Macdonald with the Prussian and Bavarian contingents; (2) in the center with the emperor were Prince Eugene, Oudinot, and the Imperial Guard; (3) in the south, Davout and Jerome; (4) in the extreme south, Charles-Philippe Schwartzenberg's Austrian corps as flank guard against Tormasov along the Pripiat Marshes.

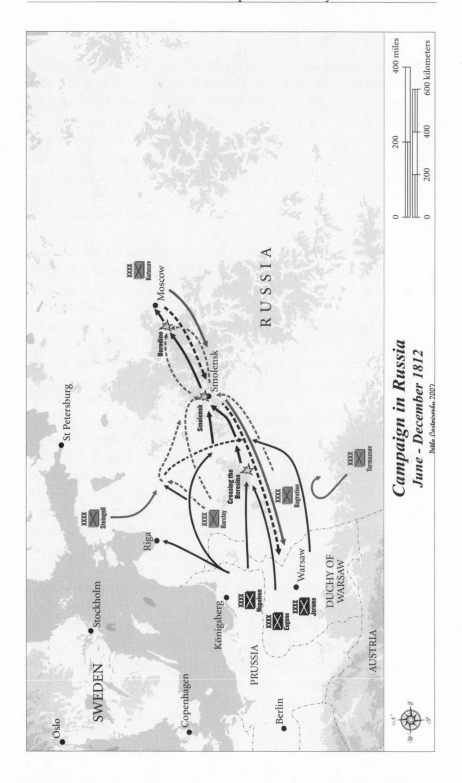

*Campaign in Russia
June - December 1812*

Delo Oostenveldt 2007

Eugene's slowness of movement permitted Barclay de Tolly to escape encirclement in the area of Vilna, which fell without fighting on June 26. The tsar sent his police minister, Balashov, to Napoleon with a message offering negotiations if the Grand Armeé returned to Poland. In full retreat, the vanquished dared to dictate unacceptable conditions to the victor. The purpose was obvious. Alexander sought only to gain precious time to permit Barclay de Tolly to recover and to complete the concentration of Tormasov's army. If he genuinely wanted peace, why did he not ask to open negotiations without preconditions? Why, at Vilna before hostilities began, did he refuse to receive Ambassador Lauriston, who was carrying a final attempt at peace?

Continuing its advance under weather conditions so extreme that they slowed its progress, the Grand Armeé occupied Vitebsk without opposition on July 27.

The heat, dust, thirst, mud, and mosquitoes inflicted an inhuman trial on the men. Unit strengths visibly declined under the effects of illness.

Barclay de Tolly and Bagration linked up at Smolensk. The city resisted an initial attack on August 16-17. Napoleon believed that he finally had found an opportunity for a great, decisive battle. Once more, however, Barclay de Tolly retreated after setting the city on fire.

The scorched earth policy of the Russian army owed more to the force of circumstances than to a deliberate choice. The Russian army's leadership was divided into two groups: those who wished at all costs to prevent the Grand Armeé from reaching Moscow, the historic and religious heart of Russia, and those who sought at any price to preserve the army from disaster by evading a great battle against the invincible Napoleon. Up until Smolensk, Russia was fortunate to have in Barclay de Tolly a partisan of the second group; otherwise, the Russian campaign would have reached its conclusion before Vilna or Vitebsk.

Barclay de Tolly's refusal to defend Smolensk set off a crisis in the Russian high command, a crisis that had been brewing from the start of the campaign. The aristocracy rebelled against a retreat that was without end and that damaged its dignity. Without doubt, the aristocrats also feared that the presence of the Grand Armeé in the heart of Russia might encourage an uprising among the serfs. Alexander eventually yielded to his aristocracy by replacing Barclay de Tolly with Kutusov, the brave vanquished of Austerlitz.

The new commander-in-chief decided to stop Napoleon at a position between Borodino and the River Moskva.

The Battle of Borodino and the Occupation of Moscow

"Never have I seen an army shine with so much merit."

—Napoleon

The great battle that unfolded on September 7, 1812, is known in France as that of the Moskva River, but in Russia by the village of Borodino.

As a good tactician, Kutusov had chosen a battlefield that limited opportunities for maneuver, forcing a frontal engagement. Napoleon disliked this type of situation, which reminded him of the slaughter at Eylau and Essling. He considered the possibility of advancing directly on Moscow while bypassing the Russian army, in the hope of forcing the enemy to leave his positions in order to defend the capital. Yet, this maneuver might well expose his communications, which in war is folly.

Mikhail Kutusov did not expect to receive such a gift. Instead, he waited firmly with 155,000 men and 636 guns, disposed in the following manner: in the north, Barclay de Tolly's army, straddling the route to Moscow on the Borodino heights, with Baggavout's, Ostermann's, Korff's, and Uvarov's corps; in the center, the Grand Redoubt, held by Rajeski's, Doktorov's and von Pahlen's corps; in the south, Bagration occupied the Three Arrows fleches with Gortchakov's and Borozdin's corps. He blocked the gap between the Three Arrows and the forest of Utitsa with Tuchkov's corps and Karpov's cavalry; in reserve, Eugene of Würtemberg's 4th division of the 2nd Corps and the Guard, under Nikolay Lavrov; on the wings, Cossack bands hovered, observing, harassing, and massacring any isolated detachment. In addition to his large numerical superiority, Kutusov benefited from the protection of numerous carefully-sited redoubts.

As a preliminary to the battle, Compans' division had seized the Schwardino redoubt at heavy cost on September 5.

The day of the 6th passed in reconnaissance, observation, and various preparations for the main attack, scheduled for the next day. The

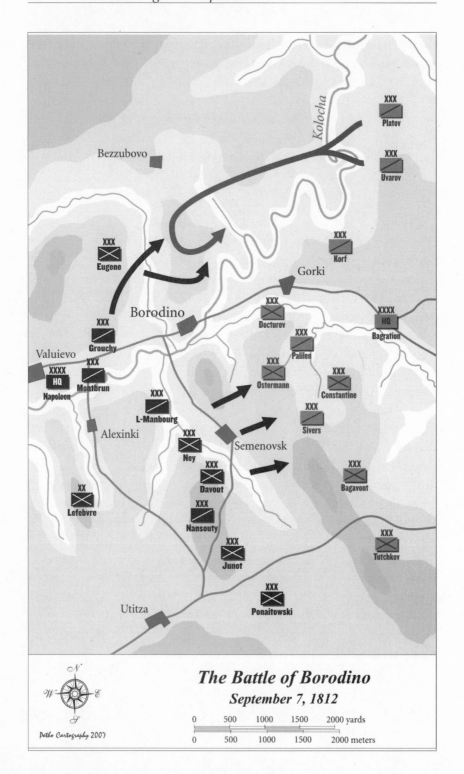

The Battle of Borodino

September 7, 1812

emperor decided on his battle plan. He had some 127,000 men and 587 cannon. He planned yet again to make up for his inferiority by the massive, well-directed fire of his artillery.

The weakest portion of the enemy line was on the southern end, on the route leading to Moscow, in the gap between the Three Arrows redoubts and the forest of Utitsa. It was there that Napoleon focused the efforts of Davout, supported by Murat. After conquering the Three Arrows in conjunction with Ney, they were to attack toward the Grand Redoubt. In their wake, Poniatowski would bypass them to attack deeper into the enemy rear.

As a diversion for the main effort, Eugene was to launch an attack in the north toward Borodino, then angle to the south toward the Grand Redoubt. At the same time, Ney, supported by Junot, Morand, and Gerard, would engage the Shevardino Redoubt, followed in reserve by the Guard and Friant's division.

Davout had suggested a flanking move farther south, through the forest of Utitsa. Napoleon thought the proposal too risky. The extension of the French line in that direction would leave it too vulnerable to an enemy counterattack. In addition, crossing the Utitsa forest without guides was likely to cause difficulties. Prudence demanded avoiding that risk. Davout came around to that analysis.

At dawn on September 7, a strong sun pierced the morning fogs, just as on December 2, 1805, but this was no longer the sun of Austerlitz! Hundreds of cannon unleashed their deadly thunder on each side.

In the north, Eugene seized Borodino and began bombarding the Grand Redoubt. In the center, Junot advanced south toward the Utitsa Woods. Ney engaged the Three Arrows in front while Davout attacked them in flank. On the sides of the Three Arrows, the melee was terrible. Bagration held firmly, waiting for the French. Davout had to draw his sword. His horse was killed under him, and he himself was wounded. Murat's irresistible cavalry charge swept across the terrain with the light brigades of Montbrun and Latour Maubourg, supported by Nansouty's cuirassiers. Ney finished the job with his habitual bravery.

The Three Arrows fell about 9:00 a.m. An hour later, it was the Grand Redoubt's turn, stunned by 400 cannon. Yet in the south, blocked by Tuchkov, Poniatowski was unable to penetrate toward Utitsa.

At that instant, Napoleon believed that he had achieved a decisive victory. The Russian line should have been close to breaking in the center, but that assessment did not allow for the extraordinary combativeness of the Russians nor the value of their leaders. About 11:00 a.m., a furious counterattack of infantry and cavalry took place all along the front and especially around the Grand Redoubt, which fell to the furor of the assault. The Three Arrows were on the point of being submerged. The emperor hurriedly dispatched Friant's division and Marchand's Württembergers there. For a time, they succeeded in stabilizing the situation. Bagration was struck in the left leg by a shell splinter, lingers for many days, and died on September 24. The Russian assault felt the effect of his loss.

By 1:00 p.m., Poniatowski had finally reached the area of Utitsa, thereby attracting various Russian units that should have supported the defense of the Grand Redoubt. It was now a question of recapturing that position, the keystone of the Russian defense. Ney and Murat implored Napoleon to commit the Guard, but he refused. He did not wish to lose his one remaining reserve to deal with the unforeseen, that constant given of warfare.

In concert with his senior subordinates, the emperor improvised a massive counter-attack on the field of battle. He concentrated the fire of 400 guns against the fortifications. Following this hammering, he launched two cavalry charges, one from each side. On the right was Caulaincourt, brother of the emperor's advisor, having just replaced Montbrun, killed at the head of his cavalry corps. On the left was Latour Maubourg. Both overran everything in their paths and enveloped the Grand Redoubt. For his part, Caulaincourt fell, mortally wounded. The artillery finished the work. The Grand Redoubt was retaken. The Russians retreated but did not break their ranks.

This would have been the moment to crown the success by launching the Guard in pursuit. The emperor again refused for the same reason as before. Blood had already flowed sufficiently in the course of twelve hours of brutal combat.

To save what remained of his army, Kutusov withdrew in a different direction from that of Moscow, toward Kaluga, offering the capital to Napoleon on a platter.

Russian propaganda attempted to present Borodino as a success. True, the Russian army was not destroyed, as it preserved about half of its effective strength. Yet, it had abandoned the battlefield and the defense of Moscow. That was hardly a success.

Caused primarily by artillery, the Russian losses were significantly higher than French losses. Russian casualties were estimated at 48,000 killed, wounded, and missing, while the Grand Armeé reportedly suffered 6,000 killed and 20,000 wounded (with Russian estimates of French losses running as high as 35,000 from all causes).

On September 14, the Grand Armeé entered Moscow, abandoned by most of its inhabitants. Beginning the next day, the sinister governor Count Fyodor Rostopchin set fire to the city, setting off uncontrolled general pillaging. In 48 hours, fire destroyed two-thirds of the city. Although the Kremlin survived, Napoleon installed his headquarters in a more remote location, the Petrovsk palace.

There he waited impatiently for a sign from the tsar. To encourage negotiations, on September 20 Napoleon wrote:

To my brother the Emperor Alexander:

> The beautiful city of Moscow exists no longer. Rostopchin has burned it. 400 arsonists have been arrested, all of whom declared that they were obeying orders from the governor or the chief of police. They have been shot. . . . I would not have written of such matters if I believed that they had been done on the orders of Your Majesty. I consider it impossible that, with your principles, your heart, and your ideas of justice, you could have authorized such excesses, unworthy of the great sovereign of a great nation. In the time it took us to bring pumps to Moscow, we could have moved 150 cannon, 60,000 new muskets, and 1,600,000 cartridges. I made war on Your Majesty without animosity: a note from You before or even after the last battle would have halted my march, and I would even have passed up the advantage of entering Moscow. If Your Majesty retains any portion of your former sentiments for me, You will take this letter in good part. . . .

The absence of any reply from Alexander did not discourage Napoleon from pursuing his efforts to open negotiations. An opportunity existed. Remaining in Moscow as director of the Foundling Hospital, Major General Toutolmin asked for help and solicited the authority to send a messenger to the tsarina, patroness of the institution. Napoleon gave him permission and asked him to "write to the tsar, for whom I have always had the highest personal esteem, that I desire peace." He was determined to renew Tilsit.

Napoleon next asked Caulaincourt, the tsar's friend, to carry a message to Alexander. Caulaincourt balked, invoking the absolute pointlessness of such a mission.

Was there still a chance to negotiate through the valorous Kutusov? He sent Lauriston to the Russian headquarters on October 5, carrying a letter for Alexander. Kutusov ignored the advice of the British commissioner not to receive the letter, but he showed himself haughty and aggressive. At least, Napoleon could be sure that his letter would reach its destination.

The tsar responded: "Peace? But we have not yet made war! My campaign has only just begun! For now, no proposition of the adversary would tempt me to stop fighting and thereby thwart my sacred obligation to revenge my outraged country."

The party of all-out war was definitely in control in Saint Petersburg.

What should Napoleon do with the harsh winter approaching? To await good weather in Moscow, Vitebsk, or Smolensk would be to enclose his army in a vast prisoner-of-war camp. The only remaining solution was to return to Poland.

Yet, the vain search for a sign of good will from the tsar had caused Napoleon to lose a month. An unusually early winter was about to entrap the Grand Armeé. The Russian "General Summer" had already inflicted a Calvary on the army. On the way home, "General Winter" would carry it down to hell.

The Atrocious Retreat

It began on October 19. Napoleon chose the route from Kaluga to Smolensk to avoid the totally destroyed route taken the previous summer. Yet, at Maloyaroslavets the Russians established a blocking position, which Eugene had great difficulty clearing, prompting Napoleon to retrace the summer route. Obviously, Kutusov was not disposed to let the French army depart in peace.

The Russian commander-in-chief had reconstituted a corps of 85,000 men, active from east to west along the French route. Admiral Pavel Chichagov's newly formed 3rd Western Army was moving up from the south. A Russian corps commanded by Wittgenstein attacked from the north. These two forces constituted the teeth of a pincers intended to close at the Berezina River. Schwarzenberg, never eager to fight to help Napoleon, remained idle. This allowed Russian forces under Chichagov to proceed to Minsk after leaving a small observation force in place to keep an eye on the Austrians. The Russians drove back the Polish troops of General Mikolai (Michal) Bronikowski and seized Minsk, with its enormous supply depots, on November 16. Gouvion Saint-Cyr was unable to prevent Wittgenstein from laying his hands on the provisions at Vitebsk. In the rear, partisan groups threatened communications and massacred stragglers and strays. And everywhere the Cossacks harassed the column ceaselessly.

The military situation was thus poor. To compound the situation, on November 4, three weeks earlier than usual, a wave of cold and snow arrived. The temperature fell to minus 25 degrees Celsius (minus 13 degrees Fahrenheit). The movement to Smolensk became a disaster. Units fell apart, with each person thinking solely of survival from the cold and famine. Only the Guard maintained its formation and discipline.

Almost all the horses perished, either of the cold or to serve as food. The only remaining cavalry was that of the Guard.

A miserable horde of some 50,000 men painfully reached Smolensk on November 7.

Bad news fell like the snow. There was no sign of life from Ney's rearguard. A significant troop reinforcement, which was supposed to support Baraguey d'Hilliers at Smolensk, did not appear at the rendezvous. Baraguey was defeated and captured.

The capture of Vitebsk by the enemy constrained Napoleon to take a more southern route by way of Orcha, Borisov, and Smorhoni, carrying the French dangerously close to the armies of Tomasov and Admiral Pavel Chichagov.

Kutusov attempted to surprise the column on November 17 at Krasnoye, 140 kilometers southwest of Smolensk. He had under-estimated the combat power of the Guard, still pugnacious despite superhuman tests suffered during the previous month. Let us render them the respect they deserve. Impeccably aligned as if on parade, impressively disciplined, unshakable under fire, advancing to the sound of bands playing "let us keep watch over the Empire," the Guard swept aside 40,000 Russians. One of those provided a flattering testimonial:

"Napoleon's Guard sailed through us like a 100-gun warship sailing through a group of fishing boats."

In a final piece of bad news, Chichagov overpowered the Polish garrison at the bridge at Borisov, the essential crossing point over the Berezina. Oudinot succeeded in recapturing Borisov on November 25, but was unable to prevent the burning of the bridge. The Russian noose tightened. The remnants of the Grand Armeé were caught between Chichagov's army on the western bank of the Berezina and those of Kutusov and Wittgenstein that clawed at them from the east. The crossing of the Berezina was a question of life or death.

A new problem came in the form of a warming trend that had replaced the bitter cold for several days. The frozen river transformed into a raging torrent, preventing the escapees from crossing on the ice. More than 120,000 Russians prepared to give the death blow to some 30,000 exhausted, starving, and freezing soldiers, carrying with them 40,000 sick, wounded, and crippled. Only a miracle could save the remnants of the Grand Armeé.

Napoleon's military genius provided this miracle. He hoodwinked Chichagov with a simulated crossing at Borisov and then crossed 20 kilometers farther north, near the unwatched village of Studianka. Thanks to the self-sacrifice of General Eblé's bridge-building engineers, the French troops crossed on November 26 to 29, leaving behind them as many as 25,000 - 30,000 unfortunate stragglers, lost through their own indiscipline.

In the realm of military art, the crossing operation over the Berezina must be considered as a masterwork of genius. Executed under such adverse conditions, it merits admiration. The French even succeeded in taking 6,000 prisoners and eight regimental colors.

This feat of arms did not completely extricate the Grand Armeé. The sufferings endured up to this point were nothing compared to what was to come. Redoubling in severity, the cold inflicted dreadful losses and gave rise to scenes worthy of Dante's inferno. The cold and famine progressively killed off those who had escaped the Berezina, and even struck Kutuzov, who was also very affected by the cold.

A sinister procession of miserable survivors reached Smorghani on December 5, again poorly prepared. Two days' march from the stocked warehouses of Vilna, Napoleon decided that his presence would be more useful at Paris, and left Murat to continue the recovery.

Yet the affair ended even more badly than anticipated. Overtaken by events, Murat was unable to prevent the pillage and sack of Vilna on December 8. Whatever remained of the Grand Armeé, including even the Guard, dissolved. Like a deserter, Murat left everything and fled to his Kingdom of Naples. Courageously, Eugene attempted to save what he could with the help of the marshals, notably Ney, who "commanded with musket in hand."

On December 15, 1812, only a few thousand escapees in the most pitiful condition recrossed the Niemen at Kovno. The disaster of Russia sounded the hunting call for a sort of gigantic fox hunt of the European monarchies against France.

The Hunting Call

In the waning days of 1812, the enemies of France could hope for the rapid collapse of the Empire. The military disaster quickly led to the diplomatic isolation of France, as we have seen in the chapter concerning alliances. Then its allies, with the sole exception of the Confederation of the Rhine, turned against it as it faced the hunting pack of the Coalition.

The Isolation of France

As might be expected, the alliance with Prussia was the first to fail. On December 30, 1812, General Ludwig Yorck von Wartenburg, commander of the Prussian corps in the Grand Armeé, signed a convention with Russia at Tauraggen. This agreement declared the corps neutral and turned over Konigsberg to the tsar's army. This touched off an anti-French insurrection, making the Vistula the defensive line of the Empire.

Never slow in duplicity, the insatiable king of Prussia pretended to disapprove of Yorck and assured Napoleon of his "scrupulous fidelity." The king added this deceit: "I am bound to you as much by loyalty as by self-interest, because I am not one of those babblers who wish to see France toppled." At the same time, he was discretely congratulating Yorck and encouraging the tsar to enter Germany. Finally, on March 17, he discarded his mask and declared war on France. Secretly prepared,

100,000 volunteers mobilized rapidly. The French army had to evacuate Berlin and fall back on the Elbe.

Several days later, Alexander made his entry into Berlin and did not leave Germany again. He claimed to be entrusted with a divine mission to liberate Europe.

Austria rivaled Prussia in the art of double-dealing. At the head of the Austrian contingent, Schwarzenberg, like Yorck, withdrew from the French army by the convention of Zeycs on January 31, 1813. The Russians were thereby able to occupy Warsaw, obliging Poniatowski to pull back.

Although he was Napoleon's father-in-law, the Emperor Francis burned to imitate Frederick William. He reinforced his armies and informed the tsar that he was not against him. At the same time, to increase the ignominy, his representative Metternich informed Napoleon in the name of his emperor that their alliance had never been more important to Austria. He was only trying to hoodwink the emperor. In the course of his contacts with Schwarzenberg, who was again ambassador to Paris, Napoleon understood that Austria was no longer an armed ally but rather an armed neutral. The protection of his marriage, whose cover Napoleon had naïvely believed sheltered him from Austria, appeared as nothing but a tragic illusion.

Elsewhere in Europe, the situation continued to deteriorate. Sweden promised to provide 35,000 men to the Coalition as an admirable contribution by Bernadotte. On March 3, Bernadotte reasserted his alliance with Britain, which promised him not only Norway but also Guadeloupe!

Hamburg rebelled on February 20, and it had to be evacuated March 12. The Russians entered the city on March 18. The Duke of Mecklenburg had no choice but to join the Coalition.

In this situation, what could the King of Saxony, grand duke of Warsaw, do? His invaded lands welcomed the Russians. He withdrew to Austria.

Throughout Germany, a strong national sentiment appeared.

The king of Denmark continued to resist what amounted to blackmail, but for how much longer? He was openly threatened with forfeiting Norway to the Swedes if he did not join the Coalition.

The Netherlands found itself prey to ferment.

Even the Kingdom of Naples was cause for some uncertainty. After having deserted the French army in Russia, the overly ambitious Murat compromised with the enemy to conserve a crown that he owed to Napoleon. Coveting the Papal States, he began to negotiate with Austria and the British governor of Sicily.

Even in France, the representatives of the regime gave indications of an understandable exhaustion. Some did not understand the gigantic stakes involved in the confrontation at hand. Others no longer had sufficient courage to continue fighting. There were also numerous opportunists who considered a restoration of the Ancien Régime. Thus Talleyrand offered his services to Louis XVIII, accommodated at Hartwell in England.

Delighting in the difficulties of the country, the royalist movement, a truly foreign party, once again raised its head. Alexander's court reverberated to the diatribes of Joseph de Maistre, Anne-Louise de Stael, Charles Pozzo di Borgo, and so many others in the pay of the British.

At this somber time, Napoleon could only count on a handful of political officials and his generals, brothers in arms. But it was always from the unalterable confidence of the nation and the touching loyalty of the people that he drew the superhuman force he needed to confront the great test that awaited him. He was willing to defend the new world to the end.

In a final attempt at peacemaking, Napoleon assured the Austrian mediator Metternich of his constant desire for peace, officially announced in a formal address to the Imperial legislature on February 14: "I want peace. . . . I will never make anything but a peace that is honorable and conforms to the interests and the grandeur of my Empire." Yet, although he mentioned various possible concessions, that did not interest the other chancelleries of Europe, and no one listened. Never had the goal of the Coalition appeared more clear, in complete fidelity to the engagement of Amiens of April 6, 1793, let us recall: destroy the new regime in France and reestablish the old. In that spring of 1813, Napoleon truly was the only sovereign who desired peace! All the others only were interested in a dishonorable capitulation, without conditions, by France.

The Campaign of 1813

The renewal of hostilities was preceded by a new prodigy of Napoleon's organizational skills, based on the unshakable patriotism of the nation. To confront the hordes of the Sixth Coalition who were preparing to crash against France, Napoleon could not draw to any great degree upon the army in Spain, which was already beset. He therefore had to form a new army in only a few months.

With regard to effectives, the contingent of 1813, already called upon in October 1812, provided 40,000 men. One hundred thousand national guardsmen also helped fill the ranks of the regular army. The contingent of 1814 was also prepared for an early call-up. To these French citizens one could add the contingents of the Confederation of the Rhine and other small allies.

The new recruits received an accelerated military training. They would perform miracles despite their inexperience and shortages in their equipment. As for the latter, in great haste hundreds of cannon had to be forged, hundreds of thousands of muskets constructed, and thousands of horses purchased to completely reconstitute the cavalry.

Because of the imperfections of his new army, Napoleon needed once again to focus on delaying the Coalition members who were preparing to invade. On April 15, 1813, he was again forced to leave his absorbing civil responsibilities to take command of the French armies in Germany. Preceded by his new army of 120,000 men, he rejoined the 120,000 troops of Eugene on the Saale River. If his 450 guns reassured him, he experienced concerns with regard to the cavalry, which had been imperfectly reconstituted.

On the opposing side, the Russian and Prussian forces were roughly equivalent. Blücher commanded the Prussians and Wittgenstein the Russians, replacing the rough Kutusov, who had died of illness in April.

Two very distinct periods characterized the development of the campaign of 1813. The first, from May to August, was marked by the striking victories of Lützen, Bautzen, and Wurschen, followed by a deceptive armistice. The second began with a new victory at Dresden after the Coalition partners violated the truce. Then, overwhelmed by numbers, the French army at Leipzig experienced a great defeat that forced it to withdraw behind the Rhine.

The first clash occurred on April 29 with Ney's brilliant victory at Weissenfels.

The Russo-Prussians responded with an attack in force at Lützen on May 2. Napoleon personally conducted the counterattack, defeating Blücher and Wittgenstein, who fell back in disorder beyond the Elbe. They were saved from disaster only by the lack of French cavalry to exploit the success.

On May 16, Metternich used the Count of Bubna as intermediary to propose to Napoleon that Metternich act as mediator to negotiate with the Russo-Prussians. Without any recompense, France was to abandon the Grand Duchy of Warsaw, Illyria, and those territories that had joined the Empire since 1811.

In more prosaic terms, this was a case of "what's mine is mine, what's yours is negotiable"! It was obvious that this unacceptable proposition had no other purpose but to force Napoleon to accept the responsibility for the renewal of hostilities. We thus see again the consistently Machiavellian conduct of the European courts in all the wars of the Empire. Although he was a man of much duplicity, Metternich did not deviate from this.

Napoleon preferred to address Alexander in person, and sent Caulaincourt to him as negotiator. The tsar did not even display sufficient courtesy to receive his former intimate friend. Once again, he demonstrated that an honorable peace did not enter into the views of the Coalition members. Napoleon eventually regretted his own desperate desire for peace. Since they wanted war, he would give it to them!

The Russo-Prussians were entrenched in a fortified position behind the Spree. On May 2, Napoleon gained a victory at Bautzen, followed on the 21st by another at Wurschen. Only Ney's failure saved the Russo-Prussians from destruction.

They retreated in disorder. The absence of reserve cavalry again hampered efforts to transform defeat into disaster as had occurred after Jena.

The defeats of Bautzen and Wurschen stirred up discord in the high command of the Coalition. Wittgenstein was dismissed in disgrace and replaced by Barclay de Tolly, who on May 29 asked for a suspension of hostilities. By this time, the French army was deployed along the Oder. In less than a month, it had pushed the Russo-Prussians more than 350 kilometers back toward their departure point and had inflicted severe losses.

Napoleon hesitated to grant a truce to an enemy whom he might face again, strengthened, in a short time. Yet, he acceded to the pressing requests of Berthier and Caulaincourt, who had become converts to the false peace. He thereby committed an operational fault that he would regret for the rest of his life. At least he would put this time to good use in reinforcing his armies, especially the cavalry that had failed him to such a degree.

An Armistice of Fools

The armistice was signed at Pleswitz on June 4, 1813, and was scheduled to run until July 20, a date that subsequently was extended. A few days later, a peace conference convened at Prague.

Britain acted promptly to encourage its Coalition partners. By the Treaty of Reichenbach on June 14, London paid more than a million pounds sterling to Russia and 600,000 to Prussia, who promised not to sign any peace treaty without British consent. This was proof that Britain was playing a game, and that the other monarchies made war only under its management, not completely as paid mercenaries but certainly only slightly more than that.

Informed of this treaty, Metternich was afraid that his efforts had been rendered moot, but he attempted to harden his negotiations. He offered to have Austria declare war on Napoleon, with whom he sought an interview, if the emperor did not accept his proposals.

The decoy armistice was about to exceed all of Napoleon's fears. From the start of negotiations, Caulaincourt, as representative of France, could already smell a trap. The Coalition partners repeatedly hardened their demands, as if they were the victors in a war in which they had in fact been thrashed. In addition to the conditions that Bubna had previously presented, they added the reestablishment of the Hanseatic cities, the dissolution of the Confederation of the Rhine, and the restoration of Prussian territory to its state prior to Jena. They wished to deprive France of all its pledges of security, stripping it naked.

Austria declared a general mobilization of its army on June 14. The Landwehr reservists were recalled.

It was under these circumstances that on June 26 Napoleon granted Metternich's request for an interview. As an opening gambit, Napoleon stated that he was not deceived by the Austrian's tricks. Metternich's demands were contrary to the honor of France. To place him in a quandary, the emperor offered to return Illyria to Austria as the price of its neutrality. Metternich pretended not to understand him. Napoleon finally stated the situation bluntly:

> You wish to humiliate me. You want me to recall my legions with musket stocks reversed [in token of surrender] behind the Rhine, the Alps, and the Pyrenees, placing myself at the mercy of those whom I have just vanquished? Ah, Metternich. How much did England pay you to play this role against me?... If you want war, very well, you shall have it!... And thus the Emperor Francis wishes to dethrone his own daughter?... In marrying an Archduchess, I wished to unite the present and the past, Gothic prejudices with the institutions of the new century. I was mistaken, and today I sense the extent of my error. But it is you who will accept the responsibility for rekindling the war.

Nothing positive emerged from this interview. In his memoirs, Metternich distorted to his advantage both the depth and the form of this conversation so as to make Napoleon solely responsible for its failure.

Metternich continued to posture for the gallery at Prague until Schwarzenberg informed him that he had completed preparations for the Austrian army. Meanwhile, Bernadotte took the final step and concluded an accord with the Coalition at Trachenberg on July 9.

Napoleon agreed to a request to prolong the duration of the truce. No one would be able to say that he had been the first to attack.

By the beginning of August, Caulaincourt and Maret, the minister of exterior relations, were no longer permitted to see Metternich. On August 11, the Coalition unilaterally declared the Congress of Prague to be closed. The next day, the Coalition completed its membership when Austria entered the war. It now included Britain, Russia, Austria, Prussia, and Sweden, in other words, all the great European powers. The hue and cry was raised for France!

Berthier and Caulaincourt, those fervent advocates of the armistice, finally realized their error. Yet one cannot leave their role there.

Considering what happened in ensuing years, their conduct was more than pernicious. If you accept the testimony of the enemy, these men had committed treason. Shuvalov and Kleist, the representatives of Russia and Prussia, respectively, reported that Caulaincourt stunned them by remarking in the course of armistice discussions, "If you are certain that Austria will cooperate with you, you would be wise not to make peace with us." Metternich himself confirmed the breach of faith. At the opening of the Congress of Prague, Caulaincourt remarked to him:

> Ask everything that is proper, and you will obtain it easily. Tell me only that you have sufficient troops to force us to be reasonable. I am as much a European as are you. Help us return to France by peace or war, and 30 million Frenchmen will bless your name.

Caulaincourt at Prague resembled Talleyrand at Erfurt. With such collaborators in whom he had placed his trust, how could Napoleon have convinced the enemy to make peace?

The war resumed.

Dresden: Another Victory Without a Future

The false Congress of Prague afforded the new members of the Coalition time to rebuild their militaries to create a crushing superiority. The 300,000 men of the French army and its allies now faced 600,000 enemy combatants.

Their initial dispositions were in the form of a pincers, reflecting a strategy to encircle the Grand Armeé between Dresden and Leipzig. In the north, Bernadotte commanded a Swedish-Prussian army of 150,000 men. East of the Katzbach, a tributary of the Oder in Silesia, Blücher controlled 100,000 Russo-Prussians. To the south in Bohemia, Schwarzenberg commanded the most important army, composed of 200,000 Austrians and 50,000 Russians. A further 100,000 Russians were en route with Barclay de Tolly. Arguing that Austria had furnished the most important contingent, Metternich had imposed Schwarzenberg as commander-in-chief, or more correctly coordinator-general. To their pincers strategy, the Coalition members added a tactic that was flattering to the military renown of Napoleon: refuse battle wherever he was located, and act offensively only against his lieutenants.

Of course, Napoleon had profited equally from the suspension of arms to increase as much as possible the Grand Armeé effectives and artillery (1,200 cannon). He had paid special attention to the cavalry, increased to 40,000 but unfortunately without experience. At their head stood the best of them, Murat, who had repented and decided to rejoin Napoleon. But he no longer had the dash and enthusiasm of yesteryear. Moreover, Napoleon was aware that Murat had not completely severed his contacts with the Austrians.

At the renewal of hostilities, the French army was in a waiting posture between Leipzig and Dresden, holding off three enemy armies: in the north, Oudinot (70,000 men) opposite Bernadotte; in the east, Ney (100,000) opposite Blücher, including Marmont's, Macdonald's, and Lauriston's corps; to the south, Gouvion Saint-Cyr (100,000), opposite Schwartzenberg. Napoleon remained in the center with the Guard (30,000 men).

Napoleon's strategy was imposed on him by the disposition of forces on the terrain. Once again, he had to compensate for his overall numerical inferiority by a succession of local superiorities, accomplished by lightning concentrations, permitting him to defeat the enemy armies in detail. The disposition of opposing forces helped him in this task. His unsurpassed rapidity of execution and his legendary coup d'oeil would do the rest.

To this general concept of maneuver, Napoleon added a diversion toward Berlin by Davout's corps, advancing from Hamburg in liaison with Oudinot's offensive. This deception story was meant to distract Bernadotte, who constituted the northern arm of the enemy pincer.

To the diplomatic infamy of a false armistice, the Coalition now added military dishonor. On August 12, Blücher violated the ceasefire that had not yet expired. He surprised Ney's units in bivouac on the Katbach, threatening to destroy them. Napoleon marched the Guard with all speed from Goerlitz to the Neisse River. As soon as he became aware of the emperor's presence, however, Blücher withdrew.

The inspiration of this violation of the law of war was none other than Jomini. This former Swiss clerk who had become Ney's chief of staff by his favor and that of Napoleon had recently passed to the enemy side. In so doing, he took a quantity of valuable intelligence concerning the

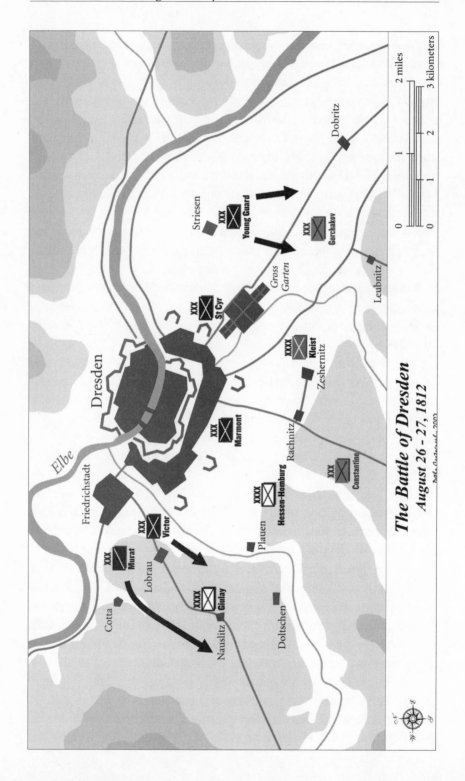

The Battle of Dresden
August 26 - 27, 1812

French army. He succeeded in persuading the Coalition monarchs to initiate hostilities before the expiration of the armistice, so as to surprise the French in the midst of their preparations. The anticipated results were supposed to eclipse the dishonor of the proceeding. These noble monarchs did not hesitate to thus sacrifice their honor and violate their oaths! Later, this criminal would push into military literature, where he obtained more success than on the battlefield, without ever convincing the true specialists in the art of war. Determined in his desire to justify his treason, his account of the Napoleonic Wars failed to conceal his bitterness at not being rewarded for his alleged merits when he was still loyal to Napoleon.

In time, Napoleon was able to detect the trap that had been prepared for him. Blücher's abortive attack was in reality only a lure to distract Napoleon's army eastward while Schwarzenberg was to seize Dresden in his rear, cutting all his communications. The infamous violation of the armistice did not achieve its purpose because of Napoleon's lightning return to Dresden, outrunning Schwarzenberg by covering 140 kilometers in three days.

The Battle of Dresden took place on August 26-27, 1813. The first day, Napoleon contained the general Coalition assault to the west of the city. The next day, he counterattacked the Austrian left in force, overthrowing it. Then he exploited the resulting penetration in a southerly direction, threatening the rear of Schwarzenberg, who rightly ordered a general retreat on Bohemia in mid-afternoon.

Thus Napoleon seized his last great victory. The Coalition left on the field 15,000 killed or wounded, 25,000 prisoners, 40 cannon, and 30 regimental colors. The French army suffered 10,000 killed or wounded.

The fruits of this victory were lost, unfortunately. Given the dispersion of the Coalition partners, the resolute pursuit of the enemy to complete his defeat could only be conducted in a decentralized manner. Left to their own devices, in several days Napoleon's lieutenants squandered the benefits of victory. To the east, Blücher severely thrashed Macdonald on the River Katzbach. In the south, Vandamme missed the opportunity for a great victory over Schwarzenberg at Kulm, and found himself a prisoner instead. To the north, Ney allowed Bernadotte to defeat him at Dennewitz.

A new and more serious period manifested itself. Allied troops began to desert en masse and turn against the French army. On August 23,

10,000 Bavarians and Saxons abandoned the ranks of Oudinot's corps, defeated by Bernadotte at Grossbeeren. This was the first tangible sign of the surge of German nationalism in European affairs, a fatal blow to the Grand Armeé.

The appearance of national sentiment in Germany dated from the uprising in Spain. Elated ideologues were its champions, including Gentz, Schlegel, and Stein, excited by French turncoats at work in European courts. The dominant idea was to oppose the French democratic revolution with a stronger patriotic counter-revolution.

Having been hostile to this movement out of fear that it might turn against them, the German monarchs embraced it once they became aware of the enormous benefits they could draw from nationalism. Napoleon's great power resided in his charismatic image as a liberator of peoples. If one could succeed in substituting an exalted nationalistic sentiment for menacing class consciousness, one could change radically the correlation of forces. What could be easier than to indirectly mobilize support to defend the monarchical classes by those who would otherwise threaten those classes? Deprived of his democratic striking force, Napoleon could not resist the rising patriotic tide. These sorcerer's apprentices risked nothing in the short run. Unpolished and unorganized, in 1813 the popular masses could not suspect this diabolical twist of consciousness. Yet, in 1848, the monarchies belatedly realized that they had played with fire.

After several years of development, German nationalism erupted sharply and helped defeat Napoleon militarily. It was too late for him to regret his failure to arouse the conquered peoples against their oppressive sovereigns.

The first defections began to spread. The German alliances weakened and then reversed themselves in a fatal sequence. On October 8, Bavaria passed to the Coalition camp. This reversal gravely threatened the communications of the Grand Armeé.

The turmoil in Westphalia caused its king, Jerome, to quit the capital, Kassel, on September 30. At Bremen, a popular uprising forced its garrison to surrender to the Cossacks on October 15. Württemberg quit the French alliance on November 2. In short, the rats departed the sinking ship.

As an added burden, on November 8 Murat offered to ally himself with the Coalition, with Rome as the price of his treason.

In these dramatic circumstances, Napoleon had only one concern: to save his army, which was surrounded on all sides and threatened with destruction.

The balance of forces having become too unfavorable, for the first time Napoleon's war aim was no longer the destruction of enemy armies, but the neutralization of them by a skillful blow, permitting him to withdraw behind the Rhine under the best conditions possible. This was the objective he chose after entrenching at Leipzig.

The Ill-fated Battle of Leipzig

From October 16 to 19, 1813, reduced to 180,000 men, the Grand Armeé occupied a defensive position at Leipzig, confronting 360,000 combatants of the Coalition.

Napoleon's mode of operations was unusual. To give the Coalition the impression that he would fight without retreat in an ultimate battle without quarter, Napoleon had concentrated all his forces in the city. He based his dispositions along the river Eister, at whose bridge he planned a surprise disengagement.

Conforming to the frontal tactics that Napoleon had enticed them to follow, the Coalition partners focused all their forces concentrically around the city. Their alignment was as follows: in the south, Schwarzenberg's Austrians; to the east, Bennigsen's Russians; on the northeast, Bernadotte's Swedes; and to the northwest, Blücher's Prussians.

Whether through a mistake in tactics, poor coordination of effort, or simple presumption, no unit blocked the escape route toward Erfurt on the west bank of the Eister.

Without even waiting for the completion of the Coalition's deployments, on the morning of October 16 Schwarzenberg attacked in force. Throughout the day, assaults and counter-assaults succeeded each other in hand-to-hand fighting. The Austrians were contained and even forced back.

The Coalition members learned their lesson from this. Thereafter, they decided to wait for all units to be assembled before renewing the attack. They spent the entire day of October 17 achieving this concentration.

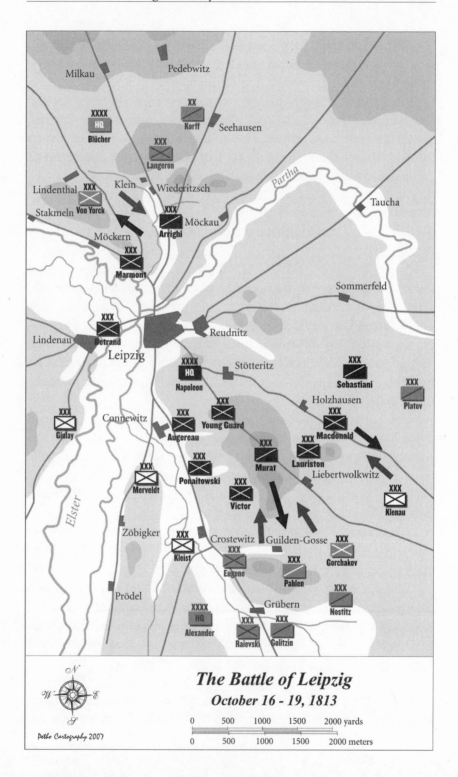

The Battle of Leipzig
October 16 - 19, 1813

Beginning at daybreak on October 18, the Coalition armies launched a general offensive. They failed to penetrate the position. In the afternoon, however, two brigades of Saxons and one brigade of Luxembourgers defected to the Coalition. Napoleon had to intervene in person with the Guard to reestablish the position, but not without difficulty. The fighting climaxed at night. The Coalition troops had not advanced a step, but the considerable casualties they suffered had calmed them sufficiently to allow the planned French disengagement under good conditions.

The retreat began at 2:00 a.m. on October 19, secretly, by the bridge over the Eister. The Coalition members did not perceive anything until daybreak. Then they quickly resumed their general attack. This resulted in the tragically premature destruction of the bridge, caused by the panic of the non-commissioned officer charged with destruction. Fifteen thousand French soldiers had not yet crossed, and found themselves thus trapped in the city. Many of them drowned while attempting to escape across the river. Without this incident, the Grand Armeé would have succeeded in withdrawing completely. It had suffered 15,000 killed and wounded and as many prisoners. The Coalition losses reached 50,000 killed or wounded.

Leaving aside the disappointment concerning the bridge, the Battle of Leipzig was thus a relative success for Napoleon. One hundred twenty thousand Frenchmen had escaped from the grip of an enemy three times as large and in the process had inflicted heavy losses. By ordinary military logic, no one should have escaped.

In the ensuing days, these harassed escapees would repulse 50,000 Austro-Bavarians at the Hanau pass before returning to their home country at the beginning of November.

In that month of November 1813, France was dramatically isolated and withdrawn behind its natural frontiers. Yet Napoleon had just demonstrated that the French army remained potent. In the interior, the political structure began to loosen and even to betray the emperor, who was admittedly much weakened but still determined. He continued to benefit from the total fidelity of the vast majority of Frenchmen. This should have made the Coalition's members reflect and incline them to moderation. An opportunity for peace existed. Once again, Great Britain stifled this opportunity at birth.

Britain Torpedoes the Last Hope of Peace

What were the Coalition's intentions? The sovereigns or their representatives gathered at Frankfurt to reach agreement on a common policy. Opinions were divided. Undoubtedly influenced by the Franco-Austrian family ties, Metternich proposed the least extreme position: the return of France to its 1792 borders, and the abdication of the emperor in favor of his son, i.e., without a Bourbon restoration. Russia and Prussia were equally in favor of an abdication without restoration, but demanded the 1789 borders instead. In Sweden's name, Bernadotte proposed himself as a candidate to succeed Napoleon! Britain again showed itself to be the most intransigent, calling for the 1789 borders plus the restoration of the Bourbons it was sheltering and counted on making into puppet sovereigns.

At first, Metternich's option appeared to be successful. On November 9, he used the Count de Saint-Aignan, a prisoner of war, to send a verbal message to Napoleon. He made this proposal in the presence of the Russian and British representatives, who raised no objection. He also suggested that Caulaincourt should negotiate for the French side.

As soon as he learned of this peace overture of November 1813, Napoleon leaped at the opportunity. He immediately informed the Coalition that he would send Caulaincourt as negotiator at a peace conference and asked his opponents to fix the date and place.

Named minister of exterior relations in Maret's place, Caulaincourt wrote to Metternich on December 1:

> It is with a lively sense of satisfaction that I am charged and authorized by my master the Emperor to declare to your excellency that His Majesty agrees to the basis that Monsieur de Saint-Aignan has communicated. These involve great sacrifices on the part of France, but His Majesty will make them without regret.

Thus, to restore peace, the emperor of the French officially agreed to abandon his crown so that France would retain both its new regime and its natural frontiers, two conditions that could not be more reasonable and legitimate. The miracle of peace almost appeared possible. Regrettably, once again it was nothing but a mirage.

The cabinet in London disavowed its representative to Frankfurt. The cabal of French émigrés at the court of Saint Petersburg, filled with hatred, persuaded the tsar to reverse his position. The British point of view carried the day. At its insistence, the Coalition partners renounced further negotiations and once again chose war. Yet, they felt forced to justify their warmongering in the eyes of public opinion. They therefore had recourse to a foul imposture to make Napoleon shoulder the responsibility. On December 1, they had not yet received Napoleon's official agreement to abdicate. To give the illusion of a negative response on his part, they backdated their December 4 declaration of war to December 1. Metternich's Machiavellianism joined with the perfidy of the British cabinet to create a minor masterpiece of ignominy.

To compound their perversity, the official decision of the Coalition on December 4 was printed in 20,000 copies of a propaganda tract and distributed across France. It read in part:

> The allied powers are not making war on France but rather on that preponderant influence that, to the detriment of both the Empire and of France, the Emperor Napoleon has too long exercised outside the limits of his empire. The sovereigns wish France to be great, strong, and happy. The powers confirm to the Empire a territorial extent that it had never known under its kings.

Knowingly confusing the effect with the cause, this insidious monument of disinformation attempted to separate the French from their emperor. The "preponderant influence" of which it accused him was due only to the fury with which the Coalition had attacked him as the incarnation of the new France. The people were not deceived by this mystification.

This fallacious concept of differentiating between a bad Napoleon and an estimable France would be revived later in the inept image of a genial Bonaparte and an odious Napoleon. Anyone who does not recognize the functional unity and continuity between Bonaparte and Napoleon has no understanding of his personality.

The attitude of the emperor of Austria antagonized even his daughter Maria-Louisa, who so informed him in an unambiguous letter:

You cannot know how painful is the thought that you could be involved in a war with the Emperor, your relation, when you both have such characters that you should be friends. May God soon grant us peace! The Emperor desires it, as do all of his people. Yet, one cannot make peace without negotiating, and up until now it appears that your side has not been willing to do so. I am sure that the English are responsible for this.

Once again, the Coalition members had erred in their presumption. They would quickly learn by painful experience the confidence that Napoleon still enjoyed from the people if not, unfortunately, from the supposed "elites."

The Campaign of France, or Fireworks Drowned in Treason

"We must pull ourselves up by our bootstraps and by
the resolution [levée en masse] of 1793."

Shamelessly violating Swiss neutrality, the Coalition armies invaded France in the first days of 1814. On January 3, they entered Montbéliard. The following day, they were at Nancy. On the 15th, Schwarzenberg occupied Langres. Four days later, Dijon fell. Almost everywhere, the invaders indulged in atrocities. Patriotic peasants attempted to oppose them by organizing guerrilla operations despite limited means and no support from the notables. They did not hesitate to fight with their scythes and pitchforks. With organization and leadership, this movement had significant operational possibilities.

Once again, Napoleon was expected to choose between capitulating unconditionally, contrary to his oath as emperor, and war. And, once again, he would show himself worthy of his reputation as a great captain.

When Napoleon left Paris for his armies on January 25, 1814, the situation of France appeared desperate. The Coalition surrounded it on four sides with more than 400,000 combatants. To the south, Wellington's British army prepared to cross the Pyrenees. To the north, Bernadotte, at the head of 150,000 Russo-Prussians, was on the frontier. He delegated his command to generals Bulow and Wintzingerode, not

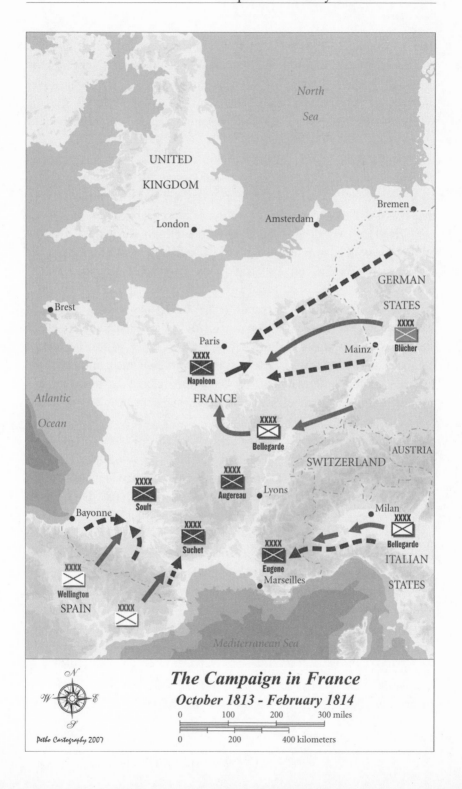

The Campaign in France

October 1813 - February 1814

0   100   200   300 miles

0   200   400 kilometers

Petho Cartography 2007

daring to fight in person the French army inside France itself. Was this a belated scruple, or fear of being executed by his fellow citizens? To the northeast, Blücher's Army of Silesia with 80,000 Russo-Prussians had crossed the Meuse and was advancing toward the Marne. To the southeast, Schwarzenberg's Army of Bohemia occupied the plateau of Langres with 185,000 Austro-Prussians.

Napoleon could only muster 110,000 first-line soldiers supported by several courageous units of the National Guard. Moreover, many were very young, with some barely 16 years old. They had been burdened with the nickname "Marie-Louise" because their enrollment had been authorized under a decree signed by the empress, and would earn the admiration of the "greybeards" of the Guard, even through they did not have peach fuzz as yet. The tsar himself rendered homage to their bravery.

Yet Napoleon could not count on the 20,000 men of the opportunist Augereau in Lyon nor on Eugene's Army of Italy, which had more effect staying where it was than moving to France. Once again, he had to compensate for a crushing numerical inferiority by a maelstrom of rapid marches and countermarches, by dazzling maneuvers and counter-maneuvers, allowing no respite to the enemy and appearing where he was not expected.

By January 26, Napoleon had overwhelmed a Russian division of Blücher's at Saint Didier. On February 1, a clash occurred at La Rothiere that proved costly because he lacked his usual numerical superiority. On February 10 at Champaubert he annihilated a complete Russian corps of Blücher's; peasants pursued the fugitives.

Rushing to Montmirail, Napoleon defeated another Russian corps on February 11. Decidedly, the Russians were not celebrating. The next day, he chased a Prussian corps from Chateau-Thierry. Here again, numerous peasants participated in the fight, armed with old muskets or simple pitchforks.

On February 14, a new and shining victory occurred at Vauchamps. Overpowered by the "French furor" that had allowed him no rest for 15 days, Blücher suffered very heavy losses: 6,000 killed or wounded and 8,000 prisoners. After four defeats in five days, the Army of Silesia was practically out of action. Now it was the turn of the Army of Bohemia!

This army was advancing southward in the direction of Moret. Its northern flank guard was surprised at Mormant on February 17. The cost was 6,000 prisoners including several generals, 15 cannon, and 50 caissons. Again the Russians had failed. The next day, an Austrian corps suffered defeat at Montereau, losing 6,000 men including another general, 15 guns, and six colors. Troyes was liberated on February 24 amidst an indescribable popular celebration.

Crippled by this avalanche of reverses, the Coalition members fell back everywhere. Their will wavered, their cohesion began to fail. Had the moment for negotiations returned?

Napoleon remained open to that as always. On February 26, he received Prince Wenceslas de Lichtenstein, sent to request a suspension of hostilities. Napoleon agreed in principle but did not wish to repeat the trickery of Pleiswitz in the previous year. He sent General Flahaut to ask for details of Schwarzenberg and to confirm that he wished to open negotiations on the basis of the Frankfurt conditions. Operations would not cease before the start of negotiations. Matters unfortunately remained there.

Meanwhile, pseudo-peace talks occurred at Chatillon, conducted on the French side by Caulaincourt, who had received full powers to negotiate on the reasonable basis of Frankfurt. Usually optimistic, Caulaincourt quickly sang a different tune. He sent Napoleon the following informative bulletin:

> What I know with certainty is that I am dealing here with men who are not at all sincere. To make concessions only encourages them to make more demands, without being able to foresee where they will stop and without obtaining any result.

This from the ardent partisan of negotiations, who finally understood!

Sensing that his Coalition partners were vacillating, the hyper-Francophone British minister Lord Robert Castlereagh hurried from London, pockets bulging with gold. A conference occurred at Chaumont, where on March 1 a treaty was signed that renewed and extended the alliance for 20 years. Austria, Russia, and Prussia each promised to furnish 150,000 men to the Coalition. They contracted to accept only the frontiers of 1789 and not those of 1792. As the price of their cooperation, the three powers shared a treasure of 150 million francs.

The stiffening of the Coalition despite its military defeats was undoubtedly due to the French traitors who continued to provide assurance and would soon manifest themselves.

The war thus inexorably resumed.

Contrasting with the prudence of Schwarzenberg, who hesitated to give up his secure positions on the plateau of Langres, the seething Blücher, who had lived only to avenge Jena, resumed the offensive toward Paris via the valley of the Aisne, with the support of the Army of the North.

Napoleon therefore conceived a strategic maneuver of great scope, consisting of defeating Blücher in the region of Soissons, rallying the garrisons of the north, pressing toward those of the east, and then attacking the area of the Army of Bohemia in liaison with an organized peasant guerrilla force. He also hoped that Augereau, reinforced by Eugene, could form the other branch of the pincers near Lyon.

Failures of execution by some demoralized generals and the disobedience of Augereau and of Eugene would compromise the execution of this plan. The capitulation of Paris by treaty would ruin it.

On March 3, the surrender of Soissons without resistance saved Blücher, who linked up with the Army of the North. After this reinforcement, the battles of Craonne on March 6 and Laon the next day were costly and indecisive.

In liberating Reims on March 13, Napoleon drove a wedge between the Army of Silesia and that of Bohemia. This latter force had renewed the offensive and threatened the southern wing of the French dispositions. Napoleon had to deviate from his path to reestablish the situation. Schwarzenberg withdrew precipitately to the Aube and reassembled all of his forces. He then attacked violently at Arcis-sur-Aube on March 20, where he was with difficulty contained.

Still following his progression into the enemy rear, Napoleon reached Saint-Didier on March 23 and gained a final victory over the Russians. This proved to be the farthest point of his offensive. The collapse of his own rear then destroyed his spirit.

A capital event had taken place. Talleyrand and the royalists had called upon the Coalition to seize Paris, guaranteeing its capitulation without resistance. It was true that, on January 1, the future Louis XVIII had sent his "subjects" an infamous proclamation: "Receive the allied generals as friends, open the gates of your cities to them, avoid the blows that a criminal and pointless resistance would cost you, and welcome their entry into France with cries of joy."

On March 25 at Fere-Champenoise, the Coalition inflicted a serious reverse on the troops assigned to defend Paris. Caught off balance, Napoleon was constrained to carry aid to the capital at top speed. Yet, he arrived too late. On March 30, near Juvisy, he learned that Marmont had signed a capitulation for the entire garrison of Paris, which was authorized to leave the capital. The inconsequential Joseph, who had been named lieutenant general of the empire for precisely the mission "not to abandon Paris without a fight," had agreed with Marmont.

The Coalition forces made their entrance into Paris on March 31, 1814, to the applause of the wealthy quarters. The noblewomen exceeded decency so far as to mount on the croppers of the horses of Cossack officers. Talleyrand accommodated the tsar in his own hotel and became head of a provisional government to prepare the restoration.

Having withdrawn to Fontainebleau, Napoleon had not yet had his final say. He still controlled 70,000 soldiers who demonstrated a touching fidelity to him, crying "To Paris, to Paris!" He had already formed a concept of operations to reconquer the capital in coordination with an uprising of the Parisian population, and he had previously recovered from equally critical situations.

However, his marshals—tired, demoralized, opportunistic, and sedentary—failed him on April 4. At least they attempted to save the regime by negotiating an abdication in favor of his son, the king of Rome. The treason of Marmont, who deserted to the enemy with his corps on April 4, dealt the final blow to the Empire and restored the monarchy. Napoleon was exiled to the island of Elba.

The Surrealistic Interlude on Elba

What a strange episode was Napoleon's exile to the island of Elba! Intended to be definitive, his banishment would last only 11 months. His return was inevitable.

First, the monarchical restoration suffered from a double illegitimacy. In the first place, the Bourbons had returned to power in the baggage train of an enemy occupier, which was unpardonable in that era of patriotic sentiment. Second, Napoleon's overthrow by the Imperial Senate constituted a flagrant violation of the Constitution, which did not permit such an action. This was also a denial of democracy. Raised to the imperial mandate by a vote of the people, Napoleon could only be legitimately removed by the people. Moreover, the Bourbons, who had learned nothing in exile, and the Coalition, which remained full of hatred, would furnish Napoleon with all the justification he needed to retake his usurped crown.

Having drawn no lessons from their past mistakes, the Bourbons never missed an opportunity to increase their unpopularity from the moment they were installed in power. In "granting" his charter, Louis XVIII began his reign well. He sensibly limited his absolute royal power. He conserved the great institutions of the Consulate and the Empire, except for the Concordat, which he repudiated under pressure from a vindictive clergy.

Louis XVIII lent himself to a pitiless purge. He seized on any occasion to humiliate the numerous followers of the emperor, designated by the supposedly pejorative label as "Bonapartists." The only minister of war he could find was General Pierre Dupont, the despicable capitulator of Bailen, who purged the army implacably. His successor, the opportunistic Soult, reserved appointments as generals solely for émigrés who had fought against the French army. He launched a national subscription drive for the construction of a monument to the glory of the Chouans and of the "martyrs of Quiberon." He imprisoned General Exelmans for the sole charge of having written to the King of Naples. To better control the numerous "half- pay Bonapartist officers," he wished to require them to live in the towns where they had been born.

Yet he could not dominate the French spirit of the veterans. If someone forced them to cry "Long live the king," they would immediately add, under their breath, "of Rome."

The usurper king formed his military retinue exclusively from officers who had fought against the armies of the Republic. He had masses celebrated for the souls of the terrorist Cadoudal and the traitor Pichegru. He honored the memory of General Moreau, the conspirator who defected to the enemy and was killed by a French cannon ball. He approved returning to the émigrés any national properties that had not yet been sold, offending all the Republicans.

Louis XVIII did not even honor his commitments under the Treaty of Fontainebleau. He withheld the stipends due to the exiled, seeking in a shabby, cheap manner to reduce them to poverty.

The sinister Count d'Artois was determined to "de-Bonapartize" the country, thereby only increasing the nostalgia for the Empire.

Public opinion soured at the anti-Napoleonic hatred of the government press. This press poured out infamous calumnies about Napoleon, accusing him of the worst sins and caricaturing him in the most grotesque manner.

Discontent increased in the country. A conspiracy developed within the army, to the point where the cautious Fouché feared a military coup d'etat.

Napoleon attentively followed the evolving situation in France. An abundant correspondence came to him from all parts of the country, confirming for him the growing unpopularity of the Bourbons. A number of his loyal followers, in particular Fleury and Chaboulon, traveled to Elba to exhort him to retake power.

Napoleon learned that, at the Congress of Vienna, the infamous Talleyrand sold out the security and the vital interests of France, being grossly compensated for his ignoble service.

It was too much! What finally convinced Napoleon to return to power were the plots to assassinate him, plots reported to him by well-placed informants. Conscious of the political danger of Napoleon's continuing popularity, the Bourbon usurpers were no longer content with merely neutralizing the emperor. Instead, they became obsessed with his assassination.

As French consul in Livorno, Talleyrand had installed a poor specimen named Mariotti in charge of an espionage network and execution of black operations. In September 1814, Mariotti proposed a scheme to kidnap Napoleon on one of the occasions he visited the island of Pianosa. Warned by Napoleon's efficient intelligence service, this affair went nowhere.

Mariotti benefited from the zealous assistance of the Chevalier de Bruslart, named governor of Corsica, to muzzle the island dwellers. He recruited Corsican killers for an assassination of Napoleon. One of these was arrested on Elba and claimed to be in Bruslart's pay for this purpose.

Even those who did not want to kill Napoleon considered deporting him farther away from Europe. The first proposal, broached before the

Congress of Vienna opened, was to move him to the Azores. Shortly thereafter, the possibility of Saint Helena arose. At Talleyrand's instigation, a secret session of the Congress on February 10, 1815, decided to move him there. This removed Napoleon's last scruple about returning to France in response to the urgent calls of the people, who were frustrated by the uprooted sovereignty of 1789.

The Hundred Days: Republican Awakening of the Nation

"The Hundred Days" describes the doleful page of the history of France extending from March 1, 1815—the date when Napoleon landed at Golfe Juan—until Waterloo on the following June 18.

Under the peaceful pressure of the French people, the illegitimate regime of Louis XVIII collapsed in 20 days, the time of the triumphant return of Napoleon to the capital. We then witnessed a new and indefensible intervention into the internal affairs of France by foreigners. Remember that the Bourbons and their confederates, the reactionary monarchies of Europe, joined together for the seventh time in a hate-filled anti-French crusade. They were about to throw all of their forces against France. Submerged and betrayed, the French army would succumb to superior numbers at Waterloo, the tragic end of the Empire.

A Popular Uprising Overthrows the Bourbons

The news of Napoleon's return, despite the vigilance of his jailers, struck like a thunderbolt, setting off a storm of enthusiasm in the country. His proclamation to the nation fulfilled its hopes. "Frenchmen, in my exile I have heard your desires and your discontent. You have reclaimed a government of your choosing, the only legitimate one," he said. "I have come among you to reclaim both your rights and mine."

Napoleon's address to the army electrified it:

> Your general, called to the throne by the people's choice and extolled by them, has returned to you. Rally under your chief's banner. His existence is identical with yours. His rights are nothing but those of the people and of you. His interest, his honor, and his

glory are the same as your interest, your honor, and your glory. The
faster you advance, the more quickly victory will come! The eagle,
with the national colors, will fly from steeple to steeple up to the
towers of Notre Dame! You will be the liberators of the country!

This appeal gave goose bumps to all of France. Never had the citizens
been so emotionally associated with their country. No other leader had so
passionately incarnated his people and his army.

Thus, after a laborious start resulting from surprise, Napoleon's
march to Paris with his tiny escort was triumphant. All along the route,
one regiment after another rallied to him amid general enthusiasm. The
inconsequential Marshal Ney, who had promised Louis XVIII to bring
"the usurper" to the king in a cage, gave way to the general euphoria and
betrayed this promise. Crowds of peasants accompanied the cortege,
demanding to enlist. All attempts by the Bourbons to halt this torrential
movement failed miserably.

The Parisians never lost their gallic humor. Scrawled on a piece of
paper on a column in the Place Vendome was the following message:
"Napoleon to Louis XVIII: My dear brother—don't bother to send any
more soldiers to me. I have enough."

Thus, on March 20, 1815, Napoleon was replaced on his throne in
every sense of the word; upon his arrival at the Tuileries, a delirious
crowd carried him between them until he reached his office. Louis XVIII
had just absconded, leaving his slippers behind, and was fleeing abroad
by the fateful route of Varennes.

Napoleon had not needed to fight—not a single shot had been fired,
not a drop of blood shed. In some ways, it was the emperor's greatest
victory. Yet nothing was finished, and the hardest part remained.

The first measures of the emperor's new government were clearly in
the nature of appeasement. At home, Napoleon was careful not to imitate
the Bourbons. He did not indulge in any vindictiveness against those who
had failed him in 1814; he limited the purge to a list of 13 obvious traitors
who had fled with Louis XVIII; and he left in place numerous prefects
and sub-prefects compromised with the previous regime. In the political
realm, he cut the ground out from under those who accused him of
despotism by issuing an "Additional Act to the Constitution of the
Empire," a document he hatched with Benjamin Constant. Who would
have believed such a collaboration? Constant was, along with the

hysterical Madame de Stael, a virulent opponent of Napoleon, having described him as "a man soaked in blood and more odious than Attila," less than two days before his return to the Tuileries. He fled but returned to Paris, proof that he did not really believe what he said. He had dared to throw himself into Attila's mouth!

Submitted to a vote, the Additional Act was approved by only 1,532,000 voters out of an electorate of more than five million. This reluctance indicated that "liberalization" of the regime was not a priority issue in national public opinion. It was in fact nothing more than an illusory political concession intended to rally an intellectual coterie to the regime and to the endangered country. In comparison to the true dictatorship of all the absolute monarchies of Europe, this imperial regime, although of necessity powerful, was not at all tyrannical. Primarily worried about social justice and material improvement, the people had never complained of a lack of liberty. Then why did they continue to give their unshakable loyalty to the emperor? In truth, it was only the intelligentsia that, in a recurring phenomenon, confused liberty with license.

In foreign affairs, the domain more relevant to our subject, Napoleon's first concern was to reassure the European monarchies. He attempted to disarm their hysterical hostility by informing them that he accepted the Treaty of Paris, thereby indicating that he renounced any claim to reconquer the frontiers of 1792 and instead engaged to respect those of 1789.

How could one better indicate a willingness for peace? All that the emperor asked of the Coalition was to leave France free to choose its own political regime, in complete democratic legitimacy. Was not that the simplest of things?

The Coalition members could not contest the fact that the overwhelming majority of the French people no longer wanted anything to do with the Bourbons. They had chosen Napoleon and the Empire by what amounted to a plebiscite, the triumphal welcome they had given him upon his return from Elba. Considering that Napoleon had solemnly pledged not to threaten his neighbors, no one could oppose him without violating the international laws regulating nation-states.

Napoleon proved his sincerity by immediately disavowing the foolish action of Murat, the King of Naples, who had declared war on

Austria on March 25. He categorically rejected the offers of service of this mythic cavalier who was aging so poorly.

In a personal letter, Napoleon attempted to convince the sovereigns of Europe that the Ancien Régime no longer suited the French nation:

> The Bourbons no longer wished to associate themselves with French beliefs or manners. France had to separate itself from them. Its voice called for a liberator. . . . Enough glory has already decorated the flags of various nations. Great successes have usually been followed by great reverses. A better arena is open today to sovereigns, and I am the first to enter it.

The only response to this peace offering was the formation of the Seventh Coalition between Britain, Russia, Prussia, and Austria, in preparation for a massive military invasion of France.

Nonetheless, the illegitimacy of this new war imposed on France agitated the British opposition party. Their spokesman in the Commons declared with a clairvoyance, an honesty, and a courage that honored him: "Bonaparte was received in France as a liberator. The Bourbons lost their throne through their own mistakes. It would be a monstrous act to make war on a nation to impose on it the government it did not want." Faithful to its noble tradition of independence, the British press did not remain idle. The *Morning Chronicle* lectured Lord Castlereagh, the foreign secretary, "English patriots think that the powers of the continent are unified not so much against Bonaparte as against the spirit of liberty."

These two citations close the loop with Part One of this study. They confirm, in the words of enemy nationals, the true reasons for this war to the knife against France.

The favorable disposition of opinion across the Channel encouraged Napoleon to attempt a final effort for peace with the British cabinet, whom he informed he was prepared to discuss any peace proposal, regardless of what it might be. He received no response. The emperor multiplied his gestures of good will and appeasement to the Coalition members, but they did not condescend even to answer his overtures out of courtesy.

The Prussian Secretary of the Congress of Vienna, Frederick von Gentz, openly avowed the reactionary ideology of the Coalition: "the wishes of the French people, even if they were formally expressed, would have no effect and no weight." There could be no cruder statement of contempt for the popular will.

Nonetheless, the Coalition members were conscious of the illegitimacy of their position and attempted to remedy it by giving the illusion of legitimacy. They had Louis XVIII address them with an official request for armed intervention. Louis was more than willing to do so, even though it was a prevarication. Still, by what right could Louis XVIII claim to speak in the name of France?

This time, the mask fell definitively. Up until 1814, the European monarchies had attempted to justify their hostility toward France by the fiction of French territorial expansionism. In 1815, this false pretext was shattered. France had withdrawn into its shell, and through the voice of its emperor had solemnly declared its desire to live in peace with its neighbors. The choice of its political regime was solely its own. Thus, the crusade being prepared for a new Bourbon restoration constituted a monstrous interference in the domestic affairs of France, according to the very description of the British parliamentary opposition. France was the victim of a triple assault, on its liberty, its sovereignty, and its independence. It was denied the right of self-determination. Who can still claim that Napoleon did not want peace in 1815?

The final war imposed on Napoleon was without doubt the most illegitimate of all. Without the incredible accumulation of misadventures affecting his operations and the unpardonable failures of execution, Napoleon would have conquered.

The Scramble

In the spring of 1815, a steamroller of 700,000 troops prepared to attack the frontiers of France on three invasion routes: the Alps (Austrians), the Rhine (Austro-Russians), and the North (British-Dutch-Prussians).

The first two theaters of operations would play a diversionary role. In the north—Belgium—everything was at risk. In this area, the Coalition members were in the process of assembling two groups of forces: (1) Wellington's army, composed of 100,000 men of whom the British provided a third, with the Dutch and Germans making up the rest. Supported by 200 cannon, it was located in the region of Brussels. (2)

Blücher's army of 130,000 Prussian soldiers and 300 guns, assembling in the region of Namur. The two armies were to regroup on the Belgian frontier at the start of July and then launch a common offensive toward Paris.

Opposite this gigantic mobilization of the Coalition, Napoleon disposed in total of only 300,000 soldiers to defend all the frontiers. He divided them as follows: (1) a principal body, known as the Army of the North, of 120,000 soldiers and 360 cannon. He assumed personal command of this group to confront the principal threat. (2) Four autonomous armies covered the other frontiers: Rapp on the Rhine, Suchet in the Alps, Brune on the Var, and Clausel in the southwest. (3) The Lamarque group was in the Vendée, where the royalists intended to re-launch the Chouannerie.

As an incomparable Minister of War, Davout had achieved a tour de force in mobilizing these forces in record time. Composed of numerous veterans and of the best units, the Army of the North was animated by excellent morale and continued to accord to the "little corporal" a moving loyalty. Yet, his choice of Soult as chief of staff was certainly not the best.

The Army of the North included five army corps, a cavalry reserve, and the Imperial Guard. Drouet d'Erlon commanded the 1st Corps, Reille the 2nd, Vandamme the 3rd, Gérard the 4th, Mouton, Count of Lobau, the 5th, and Grouchy the Cavalry Reserve. Ney supervised the 1st and 2nd Corps. The Guard was temporarily deprived of its chief, Mortier, who had fallen ill.

Why a change in the hitherto successful strategy? Following his tried and tested methodology, Napoleon would once again use speed to catch the Coalition members while they were assembling. Relying on surprise, he would insert himself like a wedge between Blücher and Wellington and attempt to defeat each one separately while holding his own forces concentrated, thereby benefiting from a local superiority.

Yet Napoleon never neglected the effect of a diversion that might disturb the enemy's dispositions and disperse his forces. In this case, a simulated attack north of Lille would cause Wellington to believe that he might be cut off from the coast, thereby delaying his support to Blücher.

After a promising start to the campaign, the god of war would abandon the emperor.

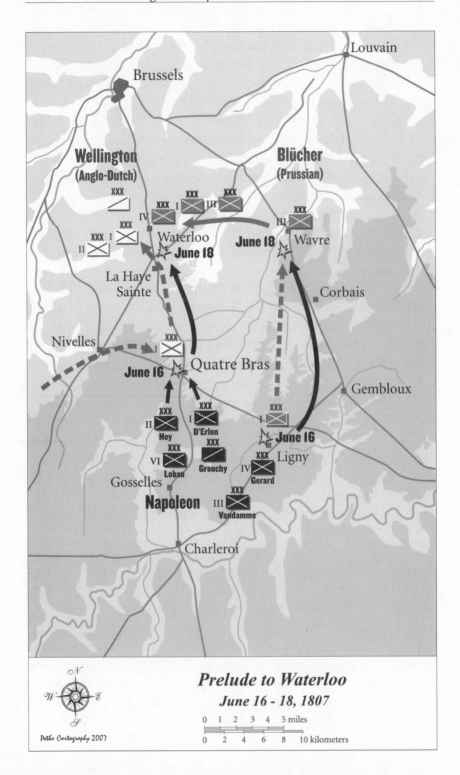

Louvain

Brussels

Wellington
(Anglo-Dutch)

Blücher
(Prussian)

Waterloo
June 18

June 18   Wavre

La Haye
Sainte

Corbais

Nivelles

Quatre Bras

June 16   Gembloux

II   Ney   I   D'Erlon   I

June 16

VI   Lobau   Grouchy   Ligny

Gosselles   IV   Gerard

Napoleon   III   Vandamme

Charleroi

Prelude to Waterloo
June 16 - 18, 1807

0 1 2 3 4 5 miles

0   2   4   6   8   10 kilometers

Petho Cartography 2007

The Victory of Ligny: A Vanished Triumph

Once again, Napoleon succeeded in surprising and destabilizing his enemy. He moved his forces to the frontier without the knowledge of the enemy, and at dawn on June 15 he seized Charleroi.

Having no inkling of this, Wellington and Blücher were shocked. The former even panicked slightly. Instead of moving toward Blücher as agreed, he took steps to move closer to the embarkation ports, a truly British reflex. The deception had produced its fruits.

The Prussian commander was less affected by the appearance of the French due to a base treason. General Count Louis de Bourmont, commander of a French division and an ex-émigré who had been generously pardoned, deserted to the enemy and revealed the entire campaign plan to Blücher, who could not conceal his contempt for the deserter. Aided by this information, Blücher assembled all his forces around Ligny, where he decided to give battle.

Napoleon's scheme of maneuver was as simple as usual: attack and fix Blücher at Ligny with Grouchy's force; take him in reverse, moving Ney's group from Quatre Bras; and exploit the results with the main reserve under the direct orders of the emperor. But things did not go according to plan on June 16.

In front of Ligny, a frontal attack commenced in mid-afternoon. Combat raged for more than three hours as counter-assaults followed assaults and Ligny was taken and retaken. Napoleon waited impatiently for Ney's attack to force the decision. Having seen no one appear by 7:00 p.m., he launched his entire reserve into the battle. The Prussian line cracked about 9:00 p.m. Fallen from his horse, Blücher was missing in action for several hours, but finally escaped from some French cuirassiers and rejoined his headquarters. The Prussians fled during the night, saved from a debacle by a thunderstorm that hindered pursuit. Ney's failure to intervene on his right flank and rear enabled Blücher to avoid total disaster.

Since June 15, the manic-depressive Ney had demonstrated that he was not at his best. The "bravest of the brave," who had been chosen for his impetuosity, exhibited an unaccustomed sluggishness and faint-heartedness. When he attacked Quatre-Bras a half-day behind schedule, the crossroads were already occupied, thanks to the fortunate initiative of one of Wellington's subordinates. Ney took advantage of his momentary superiority to seize the crossroads in preparation for executing his flanking maneuver against Blücher the next day. Yet, because of imprecise or misunderstood orders, Drouet d'Erlon did not rejoin Ney there and for a moment confusion spread in the French ranks.

On June 16, Ney waited in front of Quatre Bras until midday before launching the assault. Yet, by this time some 30,000 Anglo-Dutch held the strategic crossroads. Wellington had finally begun to move to Blücher's aid. At nightfall, the crossroads remained in Wellington's hands, preventing Ney from intervening at Ligny. As for Drout d'Erlon, he wobbled all day between Ney and Napoleon without taking part in the fighting at Ligny or at Quatre Bras. After the incomplete victory of Ligny, everything had to be done over.

Waterloo: The Unthinkable Disaster

Napoleon devoted the morning of June 17 to resting his army, physically harassed, and to preparing for the next blow.

Controlling 34,000 men and 108 cannon, or one-third of the French forces, Grouchy could, after regaining the contact with Blücher that he had unfortunately lost, do one of two things: (1) neutralize Blücher if he attempted to join with Wellington. To do this, Grouchy would have had to maneuver between the two enemy forces; or (2) add his support to Napoleon in the engagement with Wellington.

In the early afternoon of June 17, the emperor found Ney in front of Quatre Bras. Not yet completely over his strange lethargy, the Prince of the Moskva was not even aware that Wellington had begun to retreat toward Brussels. Napoleon firmly ordered Ney to pursue him aggressively.

Retrieving his customary energy, Ney advanced with great dash. Later, he was on the point of destroying Wellington's rear guard when the most inopportune of thunderstorms halted him abruptly. The roads became quagmires, the infantrymen floundered, and horses, guns, and caissons were immobilized. Just as for Blücher on the previous day, a providential rain saved Wellington from a tight spot. The rear guard was able to rejoin the main body.

Despite all this, the French army came into sight of the plateau of Waterloo, Wellington's chosen location to offer battle. Tomorrow the gods would decide the destiny of France.

Without a notable advantage in height, the site of Mont Saint-Jean, where Wellington had installed his forces, possessed military value only because of the clever tactics Wellington used there. Most of his troops were deployed beyond the military crest of the ridge. Masked in this way, the Anglo-Dutch units escaped the supposedly devastating fire of the French artillery. In addition, fields filled with grain crops, which grew high at that time of year, concealed the infantrymen until the last moment.

The British artillery was disseminated among the infantry units, in direct support and practically in the front lines. Slightly forward of the crest, the chateau of Houguemont and the farms of La Haie Sainte and Papelotte had been organized into British strong points. These three fortified outposts were intended to take the attacking French forces in reverse. Finally, the general cavalry reserve was massed behind the front line, in the center of the deployment.

Wellington deployed 70,000 combatants on Mont Saint-Jean. Prudently, he had placed 20,000 troops at Hale, 13 kilometers to the rear, to protect his line of retreat toward the coast.

Napoleon would oppose him with a roughly equivalent force, but in a manner that left him vulnerable to attack. His objective remained the destruction of Wellington's army; he sought to demonstrate that, even though he might not be sufficiently strong to defeat all of the Coalition members, they were equally unable to defeat him on the battlefield. This was Napoleon's only means of forcing them to sit down and negotiate a peace.

Napoleon therefore adopted a frontal tactic instead of a flanking maneuver to envelop Wellington to the west, as the latter might have incited Wellington to avoid battle while increasing Napoleon's own vulnerability by moving him farther away from Grouchy.

Napoleon's plan consisted of breaking the enemy line in its center, casting all his reserves into the resulting breech, and then turning to each flank to defeat the two forces in detail. To weaken the center in advance, he intended a classic diversionary attack on the British right. Lastly, to ensure numerical superiority at the crucial moment, he ordered Grouchy to march to the battlefield.

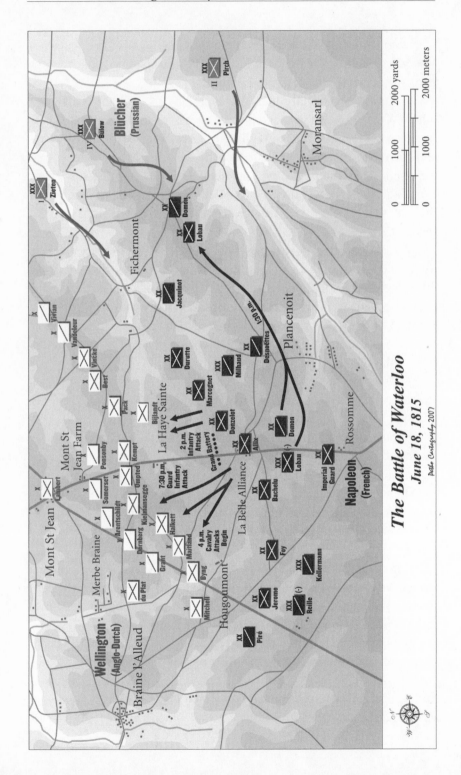

The Battle of Waterloo
June 18, 1815

Pale Cartography 2007

Yet, on that fatal day of June 18, 1815, nothing took place as planned.

Having started at 9:00 a.m., the attack was further delayed by the rain, which had continued all night and soaked the ground, thereby preventing the marshaling of forces, especially the artillery. As we shall see, this delay would prove fatal.

The diversionary operation did not begin until 11:30 a.m., when it was led briskly by Jerome Bonaparte's division, which almost succeeded in capturing the chateau of Houguement. Yet, an hour later, when the principal operation was about to begin, an event occurred that would upset everything. The leading elements of a force came into view about ten kilometers to the French right, on the Saint Lambert side. These troops were not the long-awaited Frenchmen of Grouchy, but rather Blücher's advanced guard commanded by von Bulow.

Grouchy never reached the battlefield. The orders sent to him by Soult, who was far from equal to the irreplaceable Berthier, were imprecise. The first messenger sent to Grouchy became lost. Later messages did not reach him in time. He himself demonstrated a complete lack of combativeness by failing to march to the sound of the guns at the crucial moment, as his subordinates exhorted him to do.

The result was inevitable. Forced to fight on two fronts, Napoleon's chances for success were effectively reduced to zero. Yet, he had no choice but to follow his plan, hoping always for Grouchy's arrival, however late.

The main breakthrough attack began at 1:30 p.m., after an intense preparation by 80 guns. The four divisions of Drout d'Erlon's corps engaged the farm of La Haie Sainte and the sunken road.

The first defensive line was about to be overrun when the French infantry, poorly deployed in column, sustained a fantastic counter-attack by heavy cavalry that sent it back in disorder as far as the artillery positions and threatened the emperor's headquarters. Replying tit for tat, a French cavalry counter-attack was equally furious, and reestablished the French position while destroying all that came before it.

Yet d'Erlon's planned penetration had failed. Everything had to be done over with time running out.

Napoleon ordered Ney to prepare a new attack for 4:00 p.m., even though he was already forced to fight on the east against Blücher, whose units flowed toward the battlefield. They attacked Plancenoit in force, menacing the French rear. Napoleon was forced to employ a large portion of the reserve he had intended for the exploitation of Ney's attack.

Ney now committed his second fatal error in three days. Violating all the rules of tactics, he began an assault without waiting for the artillery bombardment intended to soften up the defenders. Taking a short cut, he personally led a fantastic cavalry charge that covered him in useless glory. He dragged along with him part of the Guard that should have remained in the reserve.

The effectiveness of Wellington's tactics now began to show. He placed cannon just in front of the infantry formed in squares on the reverse slope of the ridge. The crews fired grapeshot at close range and then hurried to shelter inside the infantry squares. They returned to their guns as soon as the first French wave withdrew. Prone in the high grain, the infantrymen of the squares remained hidden until the last moment. Then, on a signal, they rose up, formed into ranks, and fired volleys. The cavaliers who survived the musketry literally impaled themselves on the first, kneeling rank, whose bayonets slanted forward with their musket butts planted on the ground. Out of instinct, the horses refused the obstacle and turned in disorder to pass around the square.

The French losses were horrible. To some extent, Ney found himself in the role of Murad Bey at the Battle of the Pyramids. With an admirable panache and unparalleled bravery, he led the units in the assault over and over again, escaping by a miracle the death he seemed to be seeking. Men lost count of the number of horses killed under him. He earned the admiration even of the British.

Around 8:00 p.m., Ney's repeated assaults finally succeeded in shaking Wellington's line, and the British left was in great difficulty after the counterattack at Plancenoit. But Blücher accelerated the movement of his units toward the British.

It was at this moment that the hours lost that morning would catch up to Napoleon. On a razor's edge, victory hesitated at that moment between the two sides. Despite Grouchy's absence, Napoleon might still seize victory by the engagement of his meager remaining reserves, thereby transforming Wellington's upset into a rupture.

Betting everything on his final card, Napoleon committed the Guard, or more precisely what remained of the Guard, less than 6,000 combatants.

It was now close to 9:00 p.m. The emperor placed himself in the midst of his "old mustaches" and was welcomed with cries of "Vive l'Empereur!" With a magnificent air and flags flying, the Guard entered the furnace to the sound of its massed drums and bands.

It was immediately shredded by artillery and assailed by a cloud of "redcoats" rising from the ground. The British line, though severely weakened an hour before, was now reconstituted. It later became apparent that another act of treason was involved.

To disengage from this situation, the Guard fell back without losing its organization. But the Guard had never before withdrawn. The units on its right and left in the attack panicked, and scattered to the cry of "The Guard is falling back—we are betrayed!"

Wellington had only to order a general counter-attack to annihilate the fugitives. The entire army was routed with the exception of what remained of the Guard and of Mouton's corps, which, acting as the rear guard, saved some portions. The defeat was complete by 10:00 p.m.

Might-have-beens will not change history. However, Waterloo might well have been another Austerlitz if it were not for the incredible accumulation of mischances that passed all understanding.

Despite Bourmont's treason, the war might have ended at Ligny on June 16 if Ney had been true to himself. The French would have been victorious at Mont Saint-Jean if Ney had not ignored tactics, and above all if Grouchy had been at his best. But even without Grouchy's help, victory might still have been assured were it not for that most inopportune of rains that delayed the start of the attack by three hours. Wellington would have been defeated before Blücher arrived. Waterloo sealed the end of the Imperial epoch.

The Abdication, or, The Ultimate Sacrifice for Peace

"I offer myself as a sacrifice to the hatred of France's enemies."

—Napoleon's Act of Abdication

Upon his return to Paris on June 21, Napoleon coldly analyzed the situation. He first examined the correlation of forces. At Waterloo, France had lost a great battle but not the war. The military losses were heavy but not fatal. The army had suffered 40,000 dead, wounded, prisoners, and missing, about the same as the Coalition. The country retained its military potential.

The remaining force lost none of its combativeness. It continued to provide shining demonstrations of glorious feats of arms.

The intrepid General Teste fought like a lion at Namur to permit the retreat of Grouchy's corps at Laon, where Soult reorganized the escapees of Waterloo. At the head of only 2,700 combatants in the garrison of Bergen-Op-Zoom, the brave General Bizanet repulsed 4,800 British to whom the population had opened the gates. The courageous General Exelmans, on his own initiative, inflicted a serious reverse on the Prussians near Rocquencourt-Versailles, without any support.

At the time of Napoleon's stay at Malmaison, prior to his departure for deportation, a line regiment operating in the area took a detour upon learning of his presence. Cries of "Vive l'Empereur" echoed outside the palace. The regiment's colonel jauntily proposed that the emperor lead his men to inflict a defeat on a strong Prussian detachment not far away.

With no more than 135 men at Huningue, the heroic General Barbanegre resisted the assaults of 30,000 Austrians for two months. And how many other, lesser, feats of arms have been forgotten by history?

The people as a whole, in particular those of Paris, continued to show a poignant attachment to the emperor at this critical time. During the last days of Napoleon's stay at the Elysée Palace, to which he had moved upon his return from Elba, a crowd appeared at the gates every day and cried incessantly, "Vive l'Empereur! Do not abandon us!" When Napoleon left that place for the last time, he had to sneak out secretly by the door facing the Champs-Elyées. The thousands of Parisians massed in the Rue of the Faubourg Saint-Honoré would not have permitted his departure.

No such unshakable patriotism could be found among those who are usually termed the "elites," a phenomenon that had recurred in the more recent history of France. Only the great Carnot, supported by Davout and by Lucien Bonaparte (who had courageously reconciled with his brother during the Hundred Days) called for the continued defense of the country. They advocated a "dictatorship of public safety" to continue fighting, not with any hope of destroying the Coalition armies, but to obtain a peace treaty that was not unconditional and above all preserved the Republican regime.

With their minds already thinking about a second restoration, the political elites and the well-to-do middle classes were categorically opposed to resisting the enemy. The legal country and the actual country were clearly divided.

What should he do? Napoleon found himself confronted by a terrible issue of conscience.

The honest and massive support of the people gave him the democratic legitimacy to continue the struggle. Yet, this would unavoidably lead to bloodshed between Frenchmen while under the eyes of the enemy, who was at the gates of the capital. Napoleon absolutely refused to do this.

Yet this popular force constituted a trump card that Napoleon could use to his advantage, in concert with his cabinet. He agreed to abdicate in favor of his son, which would guarantee the essential continuity of the regime. "If my enemies are sincere in their declarations that they only really want me . . . let us unite for the public good and to remain an independent nation," he wrote.

Yet sincerity was what Napoleon's enemies most lacked. Fearing an imminent popular uprising in favor of the emperor, the parliamentary representatives immediately supported the solution of a conditional abdication. The deputies went so far as to cry "Vive Napoleon II!"

It was then that Fouché deployed his greatest ignominy. In secret, he had already assured Louis XVIII of his devotion. He would wait until Napoleon had departed Paris and was far from the people before rendering void the conditional clause of the abdication that blocked the return of the Bourbons.

Assuming the presidency of the "Commission of Government" that was responsible for current affairs, Fouché skillfully exploited the existing vacuum in the succession. The Eaglet was only four years old and was in the hands of the emperor of Austria. The designated Regent, the Empress Maria-Louisa, did not meet the moral requirements of that function because of her notoriously bad conduct. Fouché distorted the logical devolution of the regency to Joseph Bonaparte by persuading the parliamentary representatives to favor a second restoration of Louis XVIII. Not flinching from any baseness provided that the rewards were ample, these unworthy notables violated their oaths in a cowardly manner.

The party of monarchical reaction had won. The Empire was abolished.

Even the fall of the Empire was insufficient to completely reassure the monarchies. The ghost of Napoleon continued to haunt the usurpers of the people's sovereignty, those abortionists of democracy and the hideous cohort of traitorous fellow-travelers.

To exorcise the demon, they deported Napoleon to an unhealthy island lost in the Atlantic, in violation of the code of honor. He was held there in secret while an interminable martyrdom was inflicted on him. An assassination by poison completed his sacrifice on the altar of peace.

$\mathcal{I}$n the end, we believe we have fulfilled the emperor's desire as expressed in an epigram. We have exonerated him of the accusation of "having loved war too much." We have proved that "he was always attacked," an expression that of course must be interpreted as "had never provoked a war." One must scatter to the winds once and for all the false image of Napoleon the swashbuckler, the unrepentant war monger and insatiable conqueror.

Napoleon was the worthy successor of all the rulers of France "from Clovis to the Committee of Public Safety," to use his own words. A man of order who triumphed in the midst of disorder, he first tamed the Revolution. An authentic man of the Enlightenment, he consecrated the principle of popular sovereignty and roused democracy throughout Europe. An inspired builder of a new world, he liberated the extraordinary forces of progress in France, infusing it with vitality.

The resulting upheaval shook the thrones of Europe and threatened the imperialistic hegemony of Britain. Coming from outside and from within France, an inevitable conservative reaction of all those privileged under the old order developed and survived, despite innumerable defeats. Grabbed by the throat, Napoleon's France thus found itself engaged in a spiral of incessant wars. In the 15 years of his reign, Napoleon had to deal with six implacable military coalitions, otherwise known as "crusades."

Confronted by this relentless steamroller, Napoleon was forced to base the defense policy of France on the principle of diverting war, which today is termed deterrence. The gigantic public work of rebuilding France required all his energy and was incompatible with any military adventure. War was always a terrible intrusion on Napoleon's immense labors. He never engaged the Grand Armeé except in a state of legitimate defense. In the warlike assault imposed upon him, he never ceased to treat the defeated in a more than reasonable manner, in the illusory hope of softening them. Contrary to those who insidiously attempt to differentiate between Bonaparte the Good and Napoleon the Evil, a functional unity connected the two. All Napoleon did was to defend tooth and nail the new France built by Bonaparte.

The history of the Empire has thus become confused with an interminable and glorious military resistance whose duration approached the miraculous. This longevity can only be explained by the exceptional conjunction of Napoleon's military genius and the unfailing, heroic attachment of "my people," as the emperor referred to the French. Never had a nation been in such perfect symbiosis with its representative.

Given the inequality of forces available, the final defeat was unavoidable. Nonetheless, the fall of the Empire was only an illusion. In 1815, though the standard bearer of democratic hopes was defeated, the hopes themselves were not—they only went into hibernation. After a first flourishing in 1830, they reappeared in full bloom in 1848, allowing the sovereign people of France to recover the usurped crown. Throughout Europe, the population cast off the yoke of their oppressors to cries of "Vive Napoleon!" The liberating message resounded around the planet. As "a meteor destined to burn so as to illuminate the world," Napoleon finally knew his posthumous triumph.

Napoleon, like a Titan, dominated his epoch and, indeed, all history from an amazing height. His Homeric epic seemed based in Greek mythology, and will doubtless join similar epics for the ages to come. His reforms and ideals created the basis of the modern era, and were fought by those who feared the future.

Like Prometheus, Napoleon committed the "crime" of "stealing the fire of heaven and giving it to mankind."

Index

Voted "Best Napoleonic Title of 2005" by the International Napoleonic Society

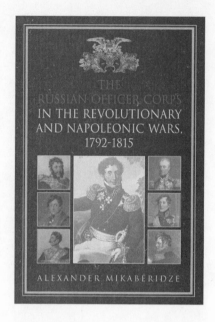

The Russian Officer Corps in the Revolutionary and Napoleonic Wars, 1792-1815

Alexander Mikaberidze, Ph.D.

440 portraits, 800 biographies, 35 graphs and charts, references, cloth, d.j., 528 pages. $64.95. (Inquire about signed copies!)

"A marvelous addition to Napoleonic knowledge and Alexander Mikaberidze should be exceedingly proud of his efforts. A real must-have." — *Richard Moore, www.napoleonguide.com*

About the book: Presented here, for the first time in any language, are more than 800 detailed biographies of the senior Russian officers who commanded troops in the Revolutionary and Napoleonic Wars. This amazing study spans the critical years of 1792 to 1815, but also includes those officers whose service fell before and after this period.

Dr. Mikaberidze's *The Russian Officer Corps* is based upon years of research in Russian archives. Each biography includes the subject's place of birth, family history, educational background, a detailed description of his military service, his awards and promotions, wounds, transfers, commands, and other related information, including the date and place of his death and internment, if known.

In addition to the biographies is an introductory chapter setting forth in meticulous detail the organization of the Russian military, how it was trained, the educational and cultural background of the officer corps, its awards and their history and meaning, and much more. Includes an annotated bibliography to help guide students of the period through the available Russian sources.

The Russian Officer Corps is a tremendous trove for historians, scholars, genealogists, hobbyists, wargamers, and anyone working on or studying late 18th and early 19th-century European history.